PAUL ROGERS is Professor of Peace Studies at Bradford University and International Security Editor for openDemocracy. He also writes a monthly briefing for the Oxford Research Group and is author of *Why We're Losing the War on Terror* and *Losing Control: Global Security in the Twenty-First Century.*

'Outstanding... *Irregular War* presents the need to establish a completely different approach to our world economic system, to the challenge of climate change and to conventional ideas of military control. The book is an essential contribution to thinking about the best way to confront the challenges of an unstable world.'

Charles Clarke, Former Home Secretary

'These stories have been told before – of inequality. environmental stress and the inability of the militarily powerful to mould the world in their own image. But they have never been told in the context of the ISIS challenge or with the historical and cultural perspective that Paul Rogers brings to bear. This book is not some important contribution to the international debate: rather, it is a masterly summary of a debate that we are emphatically not having, but which we certainly should.'

Michael Clarke, Former Director General,
Royal United Services Institute (RUSI)

'Paul Rogers identifies ISIS as symptomatic of a much broader set of developments that Western leaders have not understood. This book provides a clear and authoritative account of what is really going on and how the conventional wisdom on security needs an urgent rethink. It is compelling reading.'

Rosemary Hollis, Professor of International Politics,
City University London

'The catastrophe of the so-called "war on terror" exposed in brilliant detail by the towering intellect of Prof. Paul Rogers.'

Owen Jones, *Guardian* columnist

'Paul Rogers does it again... the picture he paints in this important book of a world of permanent insurgencies because of inequality – "revolt from the margins" – asks fundamental questions of modern armies. Are they equipped for the challenges we face? Rogers condemns our current solution of higher fences and more arms, calling for more radical measures.'

David Loyn, Foreign Affairs Analyst and author of *Butcher and Bolt:*
Two Hundred Years of Foreign Engagement in Afghanistan

IRREGULAR WAR

ISIS AND THE NEW THREAT FROM THE MARGINS

PAUL ROGERS

I.B. TAURIS
LONDON · NEW YORK

Published in 2016 by
I.B.Tauris & Co. Ltd
London • New York
www.ibtauris.com

ISBN: 978 1 78453 488 2
eISBN: 978 1 78672 006 1
ePDF: 978 1 78673 006 0

A full CIP record for this book is available from the British Library
A full CIP record is available from the Library of Congress

Library of Congress Catalog Card Number: available

Text designed and typeset by Tetragon, London

Printed and bound in Sweden by ScandBook AB

*For Benjamin
and Charlotte*

CONTENTS

PREFACE

This book has its origins in a discussion with Iradj Bagherzade about the risk of ISIS being able to develop weapons of mass destruction (WMD) and present an existential threat. In the wake of the 9/11 attacks, the disastrous wars in Afghanistan and Iraq and the emergence of ISIS from the presumed ashes of al-Qaeda, through to the attacks in Paris and Brussels in 2015 and 2016, was there the potential for ISIS or other movements to take the next steps in destructive capabilities?

While this book does indeed cover that risk, the initial discussion developed a much broader focus on the wider implications of ISIS for international security in a world increasingly overshadowed by the twin problems of a widening wealth–poverty divide and environmental constraints. The manner in which these come together with the rise of extreme political movements has scarcely been explored, yet this book argues that this is by far the most significant aspect of the rise of al-Qaeda and ISIS and the failure of the West's military responses to 9/11.

My work on this theme has been greatly helped by my involvement with two groups: openDemocracy and the Oxford Research Group (ORG). The former started soon after 9/11 in the shape of weekly analyses of the War on Terror, and I am indebted to Anthony Barnett for getting me involved, as well as to successive editors, especially Rosemary Bechler. Above all, David Hayes has added hugely to my work over the entire period, editing and improving the raw copy and adding many further links, often at very short notice, and consistently making it far more readable.

Scilla Elworthy introduced me to the ORG's work just before 9/11 and it has been a privilege to work with staff at the organisation ever since. John Sloboda, Gabrielle Rifkind, Chris Abbott, Ben Zala, Chris Langdon, Zoë Pelter, Richard Reeve and many gifted young interns and peace workers have been great to engage with. The ORG hosts the Network for Social Change's major project on remote-control warfare, and working with the staff, Caroline Donnellan and Esther Kersley, and the project's core group has been an added bonus.

Involvement with staff and students from scores of countries at Bradford University's Department of Peace Studies has been a great education and it has also been hugely helpful to have opportunities to teach at several defence colleges and other universities and to engage with many peace, development and environment groups.

I am particularly grateful to Iradj for suggesting the book in the first place and for further discussions since then, to him and Azmina Siddique at I.B.Tauris for many useful comments, suggestions and proposals as the text developed, and to Alex Middleton, Alex Billington, David Inglesfield and David Campbell for the production process.

The mistakes are all mine.

KIRKBURTON AND KYLESKU
APRIL 2016

LIST OF ABBREVIATIONS

AAAS	American Association for the Advancement of Science
AIMs	area-impact munitions
AOG	armed opposition group
AQI	al-Qaeda in Iraq
BJP	Bharatiya Janata Party (India)
BTWC	Biological and Toxin Weapons Convention
CBR	chemical, biological and radiological (weapons/warfare)
CFC	chlorofluorocarbon
CTU	Counter Terrorism Unit (UK)
CWC	Chemical Weapons Convention
EUNAVFOR Med	European Union Naval Force Mediterranean
IDF	Israel Defense Forces
IED	improvised explosive device
IISS	International Institute for Strategic Studies
ILO	International Labour Organization
IMF	International Monetary Fund
ISAF	International Security Assistance Force
ISI	Inter-Services Intelligence (Pakistani intelligence service)
JSOC	Joint Special Operations Command (US)
LTTE	Liberation Tigers of Tamil Eelam (Tamil separatist group in Sri Lanka)
OPCW	Office for the Prohibition of Chemical Weapons

ORG   Oxford Research Group
PGM   precision-guided munition
PGS   Prompt Global Strike (weapons system)
PIRA   Provisional Irish Republican Army
PMSC   private military and security companies
SAS   Special Air Service (UK)
SBS   Special Boat Service (UK)
SFSG   Special Forces Support Group (UK)
TF 145   Task Force 145 (joint US–UK special-operations
                unit in Iraq)
TTIP   Transatlantic Trade and Investment Partnership
UNCTAD   United Nations Conference on Trade and
                Development
UNEPS   United Nations Emergency Peace Service
UNSCOM   United Nations Special Commission on Iraq
USSOCOM   United States Special Operations Command
WMD   weapons of mass destruction
WTO   World Trade Organization

1

WORLD ORDER OR DISORDER: ISIS AND NEW DRIVERS OF CONFLICT

By February 2006, almost three years after the coalition invasion and occupation of Iraq in March 2003, the US Army was embroiled in a bitter insurgency, primarily against Sunni rebels who looked back to the Saddam Hussein era with pride and saw the American soldiers as occupiers of their state. One of the American reporters embedded with US units as they tried to quell the rebellion was an experienced journalist, Tom Lasseter, who was working at the time for Knight Ridder Newspapers. He was with the 101st Airborne Division when one unit was ambushed near the River Tigris at Samarra, north of Baghdad. After a violent confrontation in which several of the rebels were killed, he reported what happened next:

> Staff Sgt. Cortez Powell looked at the shredded jaw of a dead man whom he'd shot in the face when insurgents ambushed an American patrol in a blind of reeds. Powell's M4 assault rifle had jammed, so he'd grabbed the pump-action shotgun that he kept slung over his shoulders and pulled the trigger.
>
> Five other soldiers from the 101st Airborne Division scrambled down, pulled two of the insurgents' bodies from the reeds and dragged them through the mud.
>
> 'Strap those motherf——s to the hood like a deer,' said Staff Sgt. James Robinson, 25, of Hughes, Ark.

The soldiers heaved the two bodies onto the hood of a Humvee and tied them down with a cord. The dead insurgents' legs and arms flapped in the air as the Humvee rumbled along.

Iraqi families stood in front of the surrounding houses. They watched the corpses ride by and glared at the American soldiers.[1]

This incident illustrates a fundamental difference of positions. For US soldiers, the violent urban insurgency that had emerged in Iraq was by enemies that were terrorists, pure and simple. The United States had gone to war three years before because Iraq was developing weapons of mass destruction (WMD), supported terrorism, was in some way linked to the 9/11 attacks and could, in the future, provide terrorists with those WMD. From the viewpoint of ordinary soldiers in the US Army, 9/11 was, after all, an appalling attack on the world's greatest state – a powerful force for good for the whole world and a democracy in every sense. Strapping 'those motherf——s to the hood like a deer' and parading them through the town was a necessary example to deter a very dangerous enemy that threatened not just the United States but the peace of the whole world.

The feelings of those Iraqis who 'watched the corpses ride by and glared at the American soldiers' would have been completely different. Even though Iraq had fought a damaging war against Iran in the 1980s and had been repelled when it invaded Kuwait in 1990, in his 25-year rule Saddam Hussein had still presided over the development of a modern state with enviable education and health services and an economy strong enough to survive the sanctions of the 1990s. The regime drew its strength from the Sunni minority, including many of the people around Samarra, and for them the young men who had been fighting the Americans were heroic defenders of the country against a foreign invasion. To see them treated like sporting trophies was an atrocity, one that would serve to turn those watching into even stronger supporters of the insurgency and haters of America.

That episode near Samarra gives some clue to the clash of narratives that underpins so much of the conflict that has evolved since 9/11: in Afghanistan, Iraq, Pakistan, Yemen, Somalia, Libya and, more recently, Syria and Iraq once again. Moreover, this clash persists and is likely to do so for many years to come, because although al-Qaeda is less prominent than it was, the rise of ISIS since 2012 has prompted a vigorous response from the United States and its partners across much of the Middle East. It is thus essential to explore this clash, and not only in terms of the events of the past couple of decades, since it is a problem that stretches back very many years.

Furthermore, the experience of the years since 2001 and the War on Terror has a significance that goes far beyond the immediate conflict with al-Qaeda and ISIS and extends to a much more fundamental issue: whether or not that war can provide us with some indication of the global and long-term trends in insecurity that face us.

THE ARGUMENT

After 15 years of the War on Terror, there have been more than 250,000 people killed, principally in Iraq and Afghanistan, and the majority of them civilians. The bitter civil war in Syria has been at least as costly, yet the Assad regime is mentioned far less as a target for regime termination as it successfully plays on the West's greater fear of ISIS. To add to Western concerns, ISIS is now gaining support from other militant movements: in North Africa, Nigeria, Afghanistan, the Caucasus and even South Asia. Al-Qaeda may have been eclipsed, but extreme jihadist movements are growing. They are the focus of attention in international security circles and the subjects of many books and articles, and seemingly now form the greatest cause for concern.

This book takes a different view and sees ISIS and related movements as part of a much wider phenomenon: what might loosely be called 'revolts from the margins'. It does not regard Islam as the fundamental issue for the coming decades and is more concerned with the risk that we are moving into an 'age of insurgencies' – rather than one of a 'clash of civilisations' between the West and the Islamic world – and towards a global environment of fragility, instability, increasing violence and irregular war. This can be avoided, but not if the world's elites, and especially the states of the North Atlantic community, continue with their posture of maintaining control by traditional means.

The conventional view, following the expansion of the air war with ISIS, is that stable, Western states face a threat from extreme Islamists, principally embodied in ISIS, but with strong elements across many countries: from sub-Saharan Africa right through the Middle East and on to South and South East Asia. This threat may not yet be existential but, in this view, requires forceful and persistent action, no longer with tens of thousands of boots on the ground, because of the problems that arose in Iraq and Afghanistan, but by means of remote control, including air strikes, armed drones, special forces, private militaries and other 'below the radar' methods.

Given time and commitment, this approach, the argument goes, will work: advanced states will remain secure; the neo-liberal free-market system will ensure that wealth will permeate downwards; the United States and its allies will lead the way, and ISIS and its ilk will slowly wither away. As for climate change and all the other 'red/green' issues, even now the view among many Western opinion formers and politicians is that people will come to their senses and see them as annoying diversions from the road to neo-liberal progress.

This book will argue that although ISIS is certainly a major security problem, the real drivers of current global insecurity are quite different: deepening socio-economic divisions, which lead to the relative marginalisation of most people across the world, and the prospect of profound and lasting environmental constraints, caused by climate change. ISIS, in short, should be seen as a warning of what could be to come, not as a fundamental trend in its own right. The geographer and politician Edwin Brooks argued more than 40 years ago that what we had to avoid was a dystopian future of a 'crowded glowering planet of massive inequalities of wealth buttressed by stark force and endlessly threatened by desperate men in the global ghettoes'.[2]

These fundamental drivers of conflict – economic marginalisation and climate change – are exacerbated by two other factors. One is that a whole raft of welcome improvements in education and literacy is making far more people aware of their own marginalisation and unwilling to accept it, and the other is that there is an assumption in the West that security can best be assured, when other methods fail, by resort to military responses. This is greatly aided by the power and influence of what President Eisenhower called in 1961 the 'military–industrial complex', but is better described as the 'military–industrial–academic–bureaucratic complex'. At its crudest level, what is sometimes termed the 'control paradigm' might better be termed 'liddism': keeping the lid on problems rather than understanding their causes and manifestations.

The argument in this book is that ISIS is an example of a revolt from the margins, one initially specific to the Middle East but with much wider implications. Other examples include Islamist militant groups Boko Haram and the al-Nusra Front, but also the little-recognised but highly significant neo-Maoist Naxalite rebellion in India, as well as, in the recent past, the neo-Maoists in Nepal and the Shining Path movement in Peru. All in their different ways are indicators of the problems likely to be faced if that 'crowded glowering planet' is allowed to come into being. There are ways to stop it, but they go far beyond conventional thinking on security.

We will examine some of those ways in the final chapters, but our earlier concern is with how we got to where we are, not with where we might go. Why was the Western response to 9/11 so counter-productive, even leading to the emergence of ISIS? Why is there a persistent clash of narratives between Western states, with their innate belief that they are the civilised 'good guys', and so much of the rest of the world, especially in the Middle East, which takes a radically different view? Is there really a risk of nuclear, chemical or biological weapons being developed by extreme groups? How has ISIS developed and what are the underlying reasons for its gaining so much support? Is it a forerunner of the kinds of movement that are likely in the future? Finally, if we do face a 'new world disorder', how do we prevent it and use a combination of human ingenuity and wisdom to make serious progress towards a more peaceful, stable and sustainable world? If a good definition of prophecy is 'suggesting the possible', what 'prophecy' is already out there pointing the way?

WHERE WE ARE COMING FROM

In the 18 months from mid-October 2001 to April 2003, the United States and its coalition partners fought two brief and intense wars, one against the Taliban regime and al-Qaeda paramilitaries in Afghanistan and the other against the Saddam Hussein regime in Iraq. Both seemed remarkably successful – the Taliban regime was terminated and al-Qaeda dispersed in barely eight weeks, and the Iraqi regime collapsed in only three – and from a Washington perspective both were fully appropriate responses to the appalling atrocities of the 9/11 attacks.

By mid-April 2003, the Bush administration could look forward to radical political and economic change in Iraq, which would lead to a remaking of the Middle East, together with a pro-Western Afghanistan in Central Asia, curbing Chinese and Russian ambitions. More importantly, Iran, the most dangerous threat to Western interests as seen from Washington, would now be restrained by a formidable US military presence in Afghanistan to the east and Iraq to the west, pro-Western states across the Persian Gulf to the south-west and the US Navy's Fifth Fleet controlling the Gulf itself and the Arabian Sea. Iran would be surrounded, enveloped and contained.

A decade and a half later the situation looks very different. Iran is a far more influential country and is even developing better links with the United States, while Western militaries have repeatedly tried to retreat from Afghanistan, leaving a fractured country bending to substantial Taliban influence. The termination of the Gaddafi regime in Libya has left a violent, fragmented and deeply unstable country, and across south-western Asia and sub-Saharan Africa other Islamist movements, such as Boko Haram, are gaining power and territory. Iraq has been beset by violence and, above all, an extreme Islamist movement has risen from the remains of al-Qaeda to gain territory across both that country and Syria.

The sudden rise of ISIS, the most feared of the current group of Islamist paramilitary movements, in early 2014 has been the most substantial surprise. The movement's development has a significance that goes far further than the immediate wars: it is a symptom of a wider phenomenon, a clear indicator of future conflicts that will have a worldwide relevance. It represents a type of movement that will become more common over the next two or three decades: a revolt from the margins within a global system experiencing a series of drivers of conflict that will dominate international relations unless the underlying factors are faced squarely. To appreciate how and why this has happened requires us to look back at the motivations for the 9/11 attacks, and the reasons that Western states responded with wars that went well beyond the termination of the movement responsible.

Moreover, even if it eventually goes into decline, ISIS marks the emergence of a kind of paramilitary movement that is sufficiently experienced and robust to withstand the efforts of the world's most advanced militaries to contain it. It is also an example of a movement that may use a variety of forms of hybrid and asymmetric warfare, and that may seek to produce chemical, biological or radiological (CBR) weapons.

Perhaps most significantly of all, and at the heart of the problem for the West, ISIS actually seeks confrontation with powerful states as it tries to position itself not as a pariah but as a champion, with its ability to win hearts and minds and to present itself as the defender of Islam making it particularly dangerous. The very idea that this could have traction seems hugely far-fetched to Western thinking, yet that is precisely the situation. Revolts from the margins may be seen as minor irritants, but if 'the margins' represent the majority of people in a country, a region or even a continent, the resultant movements should not be regarded lightly.

Given the prominence of Islamist paramilitary movements in the early twenty-first century, there is an understandable tendency to see them as the only examples of violent revolts, but this is far from the case. In the past 30 years alone many other movements have been in evidence, including the Basque-separatist organisation ETA in Spain, the Provisional Irish Republican Army (PIRA) in Northern Ireland, the Liberation Tigers of Tamil Eelam (LTTE) in Sri Lanka, Shining Path in Peru and, most significantly in recent years, the Naxalites in India. ISIS, Boko Haram, al-Qaeda and other Islamist movements may themselves have a marked transnational impact, but in the long run it is likely that they will be seen as examples of a wider phenomenon of revolt stemming from quite different elements of human identity. As I have suggested elsewhere:

What should be expected is that new social movements will develop that are essentially anti-elite in nature and draw their support from people on the margins. In different contexts and circumstances they may have their roots in political ideologies, religious beliefs, ethnic, nationalist or cultural identities, or a complex combination of several of these. They may be focused on individuals or groups but the most common feature is an opposition to existing centres of power. They may be sub-state groups directed at the elites in their own state or foreign interests, or they may hold power in states in the South, and will no doubt be labelled as rogue states as they direct their responses towards the North. What can be said is that, on present trends, anti-elite action will be a core feature of the next 30 years – not so much a clash of civilisations, more an age of insurgencies.[3]

If this is the case, what are the major drivers of insecurity and how do they relate to the experience of the past decade and a half? If there are worldwide trends that are making for a more unstable global system, is it possible to argue that extreme Islamist groups have anything to do with them? Many would say not – that movements such as al-Qaeda, Boko Haram, ISIS and others are specific to Islam and that it is Islam that is the core problem. If so, this specific if dangerous phenomenon has no relevance to wider problems.

This book will argue against that view on six grounds. First, ISIS and its loose associates are particularly significant examples of the changing nature of conflict, and especially of the ability of movements from the margins to challenge the world's strongest and best-resourced military powers.

Second, the War on Terror has shown that those military powers, especially the United States, have taken the view that the primary means of countering such threats is the heavy use of military force. This may be understandable given the shock of 9/11, but has proved disastrous, with hundreds of thousands of people killed and more than 15 years of war.

Third, ISIS and other movements are political entities that, though rooted in a religious ideology, relate closely to a widespread perception of marginalisation across the Middle East, and have been aided in recent years by the failure to reform autocratic and deeply elitist regimes in the region, which have worked closely for decades with leading Western states. The revolts against these regimes that broke out in 2011 were certainly reactions to autocracy and the endemic suppression of rights of free expression, but they also owed much to the deep socio-economic divisions across the region, which have resulted in the entrenched marginalisation of majorities.

Fourth, although it is not uncommon to see Islam as the fundamental problem – part of a wider perception of a clash of civilisations between the Christian West and extreme Islam – such a view tends to ignore both historical experience, including the Crusades and the Thirty Years War, and, more significantly, recent experience of apparently religiously motivated violence, including the Srebrenica massacre, extreme Hindu actions in India and the Buddhist persecution of Rohingya Muslims in Myanmar. In many of these conflicts, religion has formed only part of more complex motivations; moreover, a key aspect of the wars in the Middle East is the divide *within* Islam between Sunni and Shi'a.

Fifth, given the huge publicity surrounding the wars in Iraq, Syria, Afghanistan and Libya, and the worldwide attacks of the past 15 years – from New York to Djakarta; from Madrid to Amman – there is a strong tendency to simplify, to see the challenge as the defeat of a single ideology, ignoring the many other political, social and economic trends that have added hugely to these conflicts.

Finally, there is an underlying tendency, not only but especially in the West, to see major security issues in straightforward good-versus-bad terms, something that militates against an understanding of motivations. Indeed, those analysts who do attempt to see the world through the eyes of the extreme militants are readily dismissed as sympathisers.

FUTURE DRIVERS OF INSECURITY

Prior to the 9/11 attacks and the start of the War on Terror it was already possible to identify two significant global issues: a widening socio-economic divide and environmental limits to growth. In relation to the former, the richest fifth of the world's population had increased its share of the world's wealth from 70 per cent in 1960 to 85 per cent in 1991, while over that same period the poorest fifth's share had dropped from 2.3 per cent to 1.7 per cent. There was no denying that economic development had forged ahead, including in many countries of the Global South, but it was also clear that the great majority of the investment for economic growth had gone into just a handful of countries.

The more general argument was made across the Global South that much of the unequal development since the end of the colonial era in the 1960s stemmed from a world trading system that had evolved in that era, and that as a result consistently favoured the industrialised states of the Global North. This system persisted long afterwards and involved maintaining trade relationships that were essentially unbalanced, systematically benefiting more developed countries at the expense of those whose main revenues came from producing and exporting primary commodities.[4]

This changed somewhat in the 1980s and 1990s as some states in the Global South succeeded in industrialising and providing cheap manufactured goods for export, but even this was dependent on a large pool of low-wage labour. Thus, while some countries experienced rapid economic growth, the result was that this growth was extraordinarily lopsided, with much of the benefit residing with an elite minority.

One of the consequences of this developing inequality has been an increasing resentment of the concentration of wealth, a resentment exacerbated by a greater awareness of marginalisation. In some ways this is a paradox arising out of success. One of the most welcome changes in human development since the 1960s has been a systematic improvement in educational provision across the Global South, with substantial increases in enrolment, especially but not only in primary education. Even the pernicious gender gap has at last started to close. Yet although a higher proportion of young people have gone through primary and secondary education, some even reaching universities and polytechnics, their economic prospects and life chances have not matched these changes. What used to be talked about as a 'revolution of rising expectations' has become a 'revolution of frustrated expectations'.

In its extreme form this has resulted in near-revolutionary movements, sometimes with a neo-Maoist dimension, as with the Shining Path movement in Peru, which arose directly from the work of a university philosophy professor, Abimael Guzmán. Shining Path's considerable violence and brutality were matched by that of the state, and while its power declined after the capture and imprisonment of Guzmán in 1992, neo-Maoist opposition to the economic status quo persists.

An example of a movement with wider support and more genuinely emancipatory aims is the Zapatistas, based in the state of Chiapas in Mexico. A rebellion led by this group was planned to start on 1 January 1994, the date chosen to coincide with the coming into operation of the new North American Free Trade Area (NAFTA) across Canada, the United States and Mexico. The leadership of the new movement saw this as yet another example of the rise of the unregulated free market, something that would serve the interests of richer sectors in all three countries at the expense of the poor. Their motivation was dramatically illustrated by a rebel source, who identified the reasons for the revolt:

We have nothing, absolutely nothing – not decent shelter, nor land, nor work, nor health, nor food, nor education. We do not have the right to choose freely and democratically our officials. We have neither peace nor justice for ourselves and our children. But today we say enough![5]

By the end of the 1990s, the failure of the world economic system to deliver greater emancipation and more equality was being recognised. Much of the reaction took the form of opposition to the policies of the World Trade Organization (WTO) as well as the World Bank and the International Monetary Fund (IMF), as agents and purveyors of the neo-liberal 'Washington Consensus', who were collectively seen as entrenching an unjust status quo:

The experience of mass public protests and violence at the WTO meeting in Seattle in 1999 was traumatic, not just for the organisation but for the IMF, the World Bank and other intergovernmental agencies. Bitterly criticised by citizen groups and by Third World delegations, the assumption of dominance of the WTO by elite states was seriously damaged – a crack began to appear in the edifice of Western economic control.[6]

If concern over inequalities and the innate unfairness of the world economic system developed slowly in the 1990s, this was also true of concern over global environmental trends. Back in 1972, the United Nations had called a meeting in Stockholm, the United Nations Conference on the Human Environment, to focus on what was being recognised as the growing problem of the human impact on the environment. It was influenced by the publication of the book *The Limits to Growth*, the result of a large-scale computer-modelling initiative undertaken at the Massachusetts Institute of Technology. This had concluded that the capacity of the global ecosystem – the biosphere – to handle the impact of human activity was likely to be exceeded within a few decades, perhaps by the 2020s, unless ways were found to limit it.[7]

Much of the focus of *The Limits to Growth* was on resource-depletion and problems of food security, but during the course of the 1980s and early 1990s the problem of climate disruption through the production of greenhouse gases became more dominant. In 1992 the Earth Summit in Rio put far more emphasis on this issue and by the end of the 1990s environmental awareness was widespread in some Northern industrial states. Some analysts sought to connect the two issues – economy and environment – pointing out that it was a failing economic system that was simultaneously producing greater wealth–poverty divisions and abjectly failing to come to terms with the environmental damage being done.

Moreover, there was already evidence that climate disruption would be especially damaging for many of the weakest parts of the tropics and subtropics – societies that would be least able to cope with such evolving crises. There was now a prospect of many countries across the Global South facing severe declines in food production without the resources to import, which would lead to multiple political and social difficulties as well as bitterness and resentment.

What was required was an economic transformation and a system that was both just and sustainable, but this was a far cry from the prevailing orthodoxy and remained a minority view. It was given some potency by the argument that, without such change, a combination of marginalisation and climate disruption would lead to a thoroughly unstable world that could not be controlled by minority elites, however powerful their military forces. Already the evidence from radical groups such as PIRA and the LTTE, and the activities of states determined to produce their own deterrents, such as Iraq and North Korea, pointed to a developing asymmetry in power relationships that was simply not being recognised.

Indeed, it seemed likely that if Western states were to face massive asymmetric attacks, whatever their origins and motivations, their reaction would consist of forceful attempts to regain control. The first attempt to destroy the twin towers of the World Trade Center in New York, in February 1993, would have been an example of such an attack and could have killed 30,000 people if it had succeeded. But what would have been the reaction? My own analysis, written before 9/11, argued:

> If that attack had had its intended effect, the results would have been calamitous, not just for the City of New York but for the United States as a whole. But would it have resulted in any rethinking of security? Probably not. A more likely result would have been a massive and violent military reaction against any groups anywhere in the Middle East that were thought to have had even the slightest connection to the attack.[8]

Nevertheless, and bearing in mind the growing awareness of economic injustice and environmental limits, there was still some cause for optimism:

> Whether these collective signs indicate the beginnings of a substantial change in attitudes is difficult to predict, but it is reasonable to conclude that the coming years represent a period of fundamental challenge and potential transformation. The early decades of the twenty-first century could be an era in which deep divisions in the world community lead to instability and violence that will transcend boundaries and affect rich and poor alike. They could also be an era of substantial progress in developing a more socially just and environmentally sustainable world order.[9]

THE LOST DECADE

The West has been at war for most of the period since 9/11, principally in Afghanistan and Iraq and led by the United States, with no end in sight. The 'control paradigm', which sees military force as the ultimate guarantor of security for the world's more powerful societies, remains in place in spite of the huge problems that continue to face it. On present trends, decades of war in the Middle East are in prospect.

Over the same period there has been little progress in seeking a greater degree of equity. Some of the Millennium Development Goals established by the United Nations in 2000 may have been achieved, albeit quite often after having been softened, but the wealth–poverty divide remains in place. A subtle trend is evident in the transition from what in the 1950s and 1960s was considered a rich world–poor world divide, a largely geographical construct, to a split between the transnational phenomenon of a globally interconnected elite and the rest. China now has a substantial middle class of more than 100 million people, and the Indian middle class is also growing. On a smaller scale this is true for many in what used to be called the Third World, even though the great majority of people there are still thoroughly marginalised.

At the same time, the wealth–poverty divide has got more extreme in some countries of the Global North, such as the United States and the United Kingdom, but the more important worldwide trend is of the evolution of a transnational elite of 1.5 billion people, who have benefited from the decades of growth while close to 6 billion have been left with a minority of income and wealth. A common feature of the burgeoning cities of the Global South is the emergence of highly secure compounds, some of them the size of small towns, that are protected by electrified fences and armed guards.

All this has happened as the neo-liberal free-market system has become the only game in town. Until 1990, the worldwide division between mixed-economy systems and the centrally planned systems of the old Soviet bloc and China meant that there were certain constraints preventing the wholehearted embracing of the free market. After the end of the Cold War, though, with the dissolution of the rigid Soviet system and China's cautious adoption of the market, there came the conviction that there could only be one way forward. It appeared to be self-evident that the free-market ideology of Reaganomics and Thatcherism was the clear winner and the move towards deregulation and privatisation gathered pace.

This was in spite of the experience of Russia in the 1990s, where the rapid embracing of what was aptly called 'turbo-capitalism' led to extraordinary divisions between the wealthy and the poor, not least as a handful of oligarchs creamed off the wealth of many resource-producing former state enterprises. By the tail end of the decade a third of Russian citizens were in serious poverty, while there was a huge rise in alcoholism, especially among men, and a decline in life expectancy of nearly ten years. In the West the attitude to Russia was one of little more than contempt, something that has been exploited relentlessly and to great effect by Vladimir Putin as he moves with great domestic support to try to reclaim Russia's status as a great power.

The 1997 Asian financial crisis was another warning that was ignored. The initial shock of this event rapidly receded, and in the early years of the new century the trend was very much back towards the freedom of the market, something greatly aided by the election of George W. Bush to the White House in November 2000, establishing an administration with singularly strong neo-conservative leanings.

More surprising was the even more serious crisis that developed in 2007 and came to a head in 2008. Originating with the sub-prime mortgage shortfalls in the United States and made worse initially by unregulated credit default swaps and collateralised debt obligations, the crisis led to major banks hugely over-reaching themselves. Some, like Lehman Brothers, collapsed; others had to be bailed out massively by central banks and intergovernmental institutions, leading to serious increases in government debt. This, in turn, led to the imposition of multiple austerity measures across much of Europe, although these had little effect on wealthy elites, who frequently saw their wealth increase.

By the beginning of the following decade it was almost as though nothing had happened and warnings had been ignored. There is some talk of the dangers of marginalisation, which occasionally penetrates the watering holes of the elite at Davos, meetings of the Bilderberg Group and the like, but little more than that. Two books, Pickett and Wilkinson's *The Spirit Level* and Piketty's *Capital in the Twenty-First Century*, have had some effect, but the mainstream of economic thinking has so far taken little notice.[10] To all intents and purposes the first decade of the twenty-first century was a lost decade.

This also applied to the climate-change debate, with the United Nations Climate Change Conference in Copenhagen in December 2009 being the clearest example of failure. Indeed, the eight years of the Bush administration were notable for the consistent success of the climate-change deniers, even though the overwhelming majority of scientists rejected their views. Scepticism about this issue was greatly aided by two factors. One was the determination of the fossil-fuels lobby, both transnational corporations and the main producer countries, to deny that there was a problem and to fund generously think tanks and campaigners who shared their view. Given their vested interest in maintaining successful extraction industries and the financial rewards of their exports, this was hardly surprising, but what was striking was the second factor: the link between climate-change denial and free-market ideology. The issue here was, and is, that responding to climate change requires nothing less than a transformation to ultra-low-carbon economies. The political implications are huge, since this has to be achieved in, at most, two decades, and such a time frame is far too short for market forces to be able to adapt. Governmental and intergovernmental action has to be at the centre of the transition, but this is anathema to free-market ideologues. The free market is seen as the only way forward, but since it cannot handle climate change, then climate change cannot be happening.

Given the mounting evidence of recent years, there has been a subtle change in the neo-liberal position towards the reluctant view that though the climate may be changing, this cannot possibly be due to human activity. Neo-liberals therefore argue that it is a temporary phenomenon, one that is down to natural cycles – adaptation may be required but the free market can easily cope. The central view remains deeply entrenched in neo-liberal circles that climate change is not, and never will be, a fundamental problem that requires sustained intergovernmental action. It is not a political problem.

Nor, from this perspective, is the widening wealth–poverty divide anything that will not recede naturally as wealth trickles down from the rich to the poor. Even more importantly, revolts against an effective and stable status quo are hugely dangerous and must be opposed by all necessary means, including the use of force. The problem with Afghanistan and Iraq, and again with ISIS, is that leaders such as Barack Obama have failed to exercise sufficient sustained force and are fully culpable for what has happened.

From this position, which is still prevalent across global elite communities, it is a matter of business as usual, with little or no credence given to the possibility that an unstable global system might stem from a dangerous combination of a deeply unequal economy and an increasingly constrained world, factors that disproportionately damage the lives of the marginalised majority.

We therefore have three points to consider. One is that the global economy is failing signally to fulfil human needs worldwide and must undergo a fundamental transformation. The second is that this transformation must also entail radical decarbonisation. If this is not achieved then we have the makings of a thoroughly

divided and unstable world. The lesson of the past decade is the
third point: in the face of threats, the response has repeatedly
been the recourse to considerable force, most notably in the War
on Terror.

All three issues are deeply problematic, as the analysis behind
them is opposed, or at least persistently questioned, by the prevailing forces in the current Western political system. They are
convinced that the free market is the answer to poverty and
everything else, that climate change is not a result of human action
and that threats to the status quo must be met with all necessary
force in order to maintain stability. The War on Terror may not
have achieved its aims, but new forms of control – including armed
drones and much greater use of special forces and private military
companies – will be the answer.

The main purpose of this book is to explore the third of these
points, but to do so in the wider context of an increasingly divided,
marginalised and environmentally constrained world. Seeing
the War on Terror as a problem in its own right is the common
approach and has resulted in many millions of words of commentary and analysis – yet it misses the point. The real significance of
the wars since 9/11 is their relevance to the future, not the past,
and that is what this book is about. It necessarily involves an
analysis of the main conflicts of this century, of why the wars in
Iraq and Afghanistan went so badly wrong for the United States
and its allies, and of how extreme movements are challenging
elite societies. It also involves the recognition of a remarkable
phenomenon: that elite societies do not even accept the intrinsic
instability of their own position.

THE COCOON EFFECT

This lack of acceptance is worth exploring, since it is at the heart
of so much wishful thinking or, at least, persistent misconceptions

of the state of the world. What it amounts to is the pervasive view – across the billion-plus transnational community that has benefited so much from the post-Cold War transition to free-market dominance – that there is little in the way of a real division. Looked at from a common and entrenched perspective, there may be deep poverty in some parts of the world; there may be occasional famines and other natural disasters and there may be worrying and desperate consequences of the wars in the Middle East, but across most of the world things are going quite well, all things considered.

There is a substantial element of illusion in this, which stems from the 'cocoon effect': seeing the world through a lens of well-being. The modern traveller can visit historic sites, natural wonders, safari parks, tropical beaches and all manner of comfortable destinations, travelling by air or in air-conditioned coaches, staying in comfortable hotels and dining on reliable menus, perhaps infused with just a smattering of local dishes. 'Local' gifts will be readily available, guides will provide reassuring commentary and all will seem well.

In reality, huge areas of many countries will never be visited: safe hotels may be close to shanty towns; safari parks and beaches adjacent to depressed rural environments – but little of this side of life will be apparent. Even more deluding will be the impression that many millions of people in the majority of the Global South, who are far from destitute, are in some way happy with their circumstances and, indeed, are the living proof that the free-market model really does lead to a substantial 'trickle-down' of wealth. The worst of world poverty is easing and all will eventually benefit.

The problem is not a huge gap between wealth and deep poverty. Such deep poverty certainly does persist: perhaps as many as a billion people still do not share in even the basics needed for decent existence – but it is the much larger numbers of people, often educated and literate and with knowledge of the way the world works, who might best be described as in the 'majority margins'. This very phrase, the 'majority margins', seems a contradiction in terms, but it is at the heart of what is happening. If a fifth of humanity is benefiting disproportionally from the way the current economic model works, then the 'majority margins' are the rest. They may be living in tolerable circumstances but it is the difference, and even the perceived difference, that is at the core of dissatisfaction.

Along with opposition to autocracy and to suppression of dissent, this deep resentment has been the underlying driver of much of the outburst of anger and frustration that has constituted the Arab Awakening. Moreover, it builds on a view of the world radically different from the Western notion that it is the 'developed' states of the North Atlantic community that are the guardians of civilised values. This will be explored in Chapter 3, since it is so important in the specific context of understanding the motivations of extreme movements, but suffice to say here that the cocoon effect adds greatly to the failure among the world's top 1.5 billion to understand the precarious nature of their position. Remember, too, that this is the situation *now*, before a time when climate disruption will add to the human predicament, with the risk of greatly exacerbating the relative economic marginalisation of the majority that already exists.

2

COMING OUT OF NOWHERE

In June 2001, our youngest son, Will, went on a school trip to the east coast of the United States, and one of the highlights was a visit to the top of the North Tower of the World Trade Center in New York. On his return, Will gave me a very attractive line drawing by the noted artist Bruce Arvon, showing the Brooklyn Bridge in the foreground and the World Trade Center behind. I still have it on the wall of my office.

Before Minoru Yamasaki's extraordinary complex was completed in 1987, the Empire State Building was the focus of tourist interest, but the World Trade Center was taller and much larger and soon came to represent US global economic leadership. The Pentagon in Washington was far older, having been completed in 1943, but it had a similar status to the World Trade Center, as the headquarters of the world's most powerful military force.

Less than three months after Will was there, the World Trade Center was destroyed in the 9/11 atrocity, which killed nearly 3,000 people; on the same day the attack on the Pentagon killed 189 people and damaged a third of the entire complex. In a single day, the United States had seen disastrous attacks on what can be described as its core centres of power. Moreover, most of the impact was witnessed live on TV across the world.

What happened in the decade and more after that extraordinary day determined the progress initially of the al-Qaeda movement and more recently of ISIS, both movements much influenced by how the United States and its Western coalition partners responded. While this book is about the significance of ISIS for future security in the wider context of a divided and constrained global system, it is essential to explore the experience of the wars after 9/11 in order to appreciate how the movement fits into that context and how our understanding of international security needs to change. Furthermore, analysing the growth of the original al-Qaeda movement in the 1990s, and its belief in its ability to take on the United States following the collapse of the Soviet Union, is important for our understanding of the more recent past. Unless we grasp the motives behind the West's violent responses in recent years, there is a risk that those responses will give all too clear an indication of how elite communities will react to Brooks's 'crowded glowering planet' in the future.

EARLY WARNINGS

If we are looking to understand the changing international security environment since the 9/11 attacks and the subsequent wars, it is worth noting that a decade before 2003 there was a series of events that already gave a powerful indication of the direction in which global security in the post-Cold War era was heading. In the months from February to April 1993, three events in three different cities, Washington DC, New York and London, provided pointers to what would become the global War on Terror.

In Washington in February of that year, President Bill Clinton's newly designated director of the CIA, James Woolsey, was asked at Senate confirmation hearings how he would characterise the change from the Cold War to the new security environment. He replied that the United States had slain the dragon but now lived in a jungle inhabited by poisonous snakes. That same month an audacious attempt was made to destroy the World Trade Center in New York, and two months later PIRA detonated a large car bomb in Bishopsgate in the heart of the City of London, killing one person, injuring many and causing close to £1 billion of damage.

In his response at the Senate hearings, Woolsey was pointing to the rise of ill-defined sub-state movements that might cause major problems for the United States. Although the previous administration – of President George H. W. Bush – had spoken hopefully of a new world order after the collapse of the Soviet bloc, Woolsey saw it very differently, and this was an aspect of the new world order (or disorder) that was widely recognised within the Clinton administration.

During the next few years of defence-budget retrenchment, some major elements of the US military posture were maintained and even enhanced. Many of the Cold War excesses – strategic nuclear arsenals, heavy armour in Western Europe and anti-submarine weapons – were cut back, but the most important component of US power projection, the Marine Corps, maintained almost all its budget; most of the US Navy's carrier battle groups survived; the US Army put more emphasis on special forces; and the US Air Force expanded its long-range strike capabilities. If the jungle needed to be tamed, the means were at hand.

The second event, the 1993 attack on the World Trade Center, has long since been eclipsed by the appalling events of 9/11, but the incident itself was a powerful warning – albeit one that was insufficiently heeded at the time. A large truck bomb was left in an underground car park close to support pillars of the south side of the North Tower, the aim being to bring it down across the Vista Hotel that linked the twin towers, and into the South Tower. The entire complex would be destroyed, and since the detonation was timed for just after midday, the great majority of the more than 30,000 people inside would be killed – ten times the number lost in the 9/11 atrocity eight years later.

In the event, the complex survived, though six people died and many hundreds were affected, mainly through smoke inhalation. It later became clear that although the bombers had used sufficient explosives to bring down the entire tower, these would have to have been spread across a series of smaller devices placed against a number of individual supports, rather than being concentrated in a single charge. Even though the North Tower survived, the Vista Hotel came very close to collapse, and was only saved by some remarkable emergency structural engineering, which was applied to its foundations adjoining the North Tower.[1]

The perpetrators were led by Ramzi Yousef, for whom the main motive was opposition to US military and diplomatic support for Israel, and while the group had few direct connections with the evolving al-Qaeda movement they espoused a similarly extreme Islamist outlook. Six people involved were later detained, tried and sentenced to long terms in prison. The security of high-rise buildings was reviewed right across the city and beyond, but the impact on attitudes to paramilitary violence was somewhat limited. The idea that this indicated a high degree of vulnerability for advanced industrial states was largely discounted. This is extraordinary considering what has happened since. Put bluntly, if that first World Trade Center attack had succeeded, it would have been the worst single act of violence since the atomic bombing of Nagasaki nearly half a century earlier.

Then came the Bishopsgate bomb in London – the third in a sequence of attacks by PIRA, the first two being a city-centre bomb the previous April at the Baltic Exchange and an attempt to damage a key road interchange in north-west London. PIRA had resorted to economic targeting of the City at a time when London was in bitter competition with Frankfurt to be Europe's leading financial centre. London was certainly the front-runner, but persistent bomb attacks would be well-nigh certain to drive away key international banks and to hand the prize to Frankfurt. PIRA's motivation stemmed primarily from the degree of stalemate that had developed in Northern Ireland after more than two decades of violence. While the British authorities were unable to suppress and defeat PIRA, the group itself had no prospect of achieving a united Ireland. The extensive use of economic targeting might possibly lead to a change in British political attitudes.

Three other PIRA attacks on the City were prevented in 1993 and 1994, but the political effect was still considerable – encouraging the Conservative government of John Major to engage more energetically in a negotiated settlement to the conflict. That would eventually come, but only after further PIRA attacks on London's secondary financial district at Canary Wharf and a devastating attack on the retail heart of the northern city of Manchester in 1996. That was a year before the election won by the Labour Party under Tony Blair, who then made negotiating an end to the Northern Ireland conflict one of his main priorities.

The first attack on New York's World Trade Center was a warning of what a small and determined group might be able to achieve in a mass-casualty attack. There were other such warnings in the 1990s, including an attempt by Algerian radicals to crash a passenger jet into the centre of Paris, and the bombing of the central business district of Colombo by the LTTE in Sri Lanka. In contrast, the PIRA attacks were designed to cause *economic* harm, not mass casualties, and had a pronounced political impact. Nevertheless, all these examples show the evolution of methods of asymmetric and irregular warfare, which, though still in their infancy, had the potential to enhance the power of paramilitary groups facing substantial military superiority.

Above all, though, it was Woolsey's 'jungle of poisonous snakes' that began to frame military thinking in the 1990s, though the reaction to 9/11 was as much political as military, especially given the ferocity of the US response and the fact that it went well beyond the killing or capturing of those believed to be responsible for the attacks. To explore this it is essential to examine not just the origins and aims of the al-Qaeda movement but the nature of US politics at the end of the 1990s. Today, almost a generation later, this might all seem like ancient history, something already discussed by many other people, but the strange thing is that connections are rarely made with these earlier events. Taking a long-term perspective is of great value in understanding both al-Qaeda and ISIS, and the reasons the latter has acquired and retains a surprising degree of support.

The al-Qaeda movement has its origins in late-1980s Afghanistan, in the midst of the bitter mujahidin revolt against the occupying Soviet forces. This long conflict lasted from 1980 to 1988 and was very much part of the Cold War environment. As such, it developed into a proxy war between East and West, with the United States committing substantial resources into aiding the mujahidin. In the latter part of the war foreign fighters, including Osama bin Laden and his associate Ayman al-Zawahiri, formed a small but significant part of the revolt, backed by the Pakistani Inter-Services Intelligence agency (ISI) and the CIA.

By the end of the decade the Soviets had gone, and bin Laden, al-Zawahiri and others formed al-Qaeda (meaning 'the Base'), which would take the idea of an Islamist Sharia caliphate out beyond Afghanistan. During the 1990s bin Laden and his followers moved from Saudi Arabia to Sudan and then back to Afghanistan, this time to aid the Taliban ('student') movement fighting the Northern Alliance warlords in a bitter civil war for control of the country.

By the end of the 1990s, al-Qaeda had the features of a small transnational revolutionary movement, and was unusual in that it was rooted not in political ideology, ethnicity or nationalism but in religious identity. Stemming from the Wahhabi tradition of Islam and owing much to the writings of Sayyid Qutb, the Islamic theorist executed by the Egyptians in 1966, its aims included replacing what it saw as unacceptable Middle Eastern regimes and hugely damaging the United States as part of the process of establishing a new and radical caliphate.

Two other aspects of the al-Qaeda movement were important, if little understood in the West. One was that the defeat of the Soviets in Afghanistan in the 1980s appeared to demonstrate to the movement's leaders that, given time, determined Islamists could humble a superpower. This was certainly an exaggeration given the many other factors that ended the Cold War, but there was an element of truth in it. The second was that the al-Qaeda vision embraced an unlimited timescale. Looking beyond the earthly life, the eschatological element of al-Qaeda culture meant, and still means, that revolutionary change may be measured in many decades, if not a century or more. Recognising this is fundamental to understanding the persistence of al-Qaeda and other movements, including ISIS, but it is perhaps the one element of the Islamist outlook that has been least appreciated by Western analysts used to operating on a much shorter political timescale. The leaders and dedicated followers of most secular revolutionary movements seek to achieve their revolutionary aims or at least make considerable progress in their own lifetimes – but not movements such as al-Qaeda.

By the end of the 1990s, al-Qaeda had a series of aims. A core goal was the termination of unacceptable and non-Islamist regimes across the Middle East, with the House of Saud being the worst example in their eyes: a corrupt, pro-American and entirely unsuitable 'Guardian of the Two Holy Places' (Mecca and Medina). Such regimes constituted the 'near enemy'. Beyond this aim lay an intense anti-Zionism, as well as support for other Islamist-oriented movements, whether in Chechnya, Thailand, Indonesia, Yemen, Somalia or elsewhere. The bitter opposition to Israel stemmed partly from that country's treatment of the Palestinians, but much more from its effective control of the 'Third Holy Place', Haram al-Sharif in Jerusalem. While the Six Day War of 1967 had been welcomed by supporters of Israel right across the world, it was seen as having been nothing short of a disaster by a movement such as al-Qaeda.

At a global level was a deep and abiding opposition to the 'far enemy' of the United States and its Western allies. When the Frankfurt cell conceived the idea of attacking the heartland of this enemy in Washington and New York there was a triple attraction. One was that it would demonstrate to the wider Islamic world – the *umma* – the capability of the movement; a second was that it would provoke the United States into war in Afghanistan. This apparently perverse aim had much to do with the perception that the mujahidin, aided by the groups that came to form al-Qaeda, had destroyed the Soviet Union by wearing it down in the 1980s, an operation that could be repeated with the other superpower, even if it might take a decade or more.

Finally, and this was something scarcely appreciated by Western commentators at the time, it would play very well into a narrative of al-Qaeda responding to an attack on Islam from the Western Crusaders and their Zionist surrogates. This came out in a singularly significant way in a bin Laden speech of 2004, three years after the 9/11 attacks, when the US and its coalition partners were fighting a bitter war in Iraq and facing renewed conflict in Afghanistan. In the Al Jazeera transcript he says:

> But I am amazed at you. Even though we are in the fourth year after the events of September 11th, Bush is still engaged in distortion, deception and hiding from you the real causes. And thus, the reasons are still there for a repeat of what occurred.
>
> So I shall talk to you about the story behind those events and shall tell you truthfully about the moments in which the decision was taken, for you to consider.
>
> I say to you, Allah knows that it had never occurred to us to strike the towers. But after it became unbearable and we witnessed the oppression and tyranny of the American/Israeli coalition against our people in Palestine and Lebanon, it came to my mind.
>
> The events that affected my soul in a direct way started in 1982 when America permitted the Israelis to invade Lebanon and the American Sixth Fleet helped them in that.

This bombardment began and many were killed and injured and others were terrorised and displaced.

I couldn't forget those moving scenes, blood and severed limbs, women and children sprawled everywhere. Houses destroyed along with their occupants and high rises demolished over their residents, rockets raining down on our home without mercy.

The situation was like a crocodile meeting a helpless child, powerless except for his screams. Does the crocodile understand a conversation that doesn't include a weapon? And the whole world saw and heard but it didn't respond.

In those difficult moments many hard-to-describe ideas bubbled in my soul, but in the end they produced an intense feeling of rejection of tyranny, and gave birth to a strong resolve to punish the oppressors.

And as I looked at those demolished towers in Lebanon, it entered my mind that we should punish the oppressor in kind and that we should destroy towers in America in order that they taste some of what we tasted and so that they be deterred from killing our women and children.[2]

This motive may have had some truth in it or it may have been entirely fabricated. Either way, it received little mention in the Western media, but it most certainly had an impact across the Middle East. The reason stretched back to 1982, when the Israel Defense Forces (IDF), under defence minister Ariel Sharon, launched 'Operation Peace for Galilee', ostensibly to rid southern Lebanon of Palestinian militia firing positions, which were used to launch unguided Katyusha rockets into Galilee. It began on 6 June, when the world's media was still diverted by the extraordinary war between the United Kingdom and Argentina over the Falkland/Malvinas Islands.

The IDF quickly achieved the stated objective but then continued right up to the suburbs of Beirut, in what, it became clear, was a far larger operation, designed to destroy the Palestinian paramilitary leadership in the city. But that proved to be much more difficult, and in a long and hugely damaging siege of the western part of the city the Israelis used heavy artillery and multiple air strikes to try to take control, destroying many high-rise buildings – bin Laden's 'demolished towers in Lebanon'.

Sources differ on the numbers of casualties. Early in the war, International Red Cross and Lebanese police sources stated that in the first two weeks of fighting, 14,000 were killed and 20,000 injured, and by the end of the war Lebanese sources put the deaths at 19,000, the majority civilians. Most of the civilian deaths resulted from Israeli bombardments, not least of bin Laden's 'towers', and these included Palestinians who were still refugees from the 1948 Israeli War of Independence. This huge loss of life was known and remembered throughout the Arab world, as was the subsequent massacre, in September 1982, of Palestinians by Christian Phalangist militias in the Sabra and Shatila refugee camps while Israeli troops stood by.

In his 2004 speech, bin Laden was making a direct connection between US ally Israel's destruction of towers in Beirut and al-Qaeda's destruction of the towers of the World Trade Center nearly two decades later. To a Western audience this was irrelevant, if not nonsensical, but for public opinion across the Middle East it was an all-too-appropriate response. Far from being insane, bin Laden could very easily strike a chord throughout the region and beyond.

TAMING THE JUNGLE

If that represented the thinking and motivation of al-Qaeda in its regional context, what was the political climate in the United States? In the months before the 9/11 atrocities the US political system had undergone a degree of transformation, following the end of the Clinton era. George W. Bush had been narrowly elected in November 2000 and brought in an international outlook that had strong elements of neoconservatism and what is known as 'assertive realism', taking in many of the ideas of the rightist Project for a New American Century think tank. With the Clinton administration having signally failed to demonstrate American leadership in the unipolar post-Cold War era, the deeply held view on the right was that it would be the role of the second Bush to usher in a global American century rooted in the free market.

The change in the political climate was strongest in the areas of defence and foreign policy, but they formed part of a much wider intended repositioning. The United States would take on its rightful role as world leader, a role largely avoided during what were seen as the failed Clinton years, even though the Soviet bloc had been consigned to history. Multilateral agreements were only appropriate if they were in the interests of this outlook, since the United States had a near-religious mission to bring about a better future.

The use of the term 'mission' is entirely appropriate, as the neo-conservative right's belief that the United States had a responsibility to lead the world to a truly civilised state was remarkably intense. In some respects it had its origins in the centuries-old notion of American exceptionalism, in the idea of the 'city upon a hill' as part of the Founding Fathers' escape from degenerate Europe. This new mission at the beginning of the twenty-first century would depend on strong armed forces, not least to tame Woolsey's jungle, but Bush's new secretary of defence, Donald Rumsfeld, considered that the best way to do this would be through 'war lite': the use of high-tech capabilities such as cruise missiles, rather than the deployment of thousands of troops overseas.

This was the outlook of the Bush administration when faced with the sheer shock of 9/11. At the time the disaster was compared with the Japanese attack on Pearl Harbor in December 1941, but its impact was far greater. Pearl Harbor was a military base outside the American mainland; it was bombed by a powerful state whose relations with the United States were already very tense, and all this was in the pre-TV and pre-internet age. In contrast, the attacks of 9/11 hit the heartland of the country and were witnessed live on TV. The blow was visceral and even all these years later the full impact is perhaps not recognised by many people in Europe and across the world. Significantly, the events of that day included not just the high-profile destruction of the twin towers in New York, since the attack on the Pentagon had its own huge impact on one very substantial constituency.

By 2001, a decade after the collapse of the Soviet bloc – Woolsey's 'slaying of the dragon' – the United States was without doubt the world's pre-eminent military power. No one else could touch it. As a result, it came as an appalling shock when a few young men armed with nothing more than utility knives turned a fuel-laden commercial airliner into a devastating cruise-missile attack against the Pentagon. The impact meant that any military action that the forces of the United States were ordered to take against al-Qaeda or any of its associates and supporters was an action against terrorists, pure and simple.

The provocation was intended and worked, but in one crucial respect the Pentagon did not react as the al-Qaeda strategists might have expected. Thus, instead of aiming to occupy Afghanistan with tens of thousands of troops, a process which would have taken many months and given al-Qaeda and the Taliban time to prepare, the US military planned a very different response. This involved a combination of sustained air attacks against Taliban positions, the deployment of special forces and CIA operatives, and the rearming and resupply of the Northern Alliance warlords, all undertaken in a matter of weeks.

The aim was simple: to use the Northern Alliance paramilitaries as 'boots on the ground' and assist with massive air power as these troops moved south to Kabul and beyond, surprising and defeating the Taliban forces – though in the event the latter mostly melted away, with many of their weapons intact. The al-Qaeda fighters were caught by surprise, but most of them also survived, the majority moving into Pakistan and then back to countries across the Middle East, with bin Laden and his closest advisers going to ground in north-western Pakistan.

The success of the US military approach was notable, and by December 2001 it appeared that the war in Afghanistan was over, that the country could move towards a new government under Hamid Karzai and that the Bush administration could anticipate European aid in the rebuilding of the country. In many ways the next two months would mark a pivotal period, culminating in Bush's State of the Union address to both houses of Congress at the end of January 2002, which may well come to be seen as one of the most significant speeches of the twenty-first century, given what it set in motion.

The view in the State Department, the Pentagon and the White House at the end of 2001 was that the American fighting forces had done an extraordinary job in responding to the catastrophe of 9/11. The result may have fallen short of total victory – since Osama bin Laden was still free, as was the Taliban leader, Mullah Omar – but everything else looked like a success, with the threat to the realisation of a 'New American Century' thoroughly beaten back. The expectation was that Afghanistan would make the transition to a pro-Western developing state, one that would constitute a bastion of US influence in the immediate vicinity of Central Asian republics rich in oil and natural gas. This geopolitically important region was subject to Russian and Chinese competition, and now the United States would have a much-enhanced role, not just with US bases established near Kabul and Kandahar but because of the basing agreements successfully negotiated with adjacent republics.

Even more important was the impact on Iran, long seen as the greatest threat to US interests in the Middle East and south-western Asia, but the wider issue was that the world would understand that there was a single superpower, and that it was strong enough to respond effectively to a terrible attack in a matter of weeks. This would be expressed forcefully in the State of the Union address, but even before that there were signs that hugely important factors in this complex situation were being ignored.

One such factor was postwar Afghanistan itself, where the United States expected to retain influence but with little in the way of financial commitments or efforts at security stabilisation. Washington would certainly maintain a military presence and consolidate its new regional links, but there were now other issues to deal with and the White House confidently expected that with the Taliban gone and al-Qaeda dispersed the Europeans could be relied on to aid postwar reconstruction and development. This was in marked contrast to the thinking of experienced UN officials and some senior Afghans, who saw that what had really happened was that the Taliban had melted away rather than being defeated in the conventional sense, that the warlords were vying for territory and resources, and that Afghanistan was at risk of becoming a dangerous security vacuum.

In the event, very few in Washington were concerned about this; most European states were deeply reluctant to provide any kind of substantial stabilisation force and the end result was that a security vacuum did indeed start to emerge. The half-hearted commitments made were at the level of setting up a small International Security Assistance Force (ISAF), with 5,000 troops instead of the 30,000 plus that experienced UN diplomats and Afghan analysts thought necessary. This number might have been enough to ensure a degree of security in Kabul and a few of the larger towns but was totally inadequate to prevent lawlessness and ultimately the return of the Taliban. This was of little initial concern in Washington, but it was surprising, given that some US forces in south-eastern Afghanistan, especially troops from the US Army's 10th Mountain Division, were engaged in difficult fighting with some Taliban and other armed opposition groups (AOGs) as early as the winter of 2001–2.

More generally, the underlying Western view seemed to be that what was being faced was purely a paramilitary problem, to be

dealt with by military means. For many people across the Middle
East and much of Asia it was also an indicator of Western ethno-
centrism and a persistent failure to recognise the deep perception
of marginalisation and even irrelevance, except where Western
interests might be threatened.

THE SPEECH OF THE CENTURY

This was the hidden but crucial context for President Bush's State
of the Union address of 29 January 2002, a speech that elevated
the war against al-Qaeda into a worldwide confrontation. It
was in many ways cathartic for the congressional and wider US
audiences, interspersed as it was with repeated standing ova-
tions, a perfectly understandable reaction given the deep shock
of 9/11.

At this point, the Bush administration could point to the
destruction of the forces behind the 9/11 attacks, but the speech
went much further, setting in motion a global 'War on Terror'
that continues to this day. At the centre of this was the decision
to extend the war to an 'axis of evil', a phrase harking back to
the 'evil empire' characterisation of the Soviet bloc at the time
of the Reagan administration two decades earlier. The axis consisted of three states: North Korea, Iran and especially Iraq. As
Bush put it:

> States like these, and their terrorist allies, constitute an axis
> of evil, arming to threaten the peace of the world. By seeking
> weapons of mass destruction, these regimes pose a grave
> threat and growing danger. They could provide these arms
> to terrorists giving them the means to match their hatred.
> They could attack our allies or threaten to blackmail the
> United States. In any of these cases the price of indifference
> would be catastrophic.[3]

Note, in particular, his emphasis on WMD. This remained a theme throughout the Bush era and still influences thinking, not always because of the risk of an existential attack but because of the ability of such weapons to deter US military intervention. In a key part of his address he continued:

> We'll be deliberate, yet time is not on our side. I will not wait on events, while dangers gather. I will not stand by, as peril draws closer and closer. The United States of America will not permit the world's most dangerous regimes to threaten us with the world's most destructive weapons.[4]

If the 2002 State of the Union address set out an overview of what had to be done, Bush's speech to the West Point Military Academy four months later was notable for spelling out in more detail the problem and the required response. Pointing to the probability of the existence of terrorist cells in more than 60 countries, he singled out the asymmetric nature of the new security environment:

> Enemies in the past needed great armies and great industrial capabilities to endanger the American people and our nation. The attacks of September the 11th required a few hundred thousand dollars in the hands of a few dozen evil and deluded men. All the chaos and suffering they caused came at much less than the cost of a single tank. The dangers have not passed. This government and the American people are on watch, we are ready, because we know the terrorists have more money and more men and more plans.[5]

He went on:

> The war on terror will not be won on the defensive. We must take the battle to the enemy, disrupt his plans, and confront the worst threats before they emerge. In the world we have

entered, the only path to safety is the path of action. And this nation will act.[6]

Pre-emption of future threats was essential and it was clear by June 2002 that the first target would be Iraq.

The latter part of 2002 saw a marked change of attitude to US foreign policy around the world, especially in Western Europe. Public support for the United States in the immediate aftermath of 9/11 was very high, but this began to ebb away as the full extent of an intended global War on Terror became clear. Three governments maintained their support: those of Italy, Spain and especially the United Kingdom, under Tony Blair, but public opposition to a war in Iraq grew rapidly, leading to huge demonstrations as the conflict came closer. In the summer and autumn of 2002, the United States and its likely coalition partners sought approval from the UN Security Council, but what was agreed in an initial resolution was widely considered inadequate as an international legal justification for action.

A further motion was pursued without success, but this at least gave the impression of trying. In reality, the US military was not even ready to go to war until the end of the year. This was mainly because of the urgent need to replenish stocks of armaments, especially precision-guided munitions (PGMs), due to the extensive use of such weapons in the Afghan War of the previous autumn. For some months around the middle of the year, key US weapons manufacturers were organising 24/7 production schedules in order to meet the Pentagon's need to refill the armouries, and this had been accomplished by early 2003.

The operation to terminate the Saddam Hussein regime began in late March 2003, dominated by US forces but with significant contributions from the United Kingdom and a few other countries. Most notably, neither France nor Germany was significantly involved, and Turkey not only stayed out of the conflict but refused to allow the US Army to move a division into northern Iraq through southern Turkey, immediately complicating the operation.

A WAR TOO FAR

One of the curious features of international politics in 2002–3 was the intense focus of the Bush administration on terminating the regime in Baghdad, with very little appreciation of what was happening to the al-Qaeda movement. On and immediately after 9/11, al-Qaeda had been portrayed as a narrowly hierarchical movement controlled by Public Enemy Number One: Osama bin Laden. This was never the complete picture, since although bin Laden was an important figurehead, the movement was more like a franchise, consortium or network. This was shown by the many attacks on US and other Western targets across North Africa, the Middle East and South Asia, often organised by individual groups rather than centrally.

In 2002 alone they included attacks on church worshippers in Islamabad, on German tourists visiting an historic synagogue in Djerba (Tunisia), on French naval technicians in Karachi, on the US consulate in the same city, on the *Limburg* tanker off the coast of Yemen, on the Sari nightclub in Bali and on a hotel in Kikambala in Kenya frequented by Israeli tourists. The next year, 2003, saw multiple bombings in Casablanca, Riyadh, Djakarta and Istanbul, and early in 2004 commuter trains were bombed close to the Atocha rail terminal in Madrid, killing nearly two hundred and injuring over two thousand. Many more attacks followed in 2004 and 2005, including the London Underground and bus bombings on 7 July 2005. All the while, larger al-Qaeda-linked paramilitary groups were developing in Yemen and Somalia, both of which controlled substantial territory, giving them considerable freedom of action.

Two parallel processes were therefore under way. One was the war against al-Qaeda and the Taliban in Afghanistan, together with the action to terminate the Saddam Hussein regime, and the other was the evolution of the al-Qaeda movement into a dispersed transnational entity of loosely linked groups capable of largely independent attacks. In this context, the war in Iraq began and within three weeks appeared to have achieved its aims. The purpose of this chapter is not to analyse in depth the eight-year war that followed, but rather to illuminate those aspects of the wars in Afghanistan and Iraq that were to have a substantial effect on what was to become a particularly robust and determined Islamist paramilitary movement: ISIS.

Following what appeared to be the rapid and successful termination of the regime in Iraq, President Bush was able to make his 'mission accomplished' speech on the flight deck of the USS *Abraham Lincoln* off the California coast on 1 May 2003. In many ways this was the high point of the US War on Terror, but by a remarkable coincidence that very day provided an unexpected demonstration of the fact that the mission had *not* been accomplished, since a young private in the British Army serving in Iraq, Johnson Beharry, was involved in the first of two actions that resulted in his being awarded the United Kingdom's highest military honour, the Victoria Cross.

Within a year of the apparent end of the war in Iraq in April, a bitter and hugely costly insurgency was under way that also spun off into a bitter interconfessional conflict between the Sunni minority and the Shi'i majority. Indeed, even as the US Marines and troops took over Baghdad in early April 2003 there were indications that victory was not at hand, although the rapidity of the advance suggested otherwise in the euphoria of progress. In reality, within three weeks of the start of the advance into Iraq, the US military was having to spend considerable resources in protecting its supply routes from paramilitary attack. Furthermore, while the use of area-impact munitions (AIMs) and other weapons caused huge casualties among the Iraqi Republican Guard divisions to the south and south-east of Baghdad and facing the line of US advance, these were largely expendable. What had happened in the 1990s was that the Saddam Hussein regime had largely ceased to trust these divisions and had consolidated elements known to be loyal into four brigades of the 'Special Republican Guard' and several battalions of troops directly allied to security and intelligence agencies. These forces took little or no part in the fighting, having melted away but retaining access to large quantities of munitions and equipment hidden in numerous locations.

The insurgency that developed over the first six months was aided by four key factors that did much to provide for a robust and determined paramilitary opposition. The first was the decision by Paul Bremer, head of the Pentagon's newly established Coalition Provisional Authority (CPA), to disband the Iraqi Army, sending many tens of thousands of conscripts and professional soldiers into unemployment and the margins of what remained of Iraqi society. From these ranks emerged angry and resentful young men who were only too ready to support the insurgency, which became largely rooted in those determined and well-armed elite forces that had avoided confrontation as the coalition forces had occupied the country. As we will see in Chapter 5, this element went on to fight a bitter and costly war with the US Joint Special Operations Command (JSOC), and from that conflict, in turn, many of the fighters went on to form the hardened and experienced paramilitary core of ISIS.

Closely related to this was the sacking of large numbers of public officials, many of them technocrats, who had been members of the Ba'ath Party. The fact that membership might be a prerequisite for a post did not appear to enter the calculation, and the effect was that thousands of competent professionals – in areas such as transport, energy, water resources, sewage treatment, education and local-authority administration – were left to face unemployment and a bitter future in the deeply damaged Iraqi economy. As with the military, some ended up as technocrats in the towns and cities that came under the control of ISIS a decade later.

The third factor was the behaviour of the US Army and Marine Corps personnel fighting in the country, which was rooted in an outlook that was perfectly understandable but had significant consequences. It is worth bearing in mind that the war in Iraq started barely 18 months after 9/11; these young men and women took it as read that the war was in direct response to the atrocities of that day, the implication being that Iraqis who opposed the occupation were terrorists, part of an axis of evil that represented a fundamental threat to the security of the United States.

Furthermore, these 'terrorists' turned out to be well equipped to engage in urban warfare; sometimes they were even better equipped than the US troops, given their local knowledge. What made it even worse was that within weeks of the start of the occupation the US forces were sustaining serious casualties. Moreover, the nature of these casualties had a particular effect on the morale of the troops and this, in turn, determined their response to the growing insurgency.

In conventional fighting between armed forces in the late twentieth century there was a rule of thumb that, in a well-equipped army, for every soldier killed on the battlefield, three would survive, albeit often with life-changing injuries. By the end of the century this had changed quite dramatically, especially for professional Western forces. General improvements in trauma care in the civilian health services, combined with the military becoming far more adept at battlefield trauma response, rapid casualty evacuation and skilled early stabilisation, had a positive outcome on survival rates. This was especially true for the US Army and Marine Corps, and was aided by the use of increasingly effective body armour. A major effect of this was that far more young men and women survived appalling injuries – recovering, but with lifelong consequences. By the time of the Iraq War, for every person killed on the battlefield, six or more of those wounded were surviving – a remarkable change. The *Boston Globe*, for example, reported at the end of August 2003:

> According to US Central Command, 1,111 US personnel
> have been wounded in action since the start of hostilities,

including 561 since May 1 [the date of the 'mission accomplished' speech]. Over the same period, 178 have been killed
in action, 66 since May 1. According to coalition officials
in Baghdad, allied forces are attacked on average a dozen
times a day.[7]

Perhaps perversely, given the much-improved survival rate, this
had a huge and negative impact on morale. To put it bluntly, far
more young people in the US and other Western forces were surviving with terrible wounds that were likely to lead to long-term
physical and mental disabilities, often with face, throat, urogenital
or bowel injuries, loss of limbs or mental trauma. This meant that
soldiers and marines were experiencing first-hand the effect on
their friends of an enemy made up of terrorists who were opposing
the utterly justified liberation of their country.

One of the advantages held by the coalition forces was overwhelming firepower. If a building housed a sniper who was targeting coalition soldiers, or if an improvised explosive device (IED)
were being controlled from that building, then the answer was
to call in air power and raze it to the ground. This might be an
understandable response given the circumstances, but in densely
populated cities the inevitable result was higher civilian casualties,
which in turn led to increasing bitterness from ordinary Iraqis.
This was one of the aspects of the early months of the Iraq War
that changed the perception of the coalition subtly from that of
liberators to occupiers.

The fourth and final factor concerned the political nature of
the war. From the beginning the United States and its coalition
partners were at pains to represent this as a multinational mission
to liberate a country from a tyranny that was directly implicated
in sponsoring terrorism, and that intended to develop and deploy
WMD in spite of the decade-long inspection programme of the
United Nations Special Commission on Iraq (UNSCOM). The
notion of the regime's support for international terrorism was

dubious at best, not least because the al-Qaeda movement regarded the secular Saddam Hussein regime as entirely unacceptable and part of the near enemy, even if it was itself at odds with the far enemy of the United States and its allies. The WMD issue was more plausible, at least for the first few months of the war, but even by August 2003 the United States was finding itself, along with its coalition partners, facing a singularly bitter insurgency. This required many more troops, and it was felt that it would be highly desirable if those could be supplied by another state, one not already involved, thereby confirming the multinational status of the endeavour.

Most useful would have been a division from a non-Western state, perhaps up to 17,000 troops, that would take over from US forces in the less violent north-eastern regions of Iraq, especially in the country's second city of Mosul and in Kurdish areas, allowing the Pentagon to reinforce its troops in Baghdad and the provinces at the centre of the insurgency. This was not straightforward, however, since the surprising reality of modern military practice is that only a handful of countries worldwide have that kind of capability. They include France, Germany, Russia, China, Turkey, Egypt, Pakistan and India. Of these, domestic opposition ruled out France and Germany, and neither Russia nor China would have been acceptable to Washington, even if willing. Egypt under Hosni Mubarak was far too cautious to intervene alongside the United States in an Arab country, and Turkey had not even been willing to allow a US division to pass through Turkey at the start of the war, let alone commit its own troops to the fray, given the impact on its own substantial Kurdish minority of Turks garrisoning Kurdish Iraq.

Only India and Pakistan were realistic possibilities, but the government in Islamabad was also cautious about intervening in support of the United States in a Muslim country, as well as being focused on maintaining as much influence as possible in Afghanistan, and, at home, on suppressing Islamist paramilitary groups in north-western districts and Balochistan in the south-west. India, therefore, was the one serious prospect, and the nationalist Bharatiya Janata Party (BJP) and its leader, prime minister Atal Bihari Vajpayee, were willing to consider the request. From the perspective of New Delhi, forming part of a Western coalition with the United States could serve as a demonstration that India was a significant player on the international stage. It would also send a stark message to the Pakistanis, showing that India had the spare capacity to play a global role.

The problem lay with Indian domestic opinion, which was markedly hostile to any military involvement with a coalition led by Western states. Whatever the popularity of the BJP and its appeal to nationalist sentiments, too many Indians saw collaboration with the United States, the United Kingdom and other Western powers as proof not of international status but of a willingness to go along with a country that saw itself as the only superpower and that was working towards a New American Century. Vajpayee's government faced state elections later in the year and a general election in 2004.[8]

Such was the level of popular opposition in India to involvement in a Western coalition that the idea was dropped. Though few commentators recognised this at the time, Vajpayee's decision to stay out of the Iraq War was the final factor that ensured that it became almost entirely a Western conflict, one that the Islamist propagandists were all too ready to represent as a powerful and hugely violent crusade against Islam.

A PROPAGANDA BONUS

If these factors – the break-up of the Iraqi Army, the sacking of public officials, the issue of casualties and firepower, and the Indian decision – were crucial to the development of the insurgency, one specific development was an utter gift to the propagandists of al-Qaeda in Iraq as well as in the wider al-Qaeda network. The context for this is that, in the early years of the new century, new social media were already having an impact on information distribution and jihadist groups were becoming adept in their use. These means of communication enabled propagandists to bypass the Western media, which was, in any case, being overtaken by regional 24-hour news channels.

A Western network, the Atlanta-based CNN, had started this media revolution well over a decade previously, getting a huge boost in the 1991 Gulf War, but new networks such as Al Jazeera and Al Arabiya had taken over across the Middle East and were far more potent in their coverage of the post-9/11 environment. They were much less prone to the censoring of images of war than the likes of CNN, Sky or the BBC, and were also more likely to report on output from Islamist propagandists.

What was not recognised by Western analysts was the effect of a combination of new social media, especially the ability to distribute video and audio podcasts with ease, and the opening up of discussions in the Middle East by Al Jazeera and other channels, with far less censorship than before. Taken together, these trends provided far more stimulus for radical interpretation of events and movements whose voices had previously been scarcely heard in the open. This became even more important with the growth of ISIS nearly a decade later, but even by 2003 it was already a significant factor in the increasing knowledge about the insurgency.

Into this media environment in late 2003 came the 'Israel factor'. By September–October, US forces on the ground in Iraq were facing the rapidly growing problem of how to counter the urban insurgency that was causing so many casualties. In such circumstances the US Army and Marine Corps turned to the one close ally that had decades of experience of warfare in the region, Israel, and in the latter part of the year numerous contacts were made, and renewed, with IDF counterparts.

Israel's position had military and political aspects. Of the former, most of the country's wars since independence had been primarily against armies from surrounding Arab states: Egypt and Jordan in 1948; Egypt in 1956; Egypt, Jordan and Syria in 1967; and Egypt and Syria in 1973. The 1982–5 war in Lebanon had been a part-urban and part-rural counter-insurgency, but the direct conflicts with Palestinians had been primarily about controlling dissent against occupation and fell short of urban warfare. That changed markedly with the outbreak of the Second Intifada and its rapid escalation in the early months of 2002. Thus:

> Top Israeli officials candidly admit that they had been plan-ning for the wrong next war. It is obvious, they say, that they made a mistake in ignoring the specter of urban combat while focusing for years almost exclusively on armored warfare and fielding long-range intelligence-gathering and manned strike systems.[9]

This was widely recognised at the time, but what is significant in this context is the manner in which the Israelis adapted rap-idly, retraining many of their units and investing heavily in new weapons and sensors that were directed towards urban counter-insurgency operations. This was why, barely 18 months later, the US armed forces came for advice and assistance.

For example, in early December 2003 the officer in command of the IDF Ground Forces Command, Major General Yiftah Ron-Tal, headed a series of meetings with a US Army team, including the commander of the army's Training and Doctrine Command (TRADOC), the commander of the Infantry School and other senior officers. In the words of one of the few reports of these meetings, which appeared in *Defense News*:

> The goals were two-fold: to strengthen cooperation between US and Israeli ground forces in future warfighting and

military modernization planning, and to evaluate ways in which the US military can benefit from operational lessons Israel has accrued during the past 38 months in its ongoing urban, low-intensity conflict with Palestinian militants.[10]

The journal elaborated on this by quoting a US military source:

Israel has much to offer in the technological realm, while operationally, there are obvious parallels between Israel's experiences over the past three years in the West Bank and Gaza and our own post-offensive operations in Iraq. We'd be remiss if we didn't make a supreme effort to seek out commonalities and see how we might be able to incorporate some of Israel's knowledge into our plans.[11]

Two elements of this statement are illuminating. One is the use of the phrase 'post-offensive operations', indicating that the US military had not come to terms with the reality of the situation, that is, one of ongoing conflict, in what would turn out to be an eight-year war. The other is the more immediate context and its resonance across the Middle East. Just 18 months earlier the Israeli government under Ariel Sharon's leadership was facing a determined Palestinian uprising centred primarily on the West Bank and including suicide attacks in Israeli cities. In my own contemporary analysis:

In Israel itself, the past two weeks have been traumatic, illustrating in a devastating manner the vulnerability of Israeli society to dedicated attackers who are prepared to die for their beliefs. In response to the attacks, the Sharon government has now embarked on a military campaign that is claimed to be designed to limit such attacks but, in reality, has far more substantial aims.[12]

Israel would later exert far more control over the West Bank, including by the building of the wall, but in early and mid-2002 the military campaign involved intensive urban counter-insurgency operations that also aimed to wreck Palestinian administrative infrastructure. The destruction was considerable and widely reported by the regional news media, greatly increasing antagonism towards Israel, the country now aiding the United States in its war in Iraq.

During the course of the next year the IDF worked closely with the US military in a wide range of training operations, one example being the US Army Corps of Engineers' construction of a full-scale mock Arab town, Baladia, in the Negev desert, to be used for the instruction of infantry in house-to-house combat.[13] Over the same period, a number of Israeli military companies worked closely to provide new equipment, even offering prototypes for early examination.

For Islamist propagandists this was like manna from heaven. It had long been central to their message that Islam was under attack both from the far enemy of the West and from that most pernicious manifestation of the near enemy, Israel. Here was proof that the two were working in concert in their determination to push back Islam and exercise full control over the region. The fact that Baghdad, the ancient capital of the greatest of all caliphates, that of the Abbasids (750–1258), was now under occupation was a propaganda bonus. The message was clear: Islam was facing a grievous threat from a pernicious Crusader–Zionist axis and must be resisted by all means. To many people across the Middle East this made eminent sense, but in Western capitals, especially Washington, it was scarcely noticed.

The belief that the West had to be countered by sustained violence and that the insurgents in Iraq were at the centre of this struggle might be held by a very small proportion of Muslims across the Middle East and the wider world, but that is not the point. What was more significant was that this belief was part of a much broader narrative that saw the Islamic world as being on the periphery of world power, marginalised by the United States and its allies, something exacerbated by the West's close relationships with elite regimes and always aided by the presence of nuclear-armed Israel.

A JUNGLE NOT FOR TAMING

By the end of 2005, the war in Iraq had intensified into a major conflict, one that involved around 150,000 foreign troops, drawn mainly from the United States. This was a very long way from Donald Rumsfeld's much-vaunted 'war lite', which had in practice developed, against all expectations, into 'war heavy'. At the same time, the Taliban and other AOGs in Afghanistan were slowly but surely gaining control of territory, especially in the south and south-east of the country, so much so that the NATO-led ISAF was beginning to expand, the main additional deployments coming from early 2006 onwards. As in Iraq, the warning signs had been there very soon after the initial termination of the Taliban regime but had been largely ignored in Washington given the overwhelming focus on Iraq and the remaking of the Middle East.

Meanwhile, al-Qaeda had made a transition from being a movement with a definite centre (in north-western Pakistan), but with many localised supporting groups, to being something approaching an international franchise or consortium. There were still small-scale actions involving individuals or small groups, including the quadruple London bombings of 7 July 2005, but more significant in the longer term was the development of largely separate groups, the most significant being in Yemen and Iraq. The latter, under Abu Musab al-Zarqawi, was the most formidable in terms of direct engagement with Western forces, and while the war in Afghanistan would escalate further in the latter part of the decade it is in central and northern Iraq that the origins of the ISIS movement are to be found.

The emphasis in this chapter may seem odd at first sight – why pick on a number of factors to explain the Iraq failure when only one, the disbanding of the Iraqi Army, has received much attention in the vast number of books and articles written about the war? Why, indeed, put so much emphasis on Iraq itself, largely ignoring Afghanistan, where an even longer war developed? The answer is that this book is primarily concerned with current and future par-amilitary movements and their relevance to wider global-security issues, and, in the Iraq/Afghanistan context, it is Iraq which is the more pertinent. This is partly because of its enduring impact on opinion across the Middle East; it is also because of its direct links with ISIS and its being the focus, along with Syria, of a renewed war. Moreover, the impact of the Iraq War and the mistrust of the West that it greatly exacerbated later became crucial in enabling the developing ISIS to attract far more support than most Western analysts anticipated, in spite of the stark brutality of many of the movement's actions.

Even so, Afghanistan remains relevant, and it is worth a brief discussion in order to answer the question of why the war there developed, apparently from nothing. Moreover, Afghanistan may well have a particular relevance in the future, given that there are elements linked to the Taliban and other AOGs that are now declaring their allegiance to ISIS. How can this be? After all, Bush's 2002 State of the Union address was given at a time when the war seemed over, with Afghanistan having a real chance of post-conflict peace-building supported by a potentially successful relationship with the United States and its European allies.

As discussed earlier, by the end of 2001, with the Taliban regime terminated, the Bush administration was already focused on Iraq, and its European coalition partners did not have the political will to invest heavily in a major stabilisation force. Senior UN and

Afghan analysts believed that a multinational force of 30,000 peacekeepers was necessary to support rebuilding and avoid a vacuum developing that would allow the Taliban to return. That was not forthcoming: barely 5,000 were provided by NATO's ISAF. This was not remotely enough, and by 2005–6 the Taliban and other AOGs were rapidly gaining territory. There followed a huge expansion of ISAF, which eventually numbered more than 130,000 troops. Even that failed to contain the insurgency, and by 2013 the Obama administration had finally decided that Afghanistan, like Iraq, was an unwinnable war.

That takes us back to this chapter's examination of the Iraq War and its emphasis on largely ignored factors: US casualties and their impact, the Indian refusal and the Israeli connection. On the first of these, the point of detailing it is that it is an example of a generic issue throughout the decade and a half of the War on Terror. In Iraq in 2003–4, in particular, US troops and marines on the ground were convinced that anyone opposing them was a terrorist. Their view was that the Saddam Hussein regime was hugely dangerous to the United States, was in some way implicated in terrorism, including 9/11, and was developing WMD. They also believed that the regime was hated by the great majority of Iraqis and expected to be welcomed as liberators. Not only did this not happen, but instead these young men and women were soon sustaining appalling casualties, which were inflicted on them by people who, on the evidence of their actions, were terrorists.

The point is that this was not, and is not, specific to Iraq in the middle of the first decade of the twenty-first century. It is an enduring feature of the wars the United States and its coalition partners have fought with extreme Islamists, whether in Afghanistan, Pakistan, Yemen, Somalia, Nigeria, Mali, Libya, Syria or Iraq. The United States was grievously attacked in 2001, and anyone threatening it or its military is most certainly not a professional soldier worthy of recognition but a terrorist, and must be dealt with accordingly, using massive firepower, rendi-tion, torture or long-term detention without trial. It is a culture developed especially in Iraq in the early years of that war, but one that remains endemic and explains more recent actions, not least against ISIS.

In August 2015, for example, the US defence journal *Air Force Times* reported on the intense bombing of the town of Kobani in northern Syria after it had been taken over by ISIS paramilitaries. In just five months from the beginning of the air war in August 2014, the B-1 strategic bombers of the US Air Force's 9th Bomb Squadron had dropped 1,800 bombs on ISIS targets, 600 of them on Kobani alone. *Air Force Times* quoted an Air Force major, who said: 'To be part of something, to go out and stomp those guys, it was completely overwhelming and exciting.'[14]

But what is the significance of the Indian decision not to provide peacekeepers in late 2003? The answer is that it demonstrates a wider phenomenon, one that remains very largely unrecognised, even by experienced analysts, but is utterly germane to what has happened since and, indeed, to the theme of this book. At the time, Prime Minister Vajpayee believed it was in India's political interests to back the United States, but his own people would have none of it – they simply did not see the war in Manichean terms: as a matter of good versus evil. George Bush said in the immediate aftermath of 9/11, 'Either you are with us, or you are with the terrorists,' but for vast numbers of people across the world it was not simply a matter of 'us' versus 'them'. The United States might have suffered great losses in 9/11, but what might be called the 'majority world' did not consider it to be as important as the Americans and Europeans did.

At root, the idea of the New American Century simply was not seen by much of the world as the right way forward, and the determination of the United States to ensure that this was not derailed by al-Qaeda was questioned continually. If the idea was unacceptable, so too was any part of its attempted implementation.

This is an attitude that persists well over a decade later and is part of a wider world view, yet it is something that most politicians in Europe and especially the United States have great difficulty in even beginning to understand.

Finally, there is the Israeli connection, which again has a much wider resonance than is realised. Israel may feel constantly threatened and be determined to ensure its security by all means necessary, but this determination, with its consequences for the Palestinians, is a running sore of tension right across the region. Many of the regional autocrats have long been happy to see the plight of the Palestinians draw attention away from their own repression, since the Israelis were always there to blame and therefore served a useful purpose. For Israel, too, dealing with neighbouring autocracies was in many ways preferable to responding to regimes that were representative of wider opinion. Yet the reality was that Israel's control of Islam's Third Holy Place (Jerusalem, known in Arabic as al-Quds) was a source of enduring anger, something that also encompassed deep opposition to US support for Israel. This is the reason that, when the Pentagon turned to the IDF for advice and equipment in late 2003, it had a far greater effect than was realised in the West, where it was scarcely even reported.

This factor remains relevant today, as demonstrated graphically by the reaction across the Middle East to the Israeli 'Operation Protective Edge' in Gaza in 2014. Widely seen TV footage showed buildings being attacked in two stages: first an unarmed missile would strike to warn of impending destruction, and then the building would be blown apart and collapse into rubble. Supporters of Israel pointed to the unguided rockets being fired into Israel and to the Israelis' right of self-defence, but at the root of the deep antagonism to Israel's actions was a feeling of impotence – Hamas had no direct answer to the destruction wrought by the Israelis and this led to bitter frustration and anger across the region and beyond. For many people it went further, in that Operation Protective

Edge could be seen as an American operation, with Israelis mere surrogates, flying US-built planes and firing US-manufactured missiles with Israeli markings.

Such an interpretation may seem remarkable to most people in the West, but not to people across the Middle East, where it fits in with the wider narrative of external control, one easily reinforced by seeing the Iraq War as not far short of a US–Israeli operation – a Crusader–Zionist plot. The overwhelming majority of Palestinians will have nothing to do with al-Qaeda or ISIS, but for both movements Israel is a welcome focus for anger across the region.

By 2005, the war in Iraq was well under way and was also developing into a bitter interconfessional Sunni–Shi'a conflict. It would go on to claim more than 100,000 lives, with far more seriously injured, and in many ways it was a greater gift to extreme Islamists than the occupation of Afghanistan. It helped ensure that al-Qaeda and its associates got a new lease of life, something that was aided by the destruction wreaked by coalition firepower, the fact that it came more and more to be seen as a Western war, and the way in which it could usefully be presented as a US–Israeli operation. From this environment, ISIS arose, most certainly not out of nowhere.

The war and what followed spawned a new generation of jihadist movements, but the most potent of these, ISIS, had very specific origins in the later part of the Iraq War. These, among other aspects, need to be examined if we are to appreciate the nature and significance of the phenomenon. The purpose of offering so much detail of the effects of the recent wars on wider global opinion, especially among so many Muslims across the Middle East and North Africa, is to emphasise the suspicion and distrust of the West that remains embedded. This needs a much more general examination if we are to look to the future, not just in relation to ISIS and other dangerous movements, but in the context of deeply competitive world views.

Why bother? Can we not just accept that extreme movements will arise and must be defeated, especially if they gain control of territory and have the potential to develop WMD? The answer is that we need to bother if we are to have any chance of understanding the need for radically new approaches. The War on Terror may have been a failure, but the 'control paradigm' – the imperative of maintaining control – remains at the root of the Western approach to security.

If it were the case that all we had to do was to respond to the occasional emergence of extreme movements, it might be possible to make that argument, even though we would still have to face up to the failures since 9/11. But this book argues something much more fundamental: that there are trends in world society now evolving, rooted in the dangerous interaction of socio-economic marginalisation and environmental constraints, that make the disastrous experience since 9/11 hugely pertinent to how Western states face their future.

3

CONFLICTING NARRATIVES
AND AN ENVIRONMENT FOR REVOLT

By early 2004, nearly a year into the Iraq War, the United States and its decreasing number of coalition partners were fighting a fierce insurgency, most of it centred on Baghdad and the provinces to the north and west of it. One of the key centres of opposition was Fallujah, about 40 miles to the west of Baghdad, where the US Marines had established a number of forward operating bases as they fought to gain control of the city and its surrounding countryside.

For the marines themselves, the Iraqis were not just opponents, they were terrorists who were determined to prevent a free and democratic United States from liberating their country from a regime that was implicated in the 9/11 atrocities. This was their very clear view, just as it was for most Americans back home, yet they were facing determined and violent opposition that would simply not give in to what the marines saw as a just and righteous operation. The frustration in Fallujah became intense and one illustration of the difference in outlooks came with a particular incident, or rather its immediate aftermath.

One day in April, a convoy was on its way into the city to resupply a forward base when it was ambushed by insurgents. Seventeen of the marines were separated from the main convoy and forced to take shelter from the intensive attack in a nearby building. A substantial force of marines, including four tanks and six Humvees, supported by air power, was sent to extricate them, but it was a difficult operation against determined opponents and took three hours, killing at least 20 insurgents in the process.

All of the marines were successfully evacuated, albeit with some injuries, but it was what happened next, a few hours after the incident, that was more significant, as reported by Pamela Constable, an experienced *Washington Post* journalist who was embedded with the marines:

> Just before dawn, Wednesday [...] AC-130 Spectre gunships launched a devastating punitive raid over a six-block area around the spot where the convoy was attacked, firing dozens of artillery shells that shook the city and lit up the sky. Marine officials said the area was virtually destroyed and that no further insurgency has been seen there.[1]

The AC-130, a variant of the Lockheed Hercules C-130, is fitted with powerful guns, including a howitzer, which fire sideways as the plane circles its target. It is a formidable system, one developed and used to devastating effect during the Vietnam War. As Constable makes clear, this was a punitive or reprisal raid, which 'virtually destroyed' six blocks of a crowded city. There is no way of knowing the number of civilians killed, whether scores or hundreds, but it is fair to assume that the impact on anti-Americanism was considerable. If a reprisal of this kind had been carried out by German forces during World War II there would most likely have been an attempt to bring those responsible to face a war-crimes tribunal afterwards, but to the US Marines, fighting a difficult war against a determined opponent, what they were up against were terrorists. To many Iraqis and others it was the Americans who were the terrorists.

What was in evidence in this instance in Fallujah, as so often since 9/11, was a clash of outlook, each side seeing itself as absolutely right and completely unable to see beyond its own point of view. It is a phenomenon that has to be recognised if we are to have any chance of understanding the nature of the violence that has escalated since 9/11. One of the ongoing problems for any Western observer trying to understand the sudden rise of ISIS and other extreme movements, such as al-Qaeda, Boko Haram or the Naxalites, is the difficulty with coming to terms with how 'we' (that is, the West) are perceived. There is almost always an assumption that the countries of the West are 'the good guys' who behave in a civilised way, even in the face of appalling brutality and sheer terrorism. This is not a peripheral issue, since it lies at the heart of how the major Western states see the earlier rise of al-Qaeda and the more recent development of ISIS.

There is no doubt that acts designed to cause fear and terror have been a long-term feature of extreme transnational movements such as al-Qaeda, with 9/11 being the most devastating example. Nor is there any doubt that there has been endemic brutality by the Taliban, Boko Haram and many others, including ISIS. What is therefore difficult for Western observers to understand is the popularity of such movements. It seems extraordinary, for example, that Muslim children in schools in Western Europe could paste photos of Osama bin Laden into their school books in the weeks after 9/11, or that there was even some support for Saddam Hussein after the coalition occupation of Iraq. Even more astonishing is the idea that some teenage women want to join ISIS as 'jihadi brides'. If 'we', the West, represent the civilised world, willing to aid the poor and use our armies to fight for justice against despots and terrorists, how can we possibly be so mistrusted, if not hated?

If there is to be any understanding of why extreme movements maintain support and why Western states are seen as a threat, then these issues have to be explored. Moreover, it goes further than this. As was discussed in Chapter 2, one of the main reasons Iraq ended up as essentially an American war was the inability of the Vajpayee government in India to garner enough support to aid the US in its request for troops. This meant that the majority of Indian voters saw the Iraq War as a Western venture, symptomatic of a wider attitude and a very different world view, even as the dominant economic narrative of the free market is followed in their country. Commentators within India were not at all surprised that the BJP government could not drum up the necessary support, but in Washington it was both a shock and seen as a misjudgement.

A CLASH OF WORLD VIEWS

To explore this, it is instructive to consider our own underlying assumptions before looking at the broad factors that underpin other narratives. Then it is essential to examine aspects of the War on Terror, not least in Afghanistan and Iraq, that provide specific support for extreme movements, before turning specifically to the circumstances that gave rise to the current incarnation of extreme Islamism – ISIS.

Any Western government or, indeed, society, will have a wide range of attitudes to itself and others, yet there are norms – overarching views that are acceptable to most, varying somewhat from country to country. For example, one deep-seated view, most advanced in the United States, is that the West is the core of the free world, with the United States as the leader. This view may have peaked with the idea of the New American Century, as exemplified by the Bush administration in the early years of the twenty-first century, yet the vision of the West as the custodian of civilised values resonates more widely. It is deeply embedded in political attitudes, to the extent that the values embraced by the Universal Declaration of Human Rights (1948), and by various manifestations of legislative democracy and the free-market system, are seen as essentially Western. It is a view that owes much of its origins to the Cold War, and that then got a huge boost from the collapse of the Soviet model.

Our beneficence is shown by our foreign-aid programmes and our commitments to Oxfam, Save the Children and the rest, as well as by our internationalism and our opposition to terrorism. Indeed, it is demonstrated by our willingness to act as the world's police force in Kosovo, Sierra Leone and elsewhere. From such a standpoint, extreme violent groups that oppose the West are also opposing such values. Al-Qaeda and ISIS are therefore terrorist organisations, nothing more, with no political legitimacy. They are violent, extreme and essentially nihilistic. Even talking in terms of them having political aims is giving them status that is nonsensical for groups that are basically evil.

There are gradations of this view, although in the aftermath of the 9/11 attacks it was very much the hard-line end of the spectrum that dominated. The West was under attack, and for the Bush presidency it was simply a matter of 'you are with us or against us' – there was no middle way. This is hardly surprising given the catastrophic nature of the attacks, which occurred at a time when US exceptionalism, if not neoconservatism, was the order of the day. This view of Islamist movements inevitably leads to near-incredulity about the fact that they can attract support – yet they do, and in substantial numbers.

Staying with the 'us' (the West as a whole, together with elites elsewhere who have embraced the Western outlook) and 'others' (for the purposes of this discussion those in the Middle East and the wider world who have sympathy for aspects of the Islamist outlook), a consistent surprise is the manner in which the view from 'the other' is so radically different from ours. If we are to make sense of the motivations and attitudes of supporters of extreme movements, we need to recognise and accept the existence of very different world views.

There are both general and specific reasons for the widespread and quite often intense suspicion of the West that exists in much of the world, and that stretches frequently into hatred. Some of the general views relate to the Middle East, but others are more global. These global attitudes need recognising, though, because they help frame the more specific narrative of the Islamist radical.

One reason is the legacy of the colonial era, even though that started to come to an end nearly 70 years ago, and even though it was followed in much of the Middle East and across the Global South by autocracies that were every bit as brutal as their imperial forebears. Even so, the prevailing attitude is put succinctly by an old West African quip that 'the reason the sun never set on the British Empire was that God didn't trust the British in the dark'. To crack that joke in late-Victorian London, at a time when the Pax Britannica was firmly believed to be bringing civilisation to a backward if not barbarous world, would have meant being met with blank stares, but it most certainly represented the view from below.

The belief in the colonial era as a period of progress persisted for many decades, conveniently ignoring the fact that colonialism was principally about power and exploitation for economic gain, and that the 'progress' was enforced by numerous brutal wars. Go to any regimental museum of the British Army and there you will see recorded the many valiant encounters with the 'natives' as the jungle, desert or savannah was tamed and brought into the civilising empire. You will have to search hard to find museums chronicling the appalling behaviour of Belgian forces in King Leopold's Congo, or the brutal methods used by the British, French and other colonial powers to suppress dissent. Little is made of the near-genocide of the indigenous peoples of Tasmania or, for that matter, of the ethnic cleansing that accompanied the 'opening up' of the American West. It is not a little ironic that one of the helicopter gunships available to NATO to prevent ethnic cleansing in the former Yugoslavia was called the 'Apache'. How many in the United Kingdom are aware of the British development of the concentration-camp system during the Boer War?

Fast-forward to the end of the colonial era and contrast the British view of the utter barbarity of the Mau Mau rebels and their opposition to benign colonial rule in mid-1950s Kenya with what has more recently come to light of the full extent of the violence inflicted on thousands of Kenyans as the authorities sought to suppress the uprising. Recall the opprobrium meted out to the few politicians who dared criticise the behaviour of British Army interrogators during the Cyprus emergency of the late 1950s, or note the singular lack of awareness of the French suppression of the Malagasy Uprising in 1946–8, in which the French were responsible for the deaths of more than 80,000 people.

There are some exceptions, such as the wide recognition of the extreme methods of suppression used by the United States in Vietnam, with 'gook kills', free-fire zones and the rest, but the reality is that there remains a stubborn belief that these are either exceptions or the result of the actions of 'bad apples', rather than a recognition of an endemic issue of control through violence.

As was emphasised earlier, this is in no way to diminish the violence and terror of recent and current extreme movements, but our concern is with the wider issue of how the West is perceived, and it is one that can best be addressed at two levels. One is that, in any major conflict, typically there is appalling behaviour by all sides engaged. Violence against women is endemic; prisoners are killed rather than detained; villages and towns are pounded into rubble; and napalm and its successors, the cluster bomb and multiple rocket launcher, are used to maximise the killing. This behaviour has been routine, whether American, British, French, Russian, Chinese – and so on. But national cultural norms insist that 'we' are not like that. The reality is that we are, and this is an appropriate context for trying to understand the current antagonism towards the West, especially across the Middle East.

The second, broader level concerns the widespread view in the Global South that an enduring feature of the colonial era was the creation of a world economic and trading system that was, and remains, hugely beneficial to the West. That may have altered somewhat in the past two or three decades, but in that time it has been paralleled by the 'Washington Consensus' within the world's financial organisations, especially the IMF and the World Bank. This has involved the insistence that financial and other kinds of aid from such bodies be linked to moves to ensure greater market freedom, including privatisation and deregulation, an insistence that has engendered much anger.

The perception goes further, recognising that Western control is now all too often indirect. Western corporations may contract the production of goods to local companies and any labour exploitation is, at best, hidden. The view from the majority margins is that what is increasingly seen as a transnational elite system, in which local people of power are indistinguishable from the exploiting state, must be opposed. At the root of this, though, is the deep-seated belief that whatever the involvement of local elites, the problem lies with the West, and most of all with the United States. Even though direct colonial role by the United States was relatively limited, that country is seen as the ultimate controller of the system.

NOW ADD THE WAR ON TERROR

That is the general background, to which we should add more specific factors, arising from the War on Terror. These attract little attention in the West on their own but have a considerable impact across much of the majority world, especially in the Middle East and South Asia. We can, for example, get some idea of the perspectives of people in these regions by taking just a few examples from Afghanistan and Iraq. They speak of a culture of killing and abuse that is rarely reported.

In the first few weeks of the Afghan War, as the United States sought to use its air power to destroy Taliban paramilitaries, there was much talk of using PGMs to 'take out' targets without causing civilian deaths and other 'collateral damage'. In practice, it later became clear that there had been numerous civilian casualties: one survey of just 11 sites of air attacks indicated that as many as 400 civilians had been killed.[2] Furthermore, much less discussed was the repeated use of AIMs designed to work over a very wide area, many of them based on cluster munitions or fuel-air explosives. They were effectively the successors to napalm.

To take an older example, in the first weeks of the Falklands/ Malvinas War more than 30 years ago, the media in the United Kingdom made much of the Argentine Air Force's appalling use of napalm, but virtually nothing was said about the British use of cluster munitions, which had long since replaced napalm in the RAF inventory. The standard UK cluster weapon was the BL755, made by Hunting Engineering, which was dropped from strike aircraft and programmed to dispense 147 bomblets over an area about the size of a football pitch. Each bomblet then exploded and released around 2,000 high-velocity shrapnel fragments, with anyone caught in the open being simply shredded.[3]

The United States used AIMs such as cluster weapons repeatedly in the Afghan War, and also brought in and used what was then the world's most powerful non-nuclear bomb, the BLU-82B, known as the 'Big Blue', containing 6.8 tonnes of high explosive. Hardly any news of this ever made it into the Western media, but it became well known not just in Afghanistan itself but across the region. For the West this was a fully justified response to the 9/11 atrocities, but elsewhere it could readily be seen as the use of excessive force, very often against people who had had no direct involvement in 9/11.

The second element of Western behaviour relating to Afghanistan was the rapid application of the process of rendition, frequently to countries practised in many forms of torture. Even those detained without trial at the US base in Cuba's Guantánamo Bay would be subject to tough treatment in the process, starting with a preparation phase described thus in a recent academic analysis:

[A] 'twenty minute takeout' [was] designed to reduce the detainee to 'a state of almost total immobility and sensory deprivation'. Detainees would be stripped, often by having their clothes cut from their body. They would be gripped from all sides throughout the process, and often punched, kicked or shoved. When naked, they were photographed, and be subjected to a full cavity examination. Suppositories were often administered anally, before being dressed in a diaper and a tracksuit or boiler-suit (jump-suit). Detainees were then blindfolded, sometimes after having cotton wool taped to their eyes. Headphones or ear defenders were placed on their ears, sometimes with loud music played through them. Loose hoods were then placed over the head, which reached down over the shoulders. Hands and feet were shackled, and may then have been connected to other detainees. During transfer, detainees were generally chained to a stretcher, a mattress, or the floor of these aircraft, either spread-eagled or with their hands behind their backs. No toilet breaks were provided, with detainees required to defecate or urinate into their diapers.[4]

Harsh treatment at Guantánamo often included beatings, and 'high-value suspects' were routinely tortured. Khalid Sheikh Mohammed, believed to be key to the 9/11 plot, was reportedly waterboarded 183 times. While many detainees were eventually released, especially during Obama's first term in office, of the 779 men detained from January 2002 onwards, more than 150 were still in Guantánamo in May 2011, and, in June 2013, 46 were reported to be detained indefinitely, without trial. Knowledge of treatment at Guantánamo and elsewhere eventually came to light and made it into the Western media, but long after it was known in all its detail across the Middle East.

Throughout the war in Iraq, as in Afghanistan, tens of thousands of people, mostly but not all men, were detained, often for years on end, and the abuse reported at Abu Ghraib near Baghdad was not limited to that prison, nor to the US military. Little has come out about British abuse of prisoners, although a few retired army chaplains will acknowledge it privately, some deeply troubled by what they witnessed. In the United States, the United Kingdom and other coalition powers, only a few examples have been examined in any depth and a handful of military offenders brought to court.

In Iraq, many thousands of civilians were killed by coalition air raids, while others died more directly as US troops faced unexpected opposition. One incident was cited at the beginning of this chapter, but there were others that were just as indicative – not significant to the West but hugely so in Iraq and across the Middle East. An example is an incident in the early stages of the war, as US troops got to Baghdad, which was reported in the *International Herald Tribune*:

> Reporters at the scene said the Marines had trouble distinguishing between fighters and civilians. Cars and pedestrians were spotted on the western side of the bridge, including an old man with a cane, looking confused. When he failed to heed three warning shots by the Marines, they shot him, according to an account by an Associated Press reporter. A red van and an orange-and-white taxi were also riddled with bullets after they failed to heed warning shots.[5]

In all of these examples, three aspects should be remembered. First, to repeat what was said at the beginning, none of this remotely excuses the brutality of paramilitary and other groups, but what is essential is that we recognise the impact of these and scores of other incidents on the opinions of ordinary people in Iraq, Afghanistan and other states that have experienced Western intervention during the War on Terror. For all too many of them they are confirmation that Western states do not bring freedom but occupation. In these circumstances it is only too easy for Western states to be portrayed as invaders and violent and repressive occupiers.

Second, the behaviour of Western forces owes much to the utter belief, especially among US troops in the early years of the wars, that they were fighting in response to the 9/11 atrocities and against enemies that were in some way implicated in the attacks. After all, their president and commander-in-chief had himself made clear that they were fighting an 'axis of evil' consisting of states espousing terrorism and seeking WMD. Thus, anyone opposing what were utterly legitimate military operations was necessarily a terrorist. The problem was that this was not how it was seen from the other side.

Then, finally, there is the issue of communication. The advent of multiple 24-hour TV news channels, the World Wide Web and numerous social-media outlets has been transformational, ensuring that much more is known in the region of the actions of the near and far enemies. This is how deeply oppositional attitudes have evolved, and the situation is continually exacerbated by rumour and propaganda.

One of the most difficult factors for Westerners to grasp is the impact of the Israel–Palestine conflict on public opinion across the Middle East, discussed in Chapter 2. While there is some popular support for the Palestinian cause in the West, more noticeable in Western Europe than in the United States, there is scarcely any recognition of this impact. Israel presents itself to the West as a bastion of civilised values, beset by terrorism and movements determined to destroy it. The appalling enormities of the Holocaust remain at the forefront of thinking, but Israel's attitude has been hardened by the influx of many hundreds of thousands of Russian and Ukrainian immigrants in the 1990s. They came from thoroughly insecure and marginalised environments and have been even more determined than most Israelis to place a premium on security. In a real sense, therefore, at the root of the Israeli situation is a state that is impregnable in its insecurity.

From a Middle Eastern perspective the situation is entirely different. Israel is seen as a Western construct that cannot exist without the constant and considerable support of the United States. It is regarded as an aggressive, expansionist country that has engaged in near-continual war for close to 70 years and been able to act with impunity. Moreover, it controls Jerusalem, including Haram al-Sharif, the Third Holy Place of Islam, and persistently suppresses Palestinian aspirations, leaving an entire people without a state. In this view, the century-old Zionist dream of 'a land without people for a people without a land' was fatally flawed from the start because the reality was of a people being systematically dispossessed of their land.

Any attempt at independent analysis is replete with difficulties as each narrative seems utterly reasonable to the party concerned. Opinion in the Middle East rarely acknowledges the preparedness of regional autocrats to work with Israel, or the usefulness to those regimes, at the very same time, of focusing on Palestinian travails as a diversion from their own suppression of domestic rights. Israelis see Hamas and other radical Palestinian groups solely as threats to their state's existence and cannot begin to understand the impact of the media's reporting from Gaza of successive Israeli attacks and the thousands of people killed and districts razed to the ground. Of all the elements of the 'view from the other' across the Middle East, and for all the arguments and counter-arguments, the position of the Palestinians does more to aid extreme Islamist movements than any other issue.

Much of what has happened since 9/11 – the wars across the Middle East and South Asia, the rise of extreme movements in sub-Saharan Africa and attacks on Western targets across many other countries – has stemmed directly from the vigorous if expected response to 9/11, principally by the United States.

Even so, before examining the manner in which the most recent manifestation of extreme Islamist paramilitarism has developed, it is worth noting that even as the war in Afghanistan was being prepared for in September and October 2001, there were voices advocating other approaches and warning of an era of endless war. Such voices found it remarkably difficult to be heard, especially in the United States, and that war was imminent was almost universally assumed to be the case and accepted across Western Europe and North America.

THINKING FROM THE MARGINS

There was other thinking. A detached view of the immediate reaction to 9/11 came from Walden Bello, the noted Filipino intellectual and analyst of North–South relations. Having condemned the 9/11 attacks, he wrote:

> The only response that will really contribute to global security and peace is for Washington to address not the symptoms but the roots of terrorism. It is for the United States to re-examine and substantially change its policies in the Middle East and the Third World, supporting for a change arrangements that will not stand in the way of the achievement of equity, justice and genuine national sovereignty for currently marginalised peoples. Any other way leads to endless war.[6]

Bello wrote these words as an immediate response to the 9/11 atrocities and was joined by a few other analysts who swam against the tide of a widespread demand for a fully fledged War on Terror. An early analysis from the Oxford Research Group (ORG), of which I was co-author, published a few weeks after 9/11, contrasted the views of the majority and minority worlds:

Today the majority view is of a world dominated by an elite that acts primarily in its own interests, seeking to maintain a global economic system that is deeply flawed, singularly failing to deliver economic justice, and demanding of radical change. In the context of the Bush administration, Western Europe lies somewhere in between, troubled by the seeming extremism of the current US approach, and just possibly receptive to an alternative view. It may not be a fundamental difference but it offers real prospects for positive change and certainly is the most important feature of the transatlantic divide.

What is undeniable is that the disasters of 11 September are bringing this whole class of paradigms to the fore in a wholly unexpected and specific form, giving it an immediacy that is quite remarkable. There is little doubt that the outcome of the efforts of the United States and some close allies to regain control after the recent traumatic events will affect international security for years to come. It is also clear that the present situation offers an opportunity for understanding the profound issues of our age, for wise action and for international political leadership of a high order.[7]

That opportunity was not grasped, and the War on Terror persisted with new manifestations, especially those stemming from an extreme Islamist perspective. While the origins of ISIS lie primarily in the latter stages of the war in Iraq, the escalation of the war in Afghanistan after 2005 is highly relevant, especially in the further evolution of al-Qaeda and its loose affiliates. The war there started at the end of 2001 and is likely to continue into the 2020s. Yet again, it is seen from the United States as a necessary war against a terrorist foe, but across the wider Middle East and South Asia as a continuing Western attempt to maintain control.

THE AFGHAN FAILURE

George W. Bush's first State of the Union address in January 2002 was rooted in the assumption that al-Qaeda had been dispersed and hugely weakened, even if Osama bin Laden and Ayman al-Zawahiri had not been killed or captured. Furthermore, the Taliban had been driven from power and was nowhere to be seen, even though its leader, Mullah Omar, had also escaped. The United States would maintain a presence and keep up its useful basing connections with Central Asian republics, and its European allies would step in to ensure the postwar reconstruction and development of Afghanistan. Meanwhile the Iraqi regime of Saddam Hussein was now the main enemy and the regime had to be terminated.

What was striking about the political mood in Washington in the early months of 2002 was that attention was so fixated on the coming war with Iraq that very clear warning signs from Afghanistan were either ignored or discounted. It was simply assumed that the Afghan War was over. Two incidents from that time indicated otherwise. One occurred in March 2002, when intelligence suggested that a sizeable group of Taliban and al-Qaeda paramilitaries was concentrated near the town of Gardez in eastern Afghanistan. To counter this, a large force of US Special Operations Command (USSOCOM) troops working with Afghan Army personnel was assembled and transported by helicopter to intercept the rebels and capture or kill them.[8]

This was 'Operation Anaconda', which was planned in detail over a lengthy period, but almost from the start the US forces found that their opponents were far more competent and better-armed than expected. The US forces suffered serious casualties; two helicopters were destroyed and several more damaged, and most of the guerrillas were able to escape. It is not clear from published documents whether or not the problem was poor intelligence, but another incident, in January 2002, two months earlier, had turned

out to be based on entirely false intelligence and became one of
the worst military disasters of the entire war.

Having what was considered to be reliable evidence of a substantial gathering of Taliban, a special-forces team was assembled
and dispatched and duly succeeded in killing or capturing the
suspects. Following the raid, AC-130 gunships were deployed to
destroy what remained of the compound that had been attacked.
The problem was that the intelligence on which the operation
was based was deliberately falsified by a source that wanted this
group eliminated for its own purposes, a group that included two
district governors but had no links with the Taliban. The result of
the operation was:

> twenty-one pro-American leaders and their employees
> dead, twenty-six taken prisoner, and a few who could not be
> accounted for. Not one member of the Taliban or al-Qaeda
> was among the victims. Instead, in a single thirty-minute
> stretch the United States had managed to eradicate both
> of Khas Uruzgan's potential governments, the core of any
> future anti-Taliban leadership – stalwarts who had outlasted
> the Russian invasion, the civil war, and the Taliban years
> but would not survive their own allies[9]

US counter-insurgency operations continued over the next three
years, but at a low level, and even by late 2003, while the Western
media was fixated on Iraq, there were clear indications that the
Taliban was regaining territory. The UN under-secretary general
for peacekeeping operations, Jean-Marie Guéhenno, reported to
the Security Council that many causes of insecurity remained
unresolved and that in districts close to the Pakistan border the
Taliban had been able to gain de facto control over district administration. The following August, US military sources acknowledged
that Kandahar Province's north-eastern districts were effectively
Taliban strongholds. This had little effect in Washington and was

scarcely noticed by its coalition partners, even those who had troops deployed in Afghanistan. In time, though, the coalition came to realise that it was underestimating the extent of its predicament. As so often since, the narrative of the West maintaining order in a disorderly world was dominant.

By August 2006, and with the insurgency intensifying, a substantial increase in US and other NATO forces was under way, just as another factor was becoming clear, one that may well be relevant for some decades. This was that there were now worrying indications that the experience gained by paramilitaries in Iraq was being transferred to Afghanistan, and foreign troops were facing serious difficulties:

> American commanders are troubled both by the ability of the Taliban to operate in large numbers and that the guerrilla fighters have displayed a level of tactical sophistication unseen since the US invasion of Afghanistan in 2001. Additionally worrisome has been the migration of weapons and tactics more commonly found in Iraq to the Afghan battlefield.[10]

The transfer of weapons and tactics between apparently unconnected rebellions was unexpected but became a feature of the war, not unlike the manner in which combat experience gained by the mujahidin against the Soviets in 1980s Afghanistan had fed into the Taliban's civil war against the Northern Alliance warlords in the mid-1990s. That experience fed through into Iraq after 2003 and then came back to Afghanistan as ways were found to counter the wide range of weapons, sensors and equipment available to the Americans and their allies.

During the course of the six months to November 2006, US forces mounted more than 2,000 air strikes against a resurgent Taliban as they and their coalition partners took the total overseas troop presence in the country to 100,000. These forces were held at this level for the next two years, yet it was still Iraq that was dominating the defence outlook in Washington, with the war becoming increasingly unpopular within the United States as the deaths and injuries among US troops continued to rise. The Bush administration did its best to minimise the publicity, seeking to avoid the cortèges from military airports that had such an effect in the United Kingdom, but this could not disguise what was happening. Across the United States, local news media were reporting the deaths of young men and women and the terrible injuries suffered by many more.

By early 2008 this had had a cumulative effect, and it was one factor that enabled Barack Obama to fight his presidential campaign on a policy of withdrawing troops from Iraq. Even so, if Iraq was a 'bad war' and a mistake, Afghanistan was seen by his campaign as a 'good war', primarily because it had a much clearer link with the 9/11 attacks. When Obama formed his administration in early 2009, the process began of disengaging from Iraq, but the more problematic issue was Afghanistan. After many months of consideration, some would say procrastination, the administration decided to send an additional 30,000 troops into Afghanistan, but the policy was to gain such an advantage over the Taliban insurgents that it would then be possible to negotiate a withdrawal from a position of strength.

Even with 100,000 US troops and more than 30,000 other NATO personnel in Afghanistan by 2011, it became clear that the Taliban was not being weakened, and by 2013 the Obama team determined a timetable for withdrawal by the end of 2014. A residual force of up to 10,000 troops would be retained for training Afghan Army units, and to insure against the return of al-Qaeda and other Islamist paramilitaries, but that would be all that was left of the NATO forces. By late 2014 this process was nearing completion in the face of serious worries that the Taliban would then return in force, ensuring a substantial role in the future governance of the country.

Throughout the following year, the Taliban revival continued, and by the end of 2015 the Obama administration had come to accept that its long-vaunted aim of withdrawing all US combat troops from Afghanistan before the president left office would not be achieved. Into the fifteenth year of the war, at least 5,000 and possibly many more troops would remain in the country, and it was simply not possible to say for how long.

Although the retreat from Afghanistan could be seen as a victory for Islamist extremism, the Taliban was, and is, primarily a nationalist and ethnic entity rather than one that is intentionally transnational. Because of this, the apparent success in Afghanistan so far has not proved central to the development of ISIS, which relates far more to a series of developments in Iraq stretching back to 2004. These need serious examination, because the implications of what happened, especially over the period from 2004 to 2008, are highly significant in terms of the future development of anti-Western paramilitary movements. This will be explored in Chapter 5 in assessing the current status of ISIS, its capabilities and long-term significance, a significance that goes well beyond the risk from specifically Islamist movements.

COMBAT TRAINING FOR PARAMILITARIES – COURTESY OF THE WEST

Before we do that, though, there is one point to emphasise, one that was touched on briefly above and will most likely be an enduring feature of conflict with extreme Islamists in the coming years. Indeed, it is relevant to the overall thesis of this book: that the War on Terror gives us an indication of the nature of future conflicts, which may have very different causes and little or nothing to do with extreme Islamist ideas. This is the combat training that is a fundamental part of being involved in conflict. The quotation above about combat-skills transfer from Iraq refers to the concern of US commanders in Afghanistan a decade ago about 'the migration of weapons and tactics more commonly found in Iraq to the Afghan battlefield'. This was, and is, part of a wider phenomenon, one that can be traced back over more than three decades, with various periods producing additional cohorts of paramilitary fighters.

During most of the 1980s, the Soviet Union was opposed by mujahidin insurgents, who eventually succeeded in evicting the Russians from the country. While they were aided and supported by the Pakistani ISI and the CIA, they were largely on their own in the actual combat. Some of them were motivated by religious belief, essentially radical Islam, but most were primarily nationalists or concerned with their own clan loyalties. Even from the early 1980s, though, there were paramilitary fighters going to Afghanistan to aid the fight against the Soviets, and these 'Arab-Afghans', as they were known, played a significant role almost from the start.[11]

In the latter part of the war, essentially between 1984 and 1988, the insurgency was aided by thousands more young men, who came to join the fight against the Soviets from right across the Middle East, but especially from Saudi Arabia, Yemen and Libya. They included the young Osama bin Laden, although he was primarily a logistician, and they, along with the mujahidin, gained huge experience fighting against the Soviet conscripts, mostly in rural Afghanistan. Many of these determined young men were killed and others were maimed for life, but many more retained their combat skills and technical knowledge. Though most returned to their own countries at the end of the 1980s, there was a corpus of knowledge and experience that could be passed on to others or that they could use themselves if they returned to Afghanistan in the mid-1990s.

Experience from other conflicts merged with this, such as that of those who fought in and survived the brutal Chechen wars against the Russian armed forces in the mid- and late 1990s, or those of Algerians from the long civil war in the 1990s or Pakistanis fighting in Kashmir. Many skills were passed on to new adherents who joined the al-Qaeda training camps towards the end of the 1990s, and some of these capabilities, along with those of Taliban militias, were much in evidence in the little-reported but intense battles with US and Afghan government forces, especially in 2002. Then came the renewed war in Afghanistan from 2005 onwards, as the Taliban and other AOGs began to retake territory, coming up against US, British, Canadian, Dutch and other NATO forces in the process. Yet more experience was gained, primarily by the Taliban, but it was interchangeable and readily communicated through international networks, not least between Afghanistan and Iraq.

There was a key difference between the fighting in Afghanistan in the 1980s and 1990s and that in Iraq in the first decade of the twenty-first century, and that was that the former was primarily rural whereas the latter was conducted very largely in cities and towns. The Soviet troops were well armed but the majority of them were not professionals, although the extensive Soviet use of helicopters and overwhelming firepower gave the insurgents valuable experience in guerrilla campaigning. It is true that by the mid-1980s the morale of the Soviet forces was in sharp decline, but the conflict still provided combat experience for tens of thousands of insurgents, including thousands who had come from abroad. In the 1990s, the war against the Northern Alliance was low-level and frequently exceptionally violent, but that, too, provided more experience of fighting in a very wide range of environments, from mountains, deserts and dense river valleys to some urban conflict in the few large towns and cities. From all of this came further experience, and then came the most intense environment of all – Iraq. As we shall see, this succession of generations with paramilitary experience was hugely important in the creation of ISIS, and goes a long way to explaining that movement's early successes and long-term potential.

IRAQ AS THE FOCUS

As the name suggests, Abu Musab al-Zarqawi was a native of the
Jordanian city of Zarqa, close to Amman. In his youth he was a
petty criminal, but in his early twenties he travelled to Afghanistan
to join the al-Qaeda movement, which was supporting the Taliban
in the civil war against the Northern Alliance. He arrived at the
end of the conflict in 1989 but became involved with bin Laden
and the nascent movement. In the 1990s he was back in Jordan,
where he became a leader of a group seeking the overthrow of the
king and the creation of an Islamist state, before being detained
and serving long periods in jail. After his release and a further
period in Afghanistan in the wake of 9/11, he moved to Iraq soon
after the start of the US-led invasion, and by 2004 was effectively
the leader of an offshoot of al-Qaeda, initially termed al-Qaeda
in Mesopotamia in Western parlance, having pledged allegiance
to bin Laden. This group later became more commonly known
as al-Qaeda in Iraq (AQI).

As an extreme Sunni Islamist, al-Zarqawi was strongly opposed
to the coalition but also opposed the power of Iraq's Shi'i majority.
While much of the opposition to the coalition originated with
Ba'athist elements and members of Saddam Hussein's Special
Republican Guard, AQI rapidly became a focus for Islamist-
oriented Iraqis and was joined by others from abroad. It was noted
for its extreme violence and brutality, so much so that what was
left of the al-Qaeda movement under bin Laden became markedly
critical.

As discussed in Chapter 2, almost from the start of the war in
March 2003 the US forces and the much smaller coalition contin-
gents faced considerable opposition, and by the end of that year
the problem of trying to control a deep-seated and determined
insurgency looked well-nigh insoluble. Coalition forces increased
substantially in size in the early months of 2004, especially as
opposition from Shi'i militias also increased, much influenced by

Iran, not least in eastern Baghdad and Iraq's third city of Basra at the head of the Persian Gulf.

In facing this insurgency, and after the failure of India to ease the pressure on coalition forces, the US military turned to enhanced forms of counter-insurgency warfare, with an emphasis on special forces operating with considerable independence. Over the period from 2004 to 2007 such forces became central to the conduct of the war, although with minimal publicity at the time. This period is worth examining in some detail because it is hugely relevant to our discussion, going some way to explaining three things: the origins of ISIS; why it became such a formidable paramilitary and political force by early 2014; and why the Iraq War became such a valuable recruiting force for the wider al-Qaeda movement.

In 2004, the US and its coalition partners were engaged in a wide-ranging counter-insurgency operation against a number of Sunni and Shi'i militias, but the greatest worry was AQI and its associates under al-Zarqawi, who were seen as the most dangerous. In geographical terms, the main areas of concern were central and north-western Iraq, including Baghdad and especially Anbar Province. The Euphrates valley and its hinterland stretching from Baghdad to the Syrian border were at the heart of these, with cities such as Ramadi and Fallujah being noted centres of rebellion.

Paramilitaries in Fallujah, the 'city of mosques', had prevented a US Marine Corps occupation in April 2004 (see above), and it was seen by the coalition as a city that had to be liberated. In early November of that year, President George W. Bush was re-elected, with the war in Iraq still popular in the United States. Shortly afterwards, a large force of marines, backed by air power, began a concerted assault on the city. Within days it had been overrun and the insurgents had either been killed or captured, or had fled. Indeed, it later emerged that the force of insurgents holding the city amounted to no more than 2,000, facing a combined force of 15,000 US Marines and Iraqi Army soldiers.

Although few images emerged from within Fallujah, there was copious footage of the assault from outside, with vivid pictures of missiles being fired into the city, all shown repeatedly on Middle Eastern TV networks, especially the widely followed 24-hour news channels Al Jazeera and Al Arabiya. This had an effect across the Middle East: further proof, if any were needed, that the US-led coalition was, far from being a force of liberators, actually an army of occupation determined to use maximum force to achieve its ends.

In spite of this, by the end of the month it was already clear that the insurgency was so deep-rooted and the insurgents so determined that Fallujah was simply not as significant in itself as had been thought. Rather, it was just one centre of a much wider uprising, and by the end of November the insurgency had moved on to Ramadi and, perhaps most significant of all, Iraq's second city of Mosul.

It was at this point that US military policy developed in a direction that was to lead to ISIS and its striking paramilitary capabilities. With Bush now secure at the start of his second term, the most important single foreign-policy target in the Middle East was the defeat of the insurgency and, thereby, the securing of Iraq. Afghanistan, by comparison, was of little consequence; this was at a time (late 2004) when that country had not yet fully descended into a renewed, large-scale insurgency, even if the presence of Taliban and other AOGs in rural areas was growing steadily. Iraq, therefore, was the focus, and while important in its own right it was doubly so because of the risk of increased Iranian influence if a successful and stable pro-Western regime could not quickly be established. It was well recognised among military planners and intelligence agencies that Iran was already influential, especially in the largely Shi'i city of Basra, with its strategic importance at the head of the Gulf and close to the most productive Iraqi oilfields.

Even by early 2005, the Saudis were becoming seriously concerned at the growing Iranian influence in Iraq, and were beginning to talk of a 'Shi'i Crescent' stretching from the Mediterranean to the Indian Ocean, embracing Hezbollah in Lebanon, the Alawite regime of Bashar al-Assad in Syria, Shi'i-dominated Iraq and Iran itself. Iraq was the real worry, with recognition that many leading Shi'i politicians, who had been in exile during the worst periods of the Saddam Hussein regime, had spent years in Iran. The occupation of Iraq in early 2003 had been welcomed by the Saudis and other Sunni monarchies and autocrats, but now it was becoming something of a nightmare.

The US answer to this, under the head of JSOC, General Stanley McChrystal, was a concerted and well-resourced shadow war against the insurgents, with the emphasis being on degrading and destroying AQI. McChrystal led the command from 2003 until 2008, assuming control of the ISAF and US forces in Afghanistan in 2009. During his period commanding JSOC he was engaged in the wars in both countries, but the primary concern in the middle of the first decade of the twenty-first century was Iraq.

There, the US forces, working largely on their own but with significant UK involvement, and using a network-centric model of warfare, developed an elite special-forces unit, known under various codes during the period 2004–7 but most commonly as 'Task Force 145' (TF 145), headquartered at Balad Air Base north of Baghdad. TF 145 had access to a wide range of intelligence and surveillance sources, including the use of reconnaissance drones. Its individual components developed a scheme of operations that would typically involve acting on intelligence to identify and then kill or capture presumed insurgents. Helicopter-borne night raids on compounds suspected of being the locations of the targets were the main method of interception. Intelligence already to hand would be supplemented and enhanced by robust and intense physical interrogation (torture) of captured suspects. Teams would have considerable freedom of movement and operation, enabling them, for example, to respond to new intelligence within hours and undertake more raids. Thus, one night raid might yield immediate intelligence on insurgents in another compound, which, though possibly some distance away, might be raided before dawn, before those based there even knew of the earlier raid.[12]

TF 145 consisted of four teams, each drawn from a different branch of US or UK special forces, and each working in a particular geographical area, progressively building up more knowledge of that area and the insurgents operating within it. The teams were:

- Task Force West, drawn from a US Navy SEAL Team Six squadron
- Task Force Central, drawn from a US Delta squadron
- Task Force North, drawn from a US Ranger battalion (the Rangers also providing support for Task Forces Central and West)
- Task Force Black, drawn from the UK Special Air Service (SAS), supported by the UK Special Forces Support Group (SFSG), itself drawn from the Parachute and RAF regiments and the Royal Marines.[13]

The peak period of TF 145 operations was probably the first half of 2006, including a major operation known as 'Operation Arcadia'. At this time, TF 145 was undertaking some 300 night raids each month, and in June 2006 al-Zarqawi was killed in a US air strike on a compound in the village of Hidlib near Baquba, one of the centres of the insurgency.

The combination of extensive special-forces operations, principally TF 145, a major surge in US troops in Iraq and the fostering of anti-insurgent clan groups meant that, by 2008, the insurgency in Iraq was past its peak – this was one of the factors that made it possible for Barack Obama to include a plan for withdrawal of US forces from Iraq in his presidential campaign of that year. That, though, is not the relevant point in terms of the later development of ISIS. What is relevant is one particular aspect of the entire operation, and that is the very large numbers of Iraqis detained without trial, principally by US forces, in some cases for several years.

As with many aspects of the war, it is difficult to know just how many were detained during the eight years of US involvement, but it was probably around 100,000. What is known is that JSOC was responsible for the deaths of thousands of suspects and the detaining and imprisoning of many thousands more. One huge prison camp alone, Camp Bucca, near Basra, housed more than 20,000 Iraqis at its peak, one of these being Abu Bakr al-Baghdadi, who later became the leader of ISIS. British troops were involved because of the SAS squadron that formed Task Force Black, but also in transporting prisoners to a number of the camps, including a notorious site at Balad Air Base, the subject of numerous reports concerning maltreatment. One 'softening-up' process involved housing prisoners in wire cages no bigger than large dog kennels. According to one British ex-serviceman:

> They were made of wire mesh with sloping corrugated roofs [...] They were chest high and two feet wide. There were about 100 of them, in three rows, and they always appeared to have at least one prisoner in each. They would be freezing at night and really hot during the day.[14]

By the time the United States had withdrawn its forces from Iraq at the end of 2011, the coalition-run detention camps had been closed or, in a few cases, handed over to the Iraqi government. The great majority of the detainees had been released, the only exceptions being those who were still believed to be particularly dangerous and unrepentant. Doubt is cast on how effective the decisions were by the fact that al-Baghdadi was one of those released after only a short period in detention, and it is clear that many of those who were eventually at the core of the development of ISIS had served time in the camps, a situation ripe for prose-lytising. More significantly, though, many of them had come up against the best-trained and -equipped forces of the United States and United Kingdom – the special forces of JSOC.

Thus we see the progression of paramilitary capabilities and the reason for the brief earlier discussion of paramilitary cohorts. Fighters for the Taliban in 1990s Afghanistan benefited from the experience of the 1980s cohort; paramilitaries in Iraq (and Afghanistan) after 9/11 learnt from them, as well as from Chechens and others. Finally, and most recently, although the extensive operations of TF 145 may have appeared successful, they were to provide extensive training and combat experience for people who went on to form much of the paramilitary core of ISIS – one reason why it was so successful in the first eight months of 2014, something that caught just about every Western and Middle Eastern government by surprise.

THE POTENTIAL FOR FUTURE SURPRISES

In early 2016, ISIS is facing strong opposition in the form of air strikes carried out primarily by the United States but involving some regional states and also Western ones, such as France, the United Kingdom, Canada, Australia, Belgium and Denmark. In spite of the intensity of the air war that started in August 2014, it is accepted that to 'degrade and destroy' ISIS – President Obama's words – will be problematic. This is an extreme yet very competent paramilitary force that will be very difficult to defeat. As such, and in a climate of fear, one possibility attracts attention: that ISIS will acquire WMD.

If this were possible, either for ISIS or for any future extreme movement, whatever its religious or ideological foundations, then political violence as a whole could reach a new level. The next chapter will explore this risk, focusing partly on ISIS and the next five years but also looking further ahead. Once the chances of such a development have been established, at least in broad terms, subsequent chapters will then examine the recent evolution of ISIS, why it has become the centre of what might still be called the War on Terror, the nature of its potential for further development and its capacity for serving as a model for other extreme movements.

It is this last element that is particularly significant. If ISIS represents the peak of an extreme movement that has developed from al-Qaeda but still has at least a short-term future, then its development of WMD would be a major problem. If, however, ISIS is seen as an example of a phenomenon that will become more common in the future, then the potential spread of WMD to sub-state actors becomes even more important. Moreover, the international environment in which this might develop will be determined in part by the widely differing world views explored earlier in this chapter. Given the deeply embedded nature of those views, with the Western outlook perceiving threats from the barbarian margins but so many in those margins seeing the West as always willing to use force to preserve its privilege, we have a dangerous prospect of persistent conflict.

4

WEAPONS OF MASS DESTRUCTION AND POLITICAL VIOLENCE

On 2 August 1990, the Iraqi regime of Saddam Hussein invaded Kuwait and occupied it in a matter of hours. It expected international criticism but little outright opposition, given that it had been seen as a bulwark of Western interests against Iran in the bitter war from 1980 to 1988. However, it was immediately obvious that the regime had completely misjudged the Western mood and that the George H. W. Bush administration and its UK ally under prime minister Margaret Thatcher would organise a powerful military coalition to eject the Iraqi forces and possibly threaten the very survival of the government in Baghdad.

That same month, the regime initiated an emergency programme to equip the al-Hussein medium-range ballistic missile with biological warheads, and by January 1991, at the outset of Operation Desert Storm, 13 missiles armed with botulinum warheads, 10 with anthrax and 2 with aflatoxin were ready for use, and deployed to four locations across Iraq – but well away from Kuwait, the immediate focus of the war. More than 150 spray bombs that could be delivered by strike aircraft were also available.

Perhaps even more remarkable was a decision to delegate launch authority to regional commanders, presumably in the event that the very survival of the regime was threatened, an extraordinary development that raised the possibility of the unauthorised use of these weapons during the chaos and uncertainty of a rapidly moving conflict. These actions probably took the world closer to the large-scale use of biological weapons than at any time before or since. Moreover, if the weapons had been used, President Bush would have been under serious pressure to respond with nuclear force.

It later became known that US intelligence was aware of the Iraqi biological-weapons programme and that the regime was likely to use such weapons if its own existence were threatened, this having been the subject of a US National Intelligence Estimate prepared two months before the onset of Desert Storm. In the event, the coalition defeated the Iraqi forces and evicted them from Kuwait, but did not move towards Baghdad to threaten the regime itself. The decision to cease the ground war after four days was a surprise at the time, and a contributing factor may have been the recognition that this could lead to a highly dangerous escalation of the conflict.

The relevance of this remarkable and largely forgotten aspect of the 1991 war is the fact that a singularly determined regime could develop biological weapons and present a threat to the world's most powerful military forces more than a quarter of a century ago. It is true that the Iraqi regime had control of substantial territory, a scientifically and technically competent workforce and significant financial resources, but Iraq was not one of the world's most advanced industrial or military states. It was a seminal achievement: a stark reminder of what was possible many years ago and highly relevant to any assessment of the possible use of WMD by paramilitary movements in the future.

This chapter will examine that risk, from CBR weapons to the far more devastating nuclear weapons. There is much talk of the possibility of a movement such as ISIS gaining access to WMD and even that it might represent an 'existential threat'. Is this really the case or is it a gross exaggeration? Is there far less danger than we are often told or is there real cause for concern, especially in light of the experience in Iraq?

Furthermore, this book is looking at the longer term and is especially concerned with the suggestion that ISIS will prove to be a model for the kinds of revolts that will be faced in the future. Even if we conclude that the risk of WMD falling into the hands of a group such as ISIS is low, that does not remotely mean that this will hold good for 20 or 30 years or more. If there is a longer-term risk, what are the ways of avoiding catastrophes in the future?

SUSPICIONS

In the months that followed the start of the air war against ISIS in August 2014 there were reports that the group was using chemical weapons against Iraqi troops and that it was also interested in developing biological weapons, including bubonic plague. The reports mainly originated from groups in Syria opposed to ISIS, and although there was little to back them up they did raise wider concerns.

The chemical-weapons element, in particular, struck a chord because the Assad regime in Syria had long been known to have developed and deployed such weapons. This was mainly as a deterrent against Israel's undoubted nuclear superiority, but there was also credible evidence that the regime had used chemical weapons during the course of the civil war. This was an aspect of the war that took the United States close to using air strikes during 2013, but the regime responded to the risk of attack by agreeing to give up its chemical arsenal, a process that made slow and painful progress in the months that followed.

The reports of ISIS's using chemical weapons caused concern for two reasons. The first was that they might have acquired stocks from government bases overrun by their paramilitaries; the second was that since they now controlled considerable territory they might even be able to produce such weapons without outside assistance. In the event, detailed analysis of the sparse evidence available indicated that ISIS did not have weaponised chemical agents, but it was possible that they had tried to use chlorine gas against Iraqi troops.[1] Chlorine is an unreliable battlefield weapon, though particularly dangerous when used against unprotected civilians. There were further reports, early in 2015, that ISIS had constructed IEDs that dispersed chlorine, this time for use against Kurdish Peshmerga militias in north-eastern Iraq. Once again the evidence was incomplete, but it served further to raise concerns about how far an extreme group such as ISIS might go.

Chlorine is certainly a chemical-weapon agent, but it also has many industrial uses, and in the chaos of a paramilitary conflict could easily cause as many problems for the attackers as for the defenders. As well as chlorine, the Assad regime's arsenal included nerve agents such as sarin and blister agents such as mustard gas, and there have been no indications that ISIS has these.

On the biological-weapons side, there were reports in the Israeli and European media that a laptop acquired from an ISIS paramilitary fighter contained information suggesting that the movement was seeking to develop biological and chemical weapons that might be used against large numbers of people in shopping malls or underground railway stations, but there were no indications that such work was actually being carried out.[2]

Why, then, is there concern over the risk that an extreme paramilitary group such as ISIS might acquire or develop WMD? After all, the 9/11 attacks hit the world's most famous financial centre and the headquarters of the most powerful military, killing 3,000 people, yet were undertaken without so much as handguns. Even more relevant is the example of the attempted attack on the World Trade Center in 1993, which would have killed tens of thousands of people. This would have been the most catastrophic single attack since the atom bomb on Nagasaki in 1945, yet involved less than a tonne of conventional high explosive.

In order to explore the risk of paramilitary groups getting chemical, biological, radiological or nuclear (CBRN) weapons, two issues have to be addressed first: whether any WMD can be considered to pose an existential threat, and why there is so much fear of WMD when conventional attacks can cause so much harm.

There is no accepted definition of the term 'existential threat' when applied to paramilitary violence, but it is normally held to be an action which can threaten the existence of a state, or at least a major centre of population. To be more specific, 'existential' implies, at least, catastrophic destruction to the extent that many decades, if not a century or more, would be needed for recovery.

At the height of the Cold War there really was such a threat to states. The UK government, for example, calculated that if the country were subjected to a 100-megatonne nuclear attack by the Soviet Union, 40 million would be killed out of a population at the time of 56 million people. Moreover, millions more might die in the years and decades that followed from the impact of residual radiation and a nuclear winter. Worldwide, a central nuclear exchange between the Warsaw Pact countries and NATO would have killed many hundreds of millions and been followed by a long-term nuclear-winter effect across much of the globe. For much of the northern hemisphere this was certainly 'existential'.

In opposing the 2015 nuclear pact between the 'P5+1' (the five permanent members of the UN Security Council plus Germany) and Iran, according to which Iran will reduce its nuclear facilities and stockpiles of enriched uranium in return for the lifting of economic sanctions, many critics said Iran could become an existential threat to Israel, and it is true that such a small country, with barely a dozen large towns and cities, could be devastated by perhaps 20 nuclear weapons if they could evade defences and if the attacker were confident that it would not, in return, be destroyed. One of the ironies of the criticism of Iran is that only one country in the region, Israel, has nuclear weapons, so the Iranians could consider Israel to be a threat to them and not the other way round.

As we look at the different categories of WMD, we should therefore bear in mind the actual scope for destruction before using the term 'existential threat'. Even so, that does not diminish in any way the need to explore this aspect of irregular war, since if such weapons do in the future become available to a group such as ISIS, the consequences could be massive.

We will turn now to the second issue outlined above: why are WMD feared so much when conventional weapons can be so devastating and even a carefully planned and targeted attack using guns can have an international impact? The *Charlie Hebdo* attack is a relevant example. On 7 January 2015, two French brothers of Algerian descent, Saïd and Chérif Kouachi, entered the offices of the satirical magazine *Charlie Hebdo* in Paris and opened fire on an editorial meeting with light weapons, killing eight staff members, including five cartoonists. A guest, a maintenance worker and two police officers also died. In an apparently coordinated attack, hostages were later held at a kosher supermarket, also in Paris. Four customers and another police officer were killed by Amedy Coulibaly. Both attacks ended in sieges on 9 January in which the three attackers were killed; by that time France had deployed an estimated 80,000 police, army and other security personnel in response to the original attack.

Although *Charlie Hebdo* was (before the attack) a low-circulation magazine, it was, and is, part of French political culture and represents a strand, more prominent in France than in most European countries, of vigorous political lampooning that is sometimes close to obscene. The attack was viewed immediately as an assault on freedom of expression and the response included the biggest public demonstrations of support on any issue in France for decades, which involved dozens of heads of state and government. These demonstrations were part of a reaction across Europe that also included intense arguments about what is and is not permissible for a satirical magazine to say.

Small attacks can have a huge influence, depending on the targets and the timing. Those directly involved in the attacks of January 2015 were just three people. They appear to have been well equipped and to have had some paramilitary combat training, with at least one of them spending time with an offshoot of the al-Qaeda movement in Yemen. There was also in all probability a small support group, some of whom may have been aware of what was planned. Even so, two people with a specific target and another with a more general target were able to dominate the security agenda of a major Western country for three days, with the mobilisation of tens of thousands of security personnel, and to have a major effect on the worldwide media. Later in 2015 came the multiple attacks in Paris that killed 130 people and received even more attention, yet these attacks used just firearms and explosive belts.

The French attacks of January and November 2015 help to put into perspective the possible role of WMD in sub-state political violence but do not explain the deep public fear of such weapons. The reasons behind this fear are complex. In Western states, people over 35 years of age have vivid memories of the nuclear dangers of the Cold War era and of its visions of potential destructiveness. This may be less apparent to younger generations, who have little knowledge of that period. While Cold War fears were focused on the nuclear threat, chemical weapons raise concerns partly from knowledge of the impact of gas warfare in World War I, and partly because of the intrinsically silent nature of such weapons.

This is also true of biological weapons, but they have the added element of uncertainty and what might be termed the 'presumption of multiplication'. If microorganisms can multiply rapidly they can surely set in motion epidemics that cause untold suffering. After all, the Spanish-flu pandemic that began in the final year of World War I went on to kill far more people than the war itself; the Black Death of the fourteenth century was catastrophic for medieval Europe; the plague pits of seventeenth-century London are still being uncovered; and, in the recent past, bird flu and especially Ebola have been stark reminders of the potential effects of intentional biological warfare.

This is the context for the following examination of WMD in relation to paramilitary capabilities. While one conclusion might be that the threat is commonly exaggerated, there is a sting in the tail in that there may well be circumstances in the near future in which the use of one or more of these systems becomes far more plausible as we move into an era of irregular war.

CHEMICAL WEAPONS

The most protracted use of chemical weapons was during World War I, when an estimated 100,000 tonnes of chemical agents were used, causing more than half a million casualties, including tens of thousands of deaths. They were later used by Japan in China and by Italy in Ethiopia before World War II, and then during the Iran–Iraq War of 1980–8, principally by Iraq, including a notorious attack on the Kurdish Iraqi town of Halabja in March 1988, which killed thousands of people. During World War II the US Army had plans to mass-produce chemical weapons to drench Japanese cities should the Manhattan Project to develop the atom bomb fail, and during the Vietnam War the United States made repeated use of defoliants, which had serious effects on human health. There is reasonable evidence that the Assad regime in Syria used chemical weapons in 2013, but there are so far few examples of paramilitary groups using chemical agents.

There are four types of chemical agent. *Blister agents* such as mustard gas affect the skin and mucous membranes of the mouth, eyes, nose, throat and lungs. They are lethal at high doses and if they do not kill they can lead to lifelong disabilities, including blindness. *Choking agents* such as chlorine and phosgene principally affect the tissues of the lungs and respiratory tracts, causing oedema (accumulation of liquid) and suffocation if in lethal doses. *Blood agents* such as hydrogen cyanide cause rapid death by preventing the distribution of oxygen in the blood. Finally, there are the *nerve agents*, mostly based on organophosphorus compounds, which include sarin, tabun and the more powerful 'V' agents such as VX. As well as these there is a wide range of incapacitant and neuroactive compounds, some used in riot control and public-order policing. Some of these blur the distinction between agents that are considered chemical weapons and those that are not.

In conventional warfare, chemical weapons may be more effective against unprotected military and especially civilian targets than conventional explosives. They can be deployed in many ways, including in persistent or non-persistent forms, to meet particular military requirements; their impact on opponents can be psychological as well as physical; and cumbersome and restrictive defensive measures may be required, including full-body protection. In conventional military use, though, there are also disadvantages. Older types of chemical agent may be corrosive and difficult to transport, as well as to store for long periods, and their use can be greatly affected by weather conditions, especially wind and rainfall. Furthermore, modern armies may have efficient systems of protection, and chemical weapons may not be effective in rapid-moving warfare.

In narrowly defined circumstances, chemical weapons may have a mass-destruction effect, but this is most likely to be against unprotected civilian populations, especially in enclosed environments such as covered markets, places of worship, theatres, cinemas and sports halls. It is largely for this reason that they might be used as weapons of terror, either by states or by sub-state paramilitary groups.

Chemical weapons were widely developed, produced and deployed during the Cold War era from 1945 to 1990. The United States and the Soviet Union were estimated to have arsenals of at least 30,000 tonnes each during the 1980s, with delivery by aircraft, missiles, artillery and other systems. France also maintained a chemical arsenal of around 1,000 tonnes during the Cold War. Other countries that have, or have had, such weaponry include

Iraq, Syria, Israel, North Korea, Libya and possibly Iran, though this is disputed. Israel and North Korea are presumed to maintain stocks.

After decades of failed attempts to establish an arms-control regime for chemical weapons, the end of the Cold War finally made such a thing possible. Intensive multilateral negotiations over a 12-year period resulted in the adoption of the Chemical Weapons Convention (CWC) by the Conference on Disarmament in Geneva in September 1992. It was open for signature in Paris from January 1993 and finally entered into force in April 1997, when it had been signed and ratified by a sufficient number of countries. Israel has signed but not ratified the treaty; North Korea has not signed.

There are two key features of the CWC. First, as the term 'convention' implies (in arms-control parlance), it involves a total ban on the development, deployment and use of chemical weapons. It thus seeks to outlaw an entire class of weapons. Second, the CWC established an inspection and verification system as a formal and integral part of the treaty, implemented by the Office for the Prohibition of Chemical Weapons (OPCW) based in The Hague.[3] In some circumstances signatory states can demand an inspection of other signatory states by the OPCW if they have clear suspicions of activities intended to circumvent the CWC.

Furthermore, following the signing of the CWC, a member state possessing chemical weapons has an obligation to destroy them, a process which can be expensive and difficult for some classes of arms. Progress in the destruction of existing stocks has been slower than many CWC supporters hoped, but substantial parts of the US and Russian arsenals have now been destroyed, often by specialised incineration, France has completely destroyed its smaller weaponry and most Syrian and Libyan chemical armaments have gone, as have all of Iraq's stocks.

This all looks good, but, in theory, any country with a reasonably well-developed indigenous chemical industry and its own organic chemists, chemical engineers and weapons specialists would be able to develop chemical weapons if the political leadership were to require it, although their production, storage and use all require considerable skills if safety is to be maintained. Moreover, international opinion has moved heavily against these weapons – the great majority of countries eschew their development and use and would be prepared to ensure the severe sanctioning of countries shown to be breaking or flouting the CWC. This is one of the few reasonably enduring and positive experiences in arms control of the past 70 years, but it does not, of course, apply to countries that have not signed or ratified the convention, or to sub-state actors that may control territory.

Some agents that in certain circumstances can be used as chemical weapons, such as chlorine and cyanide, are in sufficient industrial use to be potentially available to a paramilitary group, if that group were able to obtain them by theft, threat or subterfuge. A particularly well-equipped and well-trained group might be able to develop the means to produce more complex agents, such as sarin, from its own resources, a task made easier if it had stable control of territory. Unless chemical-agent supplies were available from a supporting state or powerful foreign group, this is probably the main way in which a paramilitary movement would be able to acquire chemical weapons.

Even so, the safe manufacture and dispersal of an agent such as sarin by a sub-state group is not easy, as is illustrated by a well-known case. On 20 March 1995, members of the Aum Shinrikyo religious sect in Japan released quantities of sarin at a number of points on the Tokyo subway system, affecting three lines and 15 stations over a distance of eight miles, mostly around downtown Tokyo. Aum Shinrikyo was an apocalyptic religious cult that believed in an impending end to the world, its leader, Shoko Asahara, having prophesied World War III. The cult had been particularly adept at bringing in scientists, and equipped and ran its own laboratories, where it sought to produce chemical and biological weapons. At the subsequent trial of Asahara on murder charges the prosecution claimed that the aim of the subway attack was to start the process of bringing about the collapse of the Japanese government and its replacement by Asahara as the new emperor of Japan.

The attack led to the deaths of 12 people, and up to 5,500 were made ill, some of them seriously, though panic is thought to have played a major part. While it was a serious incident that brought worldwide attention to the sect, the human effect fell far short of what the perpetrators had expected, since they had anticipated a much higher death toll. The reasons for this appear to have been twofold: the sarin nerve agent produced was insufficiently pure, and the mode of distribution did not take account of the air-circulation and ventilation patterns of a modern subway system. This was despite the professional expertise available to the sect and the fact that small-scale experiments had already been undertaken in preparation for the strike.

While only one incident, the Aum Shinrikyo attack lends some credence to the view that the use of chemical weapons by sub-state actors is unlikely to be a major element of paramilitary actions. This does not mean that it will not happen – and if it does the overall public effect could be disproportionate to the number of casualties – but that there are few indications that this class of WMD should be the greatest cause for concern. It is appropriate, though, to analyse whether this is also true for biological, radiological and nuclear weapons.

BIOLOGICAL WEAPONS

Biological-warfare agents include a wide range of microorganisms capable of infecting humans, animals and plants, as well as toxins produced by microorganisms and chemicals based on such toxins. There is a worldwide arms-control convention covering all of these that dates back to 1972: the Biological and Toxin Weapons

Convention (BTWC). This has been signed by the great majority of countries and remains in force. While this agreement has the status of a convention – involving a ban on the production, deployment and use of such weapons – it has three weaknesses.[4] One is the considerable overlap in definitions, particularly regarding where the line is drawn between naturally occurring toxins and synthetic versions, and a second is that the BTWC lacks any kind of monitoring or inspection process, unlike the CWC. Finally, it remains fully acceptable to undertake research into disease agents that present a risk to health, especially in relation to infectivity and epidemiology, yet the dividing line between defence preparedness and offensive use can be tenuous at best.

Even so, while there is a widespread anxiety that biological warfare would present a huge problem if practised by violent sub-state groups, with the 2014–15 Ebola outbreak causing additional fears, there are significant difficulties with trying to produce and use a successful agent. These may be summarised as follows:

- The agent should spread the disease rapidly even when present in low concentrations, and should be highly contagious, preferably most readily spread by airborne dispersal and respiratory infection.
- Its effects on the target population should not be easy to treat with chemotherapy, vaccines or other means, yet the attackers should be able to be protected and it should not spread too easily among their own community.
- It should be easy to produce in bulk, preferably in small facilities that can be hidden.
- There must be an efficient way of delivering it.
- If it is an airborne agent then weather conditions must be right.

All of these conditions apply to the development and use of biological warfare by a state, and they make its use by a sub-state actor even more unlikely, except that the willingness of attackers to give their own lives might make dispersal less difficult. They do much to explain why biological-warfare agents have not featured significantly in war in the modern era, but there are several elements that need to be explored if we are specifically concerned with paramilitary groups.

One is that the number of organisms that are amenable to airborne dispersal, rapid infection and limited treatment is actually very small. Most microorganisms that are spread through the air, and that therefore can be distributed widely, actually degrade rapidly, especially when exposed to solar radiation. Among the few exceptions is anthrax, a bacterial disease caused by *Bacillus anthracis*. This can be spread by ingesting contaminated food, by infection of wounds and by breathing in spores. The anthrax organism is one of the few bacterial species that forms resting spores that are resistant to sunlight, yet if inhaled can cause a lung infection that is highly lethal unless treated early with antibiotics. Anthrax can be produced in bulk given appropriate culturing equipment, but must then be weaponised to a form more suited to aerial dispersal. There is some evidence that the Japanese cult Aum Shinrikyo tried to produce weaponised anthrax but failed in attempts to cause infections.

A second issue is dispersal. For a biological agent (or 'bio-agent') such as anthrax to be used for a mass-casualty attack requires some sort of dispersal mechanism, such as an aircraft flying tangentially to wind direction, upwind of the target population and therefore able to create a cloud of spores spreading across an urban area. Dispersal of bio-agents via water supplies is difficult because of the very large quantities of inoculum required.

Finally, the safe production of bio-agents requires considerable knowledge and experience of how to avoid infection of operators during the process. Biological containment of a dangerously infectious organism under any circumstances requires skill, but if it has to be maintained during the process of bulk production, storage, weaponisation and delivery, the problems are much greater.

None of this means that biological warfare is outside the remit of a paramilitary group, especially if it has an extreme and even apocalyptic vision, but rather that it will only be feasible in narrow circumstances. Furthermore, as with chemical weapons, even the small-scale use, or threatened use, of such weapons is likely to instil considerable fear. One small attack, such as anthrax spores sent through the mail, could be enough.

RADIOLOGICAL WEAPONS

Radiological weapons are not nuclear weapons – their purpose is not to produce a devastating nuclear blast but to use conventional explosives to disperse radioactive material. If a radiological attack were to take place, and the nature of the attack were recognised quickly, then the death toll might be very low or even zero. The aim would not be to cause high civilian casualties but to contaminate an area, rendering it unusable for months or even longer.

It is possible that nuclear-reactor waste might be hijacked and used to great effect, but more likely would be the use of isotopes such as Cobalt-60 or Caesium-137 obtained from medical or industrial facilities. Indeed, if a paramilitary group had control of cities for any length of time and had dedicated people with sufficient technical competence, then such weapons would be possible, even more so if the people concerned were prepared to risk their lives in the process.

A paramilitary organisation with access to radiological material could have a wide range of targets, many of them designed to cause maximum economic disruption. One possibility would be the detonation of a radiological weapon (more correctly termed a radiological dispersal device) in a financial district. Such a device could render the financial heart of a state inoperable and cause considerable chaos lasting many weeks or months. Another example is a major international airport, especially a significant hub.

There have been no known substantial uses of radiological weapons, but two of the many nuclear accidents of the Cold War era give an indication of the problems of decontamination, even though such accidents took place in remote and unpopulated places. In January 1966 a B-52 strategic nuclear bomber collided with a tanker aircraft near Palomares in Spain. The latter plane exploded in mid-air; the B-52 crashed and its four bombs were scattered. One was recovered intact on land; a second was recovered off the coast after a 15-week search. In the case of the other two, the explosives designed to set off a nuclear detonation did themselves detonate but only dispersed the radioactive material without causing nuclear blasts. There was widespread contamination, but fortunately of soil and vegetation, not of towns or villages. Even so, a massive clean-up operation had to be mounted in order to render the contaminated material safe for transit to long-term storage in Texas. In all, 1,400 tonnes of material was moved. Only four days after the Palomares incident, another nuclear-armed B-52 crashed, seven miles short of the Thule Air Base in Greenland. This time all four nuclear bombs dispersed their contents and 1.5 million gallons of snow, ice and water had to be removed in the decontamination process.

CBR WEAPONS AND POLITICAL VIOLENCE

If an extreme paramilitary organisation were to acquire or develop CBR weapons, it might utilise them for two quite different purposes. One would be to create a deterrent: to discourage attacks on its organisation or the territory that it controls. Given the way in which modern armies are able to protect themselves from CBR warfare, this might not have much effect unless the movement were able to use such weapons against the civilians of the state threatening it. Under those circumstances it might be effective as a deterrent but would need some means of delivery.

The other purpose would be as a direct means of projecting its own power and authority in the form of terror attacks, most likely against unprotected civilians. Yet as this brief summary of CBR agents suggests, unless very large quantities are used, the effects would not exceed those of some of the attacks already undertaken using conventional high explosives, such as the destruction of airliners, the use of large truck bombs or the 9/11 attacks. It is just possible that a paramilitary group could cause very large casualties if targeting an indoor arena or vast shopping mall, but the real effect would actually be fear, based on a pervasive worry about weapons that, in some difficult-to-define way, are 'different' from conventional bombs.

For a group such as ISIS, this second purpose is important because it has shown itself to be capable of using brutal methods to incite and provoke particular courses of action. The acts of beheading hostages or burning alive a young Jordanian pilot were designed not just to cause anger but also to frighten military personnel and others who would know all too well what would happen should they be captured. Similarly, the wider effect of even the small-scale use of CBR weapons would be disproportionate to the direct impact.

At the root of the fear of the use of such weapons as an instrument of terror is the belief that if epidemics can happen naturally then surely the deliberate use of bio-agents would be very much worse. It doesn't really help that this is probably not the case, at least in most circumstances, since disease agents such as the Ebola or bird-flu viruses are so difficult to control that they would be as likely to cause havoc among the groups spreading them as among any intended victims. Yet this does virtually nothing to reassure people, which is the main card that an extreme group can play. Even if it seeks to stage a biological-warfare attack that is quickly brought under control, the fear factor will be extreme. As with chemical weapons, it is the fear of the unknown that has its own perverse value.

Even so, there are some caveats to what seems an unexpectedly reassuring prognosis. One is that under some circumstances an attack with bio-agents could be directly effective. Not long after the 9/11 attacks, US authorities modelled the release of anthrax spores into the ventilation system of the New York Stock Exchange, and this exercise highlighted one particular vulnerability: the anthrax bacterium, if dispersed as spores, is virtually impossible to detect in the air unless you are looking specifically for it using specialist equipment, which would not normally be available at an average threat level. Anthrax in aerial form spreads through inhalation; a person affected will begin to show symptoms many hours later, with these varying from person to person depending on his or her health, the quantity of spores inhaled and so on. Once those symptoms become apparent, and provided the cause is diagnosed promptly, then treatment with antibiotics combined with intensive care is feasible. Prophylactic treatment of people exposed to anthrax spores but before symptoms appear is much more effective. What this means, though, is that if sufficient anthrax spores were introduced and dispersed in a crowded cinema, theatre, shopping centre or, worse still, large indoor arena, then thousands could be affected. However many people were killed the impact would be huge.

A second issue is the ability to produce anthrax in quantity. One state, Iraq, did this in the late 1980s as part of an extensive weapons programme that even now is little known. It would be possible for an established state to provide bio-agents such as anthrax to a sub-state group, but the risk to that state if this were proved would be considerable. Of greater concern is a situation in which an extreme group is able to take over and maintain control of substantial territory for long enough to bring together the expertise and technical competence necessary to establish a chemical- or biological-weapons programme. This is far from being beyond the bounds of possibility, and it is by no means impossible that ISIS, which by mid-2015 controlled a territory the size of the island of Britain and a population of well over 6 million, could seek to do this.

The key point here is what it might then do. To initiate the use of chemical or biological agents against a regional state or against some element of the far enemy would almost certainly result in such an assault on ISIS that its prospects for a caliphate would be hugely damaged. Such an attack cannot be ruled out, but more likely is the development of a weapons capability designed as a deterrent to a comprehensive assault by other powers.

Finally, when discussing bio-agents, specialists have emphasised anthrax as the one current disease that is readily amenable to use in an attack. There are others, such as tularaemia (rabbit fever) and botulinum toxin, but they are few in number. This might change if a sustained programme of advanced genetic manipulation is undertaken, aiming to increase the pathogenicity, survival and resistance to treatment of other disease agents. This would require a level of sophistication that is almost certainly beyond any paramilitary group currently in existence or likely to exist in the near future, but perhaps not impossible for a determined group in one or two decades' time. It is one of several reasons why there is an urgent need to strengthen the BTWC of 1972, but there simply isn't the political interest or will to do so at present.

So there is a potential threat of the use of some chemical- or biological-warfare agents, and also from radiological devices, from a group such as ISIS, although at its worst this might involve deaths in the hundreds or possibly low thousands rather than an existential risk to a state. The greater issues are the fear factor and what such use would mean for a political commitment to act against ISIS.

That leaves us with the much bigger issue of nuclear weapons. In this case, we are dealing with forms of destruction at least an order of magnitude greater than that possible with CBR weapons systems. To look at such risks it is necessary to provide a reminder of the origins, development and pervasive distribution of nuclear weapons before going on to discuss their current status. As a result of the ending of the Cold War a quarter of a century ago, there has been something of an assumption that we are moving beyond the nuclear age. Although there were reasons for making this assumption for the first 20 of those 25 years, there are far fewer now, and while we may be at much less risk of an all-out global nuclear war – looking over the abyss, so to speak – we are now on something of a slippery slope towards a proliferating world, which does have serious long-term implications for paramilitary violence.

NUCLEAR WEAPONS: DEVELOPMENT AND PROLIFERATION

Two forms of atom bomb had been developed in the Manhattan Project by July 1945: an impact device utilising the uranium isotope U-235, which was used against Hiroshima on 6 August 1945 without first being tested, and an implosion device utilising the plutonium isotope Pu-239, which was tested at Alamogordo in the New Mexico desert on 16 July 1945, and then used against Nagasaki on 9 August. Between them, the bombs dropped on the two cities caused 185,000 deaths and tens of thousands of injuries.

The Hiroshima and Nagasaki bombs were equivalent in destructive power to many thousands of tonnes of conventional explosive, and the term 'kilotonne' quickly came into use as a measure of nuclear capability, with one kilotonne equalling 1,000 tonnes of high explosive such as TNT.[5] Both the bombs used against Japan exploded in the range of 10 to 20 kilotonnes.

Before the attacks and Japan's subsequent surrender, the US had already started a production line for atom bombs, and would have been able to use two per month against Japan for the rest of 1945. There was also a back-up plan had the Manhattan Project failed to produce nuclear weapons, which was the rapid mass production of chemical weapons for attacking Japanese cities, something that would have caused up to 5 million deaths.

After the end of the war the United States proceeded unilaterally to develop a nuclear arsenal, producing 50 bombs by 1948 and 370 by 1950. The Soviet Union put huge effort into its own postwar nuclear programme, testing a device in 1949 and producing five bombs by 1950. A decade later the US arsenal had grown to 20,400 and the Soviet Union's to 1,600; there then followed a determined effort by the Soviets to catch up, so that by 1980 their arsenal had risen to 30,100, compared with 23,900 for the United States. Some of these nuclear weapons were massively more powerful than the Hiroshima and Nagasaki bombs. The United States had weapons close to 1,000 times the strength of the Hiroshima bomb, and the largest Soviet device was twice as powerful as that. Each side was prepared to destroy the other, and much of humankind too.

Meanwhile, other states were seeking to gain nuclear weapons, with the United Kingdom succeeding in its first nuclear test by 1952, France by 1960, China by 1964, Israel by the end of that decade and India in 1974. Since then, Pakistan and North Korea have joined the nuclear group; other countries, such as South Korea, Taiwan, Sweden, Switzerland, Brazil and Argentina, may have had nuclear aspirations, but have not pursued them to completion. Four countries have actually got rid of their nuclear weapons: Ukraine, Belarus and Kazakhstan returned Soviet-era weapons to Russia after the end of the Cold War, and South Africa gave up its small arsenal, believed to have consisted of six bombs, around the end of the apartheid era in the early 1990s. Others, including Canada and the United Kingdom, no longer have US nuclear weapons based on their soil.

Beginning in the early 1990s, with the end of the Cold War, there was a period of nearly two decades in which the salience of nuclear weapons diminished, in spite of French tests in the 1990s,

Indo-Pakistani nuclear rivalry and the slow progress made by North Korea. Back in the mid-1980s, the world's nuclear arsenals had peaked at nearly 70,000 weapons, but a series of cuts, principally by the United States and Russia, brought this down to a little more than 10,000, albeit with the fissile cores of thousands of the others placed in storage.

As to the future, though, a good starting point for what might be achieved is a surprising statement by four former US politicians who had occupied very senior positions in both Republican and Democrat administrations. They were: Henry Kissinger, George Shultz, William Perry and Sam Nunn, respectively two former Secretaries of State, a former defence secretary and a former chair of the Senate Armed Services Committee. In January 2007, they called for a worldwide programme to reduce the salience of nuclear weapons, leading eventually to a nuclear-free world.[6] People suspicious of such a statement from senior US figures pointed out that such a world would benefit the country with the most substantial conventional weapons, which just happened to be the United States, but it was also clear that their call was genuine and may well have been motivated by their inside knowledge of many of the crises and accidents of the Cold War era, some of which may have taken the world far closer to nuclear disaster than would ever have been admitted.

Whatever the motivations of Kissinger and the others, 2007 probably marked the high point of a less nuclear-fixated era, and it has most definitely been downhill ever since. Even under Barack Obama, the United States is set on modernising a range of nuclear systems, and Vladimir Putin's Russia is positively relishing its nuclear status and spending a singularly large part of its defence budget on new systems.[7] Although China has far fewer nuclear weapons and has been prioritising the modernisation of its conventional forces, it is now upgrading its long-range land-based missiles and has started to produce missile submarines as well.

Two other, middle-ranking nuclear powers, the United Kingdom and France, still harbour their delusions of post-imperial grandeur and are intent on modernising their nuclear forces, while a small-scale but potent mini-nuclear arms race is very much under way in South Asia. Pakistan, with its perennial fear of its far larger neighbour, India, is leading the way, with a range of missile and aircraft delivery systems being developed, while India now has the Agni-V land-based nuclear missile with a range of 5,000 miles. India's nuclear ambitions may be very much related to its concern over China, but the impact on Pakistan is inevitable – from Islamabad's point of view, it is India, not China, that is the state of concern.

Then we have two maverick states: North Korea – with perhaps a handful of crude but usable nuclear warheads – and Israel, which would object strongly to being described as 'maverick'. In the nuclear context, though, it is the country that is simply not discussed in polite circles, yet it has had nuclear weapons for at least 40 years. It is highly secretive about its nuclear capability, but was most likely aided by France in initially developing it in the 1960s, and now has at least 80 weapons and probably many more. Delivery systems include US-produced F-15 and F-16 strike aircraft and also the mobile Jericho III ballistic missile, which has a range of more than 4,000 miles.

Thus, the nuclear-weapons world may not yet involve substantial proliferation, and Iran's ambitions may eventually be limited by agreement, but the point here is that we are simply not moving towards a nuclear-free world or anything like it. At least for now, the post-Cold War momentum has been lost. Moreover, with Russia seeing its nuclear forces as key indicators of a hoped-for return to great-power status, there is even the risk of a new East–West nuclear arms race, a circumstance that most analysts would until recently have thought highly unlikely and a throwback to a past era. With nuclear weapons here to stay, that means that the risk of their proliferating beyond possession by states to possession by sub-state actors remains, and while the obstacles may be substantial for now, that may not always be the case. Where do the risks lie?

NUCLEAR WEAPONS: PARAMILITARY RISKS

Nuclear weapons require uranium that has been enriched so that at least 85 per cent of it consists of the U-235 isotope, known as weapons-grade uranium. Only 0.7 per cent of natural uranium consists of this isotope, the great majority being U-238, which under normal circumstances is inert. U-238 is so similar in chemical and physical nature to U-235 that they are very difficult to separate. Enriching naturally occurring uranium therefore requires substantial industrial capabilities and expertise. Low-enriched uranium, about 4 per cent U-235, can be used to fuel nuclear reactors producing electricity; enrichment to 20 per cent is not uncommon for reactors producing radioisotopes for use in medicine and industry, and some naval nuclear reactors use even more highly enriched uranium. Reactors may be used to produce Pu-239, which is fissile like U-235 and does not occur naturally, but separating it out is a difficult and dangerous chemical process. The 'value' of Pu-239 is that it is more effective as the core component of a nuclear weapon, and therefore most weapons use this.

A great many of the intellectual capabilities, skills, techniques and instruments required to produce reactor-grade U-235 for a civil nuclear industry are the same as, or similar to, those required to produce weapons-grade U-235. Indeed, the same enrichment plant can be used, with some modifications, to continue enriching 4 per cent or 20 per cent uranium to weapons-grade level. This is at the root of fears about civil nuclear industries, and has also been at the heart of the controversy over Iranian intentions.

For a paramilitary group to produce even a crude uranium weapon, it would require a supply of processed uranium ore, and for that ore to be fed into a substantial and expensive enrichment plant and then converted into metal. Even then, to make the weapon itself would require considerable metallurgical skill and some means of delivery. The same applies to a weapon using plutonium, except that it would also require a sophisticated reprocessing facility to separate it out from reactor waste. To this extent, producing nuclear weapons from scratch is beyond the capability of any sub-state group that currently exists. If, in the future, an extremist group were to maintain control of territory that included reasonably advanced industries, and were able to bring together the expertise necessary and to identify a source of uranium, then it might be possible to produce nuclear weapons, but that is still a long way off.

There remain two other ways. One is to buy or steal weapons-grade uranium or even a complete weapon. While there were concerns about this in the chaos that followed the collapse of the Soviet economy in the early and mid-1990s, these have diminished substantially, although if societal breakdown were to occur in an existing nuclear-weapons state such as North Korea or Pakistan, there would be huge fears for the security of nuclear arsenals. The other risk is that a state could supply a sub-state group, possibly because it was of political value to that state to do so. While highly unlikely, this has to be considered given the very existence and continued development of nuclear weapons.

This is perhaps the real issue. Nuclear weapons are here; they are held by only a handful of countries, although some more are based in client states, as in the case of US nuclear weapons in some NATO countries; and none of the existing nuclear powers shows any sign of a serious commitment to a nuclear-free world. In fact, quite the reverse, since we have seen how committed all nuclear states are to the modernisation of their arsenals. The brief period of potential movement towards a nuclear-free world has gone, at least for now, and the 2015 review conference of the Nuclear Non-Proliferation Treaty, originally signed in 1968, was widely considered a failure.[8] Over the coming decades, therefore, we should expect further proliferation to occur, even if it seems unlikely at present. Thus, there is a serious long-term issue, especially since one of the arguments of this book is that on present trends we are moving into an era of considerable international instability and uncertainty.

Looked at overall, the chances of nuclear weapons being used by groups like ISIS are very low, at least for now, though that may not remain the case in the coming decades. The risk of the use of CBR weapons is much higher, and while they would be unlikely to cause very large numbers of deaths, the fear factor with chemical and biological weapons and the potential economic chaos rendered by a successful radiological attack would be substantial.

CAUSE FOR CONCERN?

The 9/11 attacks on the World Trade Center and the Pentagon killed 3,000 people yet did not even involve firearms. The 1993 World Trade Center attack, if fully successful, would have been close to the area bombings of Hamburg and Dresden during World War II in terms of destructiveness, and within reach of the impact of the 1945 Tokyo firebombing – a raid by US B-29 bombers that killed more than 100,000 people – and the two nuclear attacks on Hiroshima and Nagasaki.

That is the perspective that we should have in mind when we raise the question of whether WMD could give a group such as ISIS the capacity for an existential attack. The very term 'existential' implies threatening the survival of a country or even a people, and that would require nothing short of a sustained nuclear attack with many warheads, an attack likely to be beyond the capability of any paramilitary group at present and also in the foreseeable future. If we restrict 'existential' to a threat to the existence of a single large city, then even that would require the use of a single massive weapon in the multi-megatonne range or of a cluster of smaller nuclear weapons. That, too, is beyond the capabilities of any known or likely group.

This would seem to imply that the idea of an existential threat, whether country- or city-wide, is somewhat overhyped and more likely to be used as a political device to raise the impact of a given paramilitary group such as ISIS. This might be done by propagan-dists for ISIS, by future extreme groups seeking to exaggerate their own power, or by states whose interests are threatened by ISIS and who wish to increase the perception of risk so that they can take stronger action against it. This last tactic may have been used to persuade Western electorates to accept the need to terminate the Saddam Hussein regime back in 2002–3, and there have been regular press reports of ISIS seeking WMD, albeit mainly in the form of chemical and biological weapons.

Remember, though, the demonstrated abilities of sub-state movements to have a considerable effect without WMD. Apart from 9/11 itself, there was PIRA's use of economic targeting in the United Kingdom in the 1990s and what would have hap-pened if the 1993 attempt to destroy the World Trade Center had worked as planned. There are many other examples, some that succeeded and others that didn't. For instance, in December 1994 an Air France Airbus A300 was hijacked en route from Algiers to Paris by four members of an extreme Algerian group. Their intention was to crash in the centre of Paris, but the plane was stormed by counter-terrorism forces during a refuelling halt at Marseilles airport. Just over a year later, in January 1996, the Sri Lanka Army captured the LTTE stronghold of Jaffna, at great cost to its own men, with more than 600 killed. Many of the LTTE paramilitaries melted away, but the movement retaliated with a devastating attack in which a large truck bomb was detonated at the entrance to the Central Bank in the heart of Colombo's business district. Nearly 100 people were killed and more than 400 were injured.

Many of the al-Qaeda attacks in the early years of this century had huge impacts, including the London and Madrid attacks and the Sari nightclub bombing in Bali. Looked at more broadly, the collective result of the al-Qaeda campaign has been a massive worldwide expenditure on protection and security procedures, especially at airports, as well as a huge expansion in the resources committed to intelligence, policing and counter-terrorism. All of these and many other incidents involved conventional explosives; the impact of the *Charlie Hebdo* attacks using nothing more than light arms was huge, and there remains the potential for cyberattacks.

Concerns over cybersecurity have increased hugely in recent years, though the main emphasis has been on the capabilities of states, as shown by the 'Nashi' incident in Estonia in 2007 (which was blamed on Russian government agencies) and the Stuxnet attack on Iranian nuclear facilities in 2010 (widely believed to be the work of the US and Israeli governments), and also of well-resourced groups engaged in commercial espionage.[9] In relation to extreme paramilitary groups such as ISIS, a recent analysis pointed out that

> no cyber attack has ever demonstrated the ability to inflict physical damage on the scale of a military or terrorist attack and many cyber security experts have reacted to the prospect of an upcoming 'cyber 9/11', or even a 'cyber Hiroshima' with more pragmatism and less panic.[10]

One reason is that experience so far, with Stuxnet for example, suggests that such an attack 'requires great expertise, significant resources and a profound knowledge of the target'.[11] That, at least, is the situation at the time of writing.

So if the threat of paramilitaries with WMD or cyber capabilities is exaggerated, is there any cause for concern? The answer, almost certainly, is yes, and at two levels. The first is that an existing group such as ISIS might find the means to produce and then use a crude chemical or radiological weapon or even attempt an attack with anthrax or another bio-agent. Given the brutality of the movement, it is right to think that if it develops the ability it may use it, but the main effect would be fear. Even if an attack had a substantial human impact with casualties at the level of the Colombo, London or Madrid atrocities, the psychological effect would be very much greater, based primarily on the fear of the unknown.

This limited threat from WMD cannot be described as 'existential' in the proper sense of the word, but in a narrower sense it might be. Given the far greater fear of chemical and especially biological weapons, the use of such weapons by a group such as ISIS would lead to a hugely increased demand for tighter security, far more surveillance, less acceptance of difference and a severe escalation in Islamophobia. It could impact and alter current political systems, including what in other circumstances would be seen as wholly unacceptable infringements of human rights. In other words, the existential threat to our more or less liberal democratic societies would come not from the actions of extremists but rather from the reactions of our own politicians and media.

The second level concerns what might be developed or acquired by extreme paramilitary movements in the longer term, perhaps over the next two or three decades, especially if they are movements that have been able to take and maintain control of substantial territory and populations. This would enable them to assemble the resources and expertise necessary to develop far more powerful weapons. Because of the sheer destructiveness of nuclear weapons, it is these that have to be taken most seriously. As I have emphasised, the indigenous production of nuclear weapons, even by an extreme movement that has controlled significant territory for some years, would still be very difficult and probably detectable. This suggests that the risk is small, even in the long term.

Perhaps – but perhaps not. After the end of the Cold War there was a real chance that the contraction and downgrading of nuclear arsenals might continue to the point where they would become marginalised as instruments of strategy, one key effect being to reduce the probability of proliferation. This, combined with the decline in the development of nuclear power, would mean that the nuclear fuel cycle would itself decline, the two aiding the process of reducing the risk of knowledge, technologies and fissile material being available to extreme groups.

Nuclear-power generation is less favoured than it was, not least because of the Fukushima catastrophe in 2011, but given the deterioration in NATO–Russian relations since 2010, there seems little or no prospect of the existing nuclear powers reducing their commitment to nuclear weapons. They are here to stay, at least until the next nuclear war. With their persistence comes the continuing risk of proliferation and also of their diversion into the hands of extreme groups. However, this is unlikely to be imminent, and we are talking most likely about circumstances towards the middle of this century.

THE IRAQ EXAMPLE

Much of this chapter leads to the conclusion that it is overly pessimistic to suggest that extreme movements such as ISIS may gain the capacity to launch existential or even catastrophic mass-casualty attacks. While that is a reasonable summary, there is a very significant caveat that takes us back to the beginning of the chapter, where I pointed to the experience of the 1991 Gulf War and how close that took us to the use of biological and chemical weapons. The context of this is important to examine because it is a reminder of what can happen when a determined regime decides to follow this path.[12]

Under Saddam Hussein, Iraq had developed into a powerful regional force by the end of the 1970s, utilising its considerable oil wealth to advance its education system and industrial base. With aspirations to be a major power and a leader of the Arab world it worked systematically to develop a wide range of conventional armaments, but also looked to produce nuclear, chemical and biological weapons. This particular effort continued after it attacked Iran in 1980, which it had assumed to be in a vulnerable state in the wake of the violence and disruption that followed the revolution of 1979. Indeed, the failure of that attack and the bitter and protracted war that followed made it an even higher priority for the Saddam Hussein regime to have major deterrent systems.

Even by 1979, the year Saddam Hussein finally consolidated power, Iraq already had stocks of chemical weapons, including mustard gas and nerve agents such as sarin. A nuclear-weapons programme was reported to be well under way, based on the plutonium route, which required an experimental nuclear reactor, the Osiraq plant, being built near Baghdad. Israel, aware of this programme, was not prepared to see any other state in the region challenge its nuclear monopoly, and destroyed the reactor in an air raid in 1981. It is not now certain that the Osiraq plant was part of a nuclear-weapons programme, but it is clear that an effect of the Israeli attack was to increase the determination of the regime to develop nuclear weapons.

Dependent normally on a single facility – an appropriate nuclear reactor and reprocessing plant – the plutonium route to nuclear weapons is clearly vulnerable to pre-emption, and so the regime opted for the uranium route, which could be dispersed to a number of sites. It also established a much more substantial series of chemical-weapons plants. In addition, the regime put far more resources into developing delivery systems based partly on imported strike aircraft and locally modified surface-to-surface missiles using the old Soviet Scud design.

In spite of committing some $10 billion and employing 7,000 people, Iraq's nuclear programme made slow progress in the 1980s, but its biological-warfare effort, begun in 1985 with work on anthrax, was a different matter. Within two years the decision was taken to move to a full-scale biological-weapons-production programme, and by March 1988 a plant and a parallel research centre were established, the plant concentrating on the production of anthrax and also on botulinum toxin, a particularly lethal poison produced by the microorganism *Clostridium botulinum*.

The entire programme included fermentation equipment imported for supposed use in acceptable processes such as antibiotic production, coupled with equipment commandeered from across Iraq. By May 1989 Iraq had started mass production of both of these biological-warfare agents, producing 6,000 litres of concentrated botulinum toxin and 8,425 litres of anthrax in 1990 alone. While this was happening, research was conducted into other agents. One of these was *Clostridium perfringens*, which is the causal agent of gas gangrene. The thinking was that if cluster munitions were impregnated with this agent, resulting wounds among enemy military forces would be more likely to become gangrenous, stretching medical resources as well as causing great fear and anxiety among the military.

Another research track was looking at mycotoxins (toxins produced by fungi), including one that caused cancer and others that caused vomiting and diarrhoea, as well as a virus that caused haemorrhagic conjunctivitis, involving extreme pain and temporary blindness. The regime even investigated anti-crop warfare, producing large quantities of the organism that causes 'covered smut' in wheat, a potentially devastating plant pathogen that could have been used against Iranian crops.

In parallel with this work, the regime invested heavily in a range of delivery systems, including 122-mm rockets and aircraft-delivered bombs and spray tanks. Experimental field trials commenced as early as 1988 and were sufficiently successful that by 1991 166 bombs had been produced, ready for use – 100 filled with botulinum, 50 with anthrax and 16 with aflatoxin – as well as 25 al-Hussein medium-range ballistic missiles.

ISIS and other extreme movements may not be in the same league as Iraq in the 1980s, but the Iraqi example is still worthy of attention. It is an indicator of what could be achieved many years ago and what might be possible on a much smaller scale in the near future. At the very least it should provide food for thought in any analysis of the potential for extreme paramilitary movements to cause far greater problems than security specialists tend to assume, and a spur to redouble efforts to promote arms control, especially after the failure of the 2015 Nuclear Non-Proliferation Treaty Review Conference to make any progress.

That, though, is a very good reason to pay more attention to the nature of current extreme groups, the subject of the next two chapters, and then to look at the global security environment, in order to assess whether movements such as ISIS will themselves endure, or whether they should be seen as symptoms of a wider malaise in a global system with serious economic failures and environmental constraints likely to spawn more revolts from the margins. In such circumstances, a concern with WMD – CBR and especially nuclear – should be high on the agenda as a particularly strong motive for avoiding such a dystopian global environment.

This is an added motivation for addressing the underlying causes of current and potential conflicts. If this does not happen, there may be an argument that robust military responses to movements such as ISIS are necessary actions that Western states simply have to learn to live with. Even with all the failures since the 9/11 attacks there is still an embedded resistance to accepting the idea that the control paradigm, with heavy reliance on military force, is now becoming obsolete. The risk from the potential development and use of WMD by extreme movements may not be the only reason for seeking an alternative path to a more sustainable security system, but it is a powerful reason for doing so.

5

ISIS AND ITS FUTURE

In June 2014 a force of barely 1,000 paramilitary jihadists easily overran Iraq's second city of Mosul, driving out a far larger Iraqi Army force and taking control of a huge quantity of vehicles, weapons and ammunition. Much of this was rapidly moved across north-western Iraq, over the border into Syria and to the centre of ISIS's power – the city of Raqqa. The rapidity of the advance caught almost every analyst and intelligence specialist by surprise, especially as the movement went on to add to its existing control of substantial parts of Iraq's Anbar Province, having already taken control of the key city of Fallujah six months earlier.

Together, these advances, and the shock of the change in the status of the movement soon to call itself ISIS, led to Western and regional countries recognising that an extreme Islamist group now controlled substantial territory in the heart of the Middle East, far more than was achieved by al-Qaeda in the previous two decades. While the territory did not include major oilfields, many smaller oilfields and local refineries were under ISIS's control, as were some hydroelectric plants and irrigation dams. By July 2014 ISIS controlled land similar in size to the island of Britain and with a population of around 6 million. Much of the territory was desert or semi-desert scrubland, but the valley of the Euphrates and some of its tributaries was rich agricultural land, with the food produced there readily amenable to taxation.

Of even greater use to ISIS was the fact that, in recent times, the whole region had become a haven for smuggling, with a huge array of produce and consumer goods as well as oil and processed petroleum products, moving between northern Syria, northern Iraq and Turkey, with Iran also involved. Most if not all of the borders were porous, with numerous back routes available, but smuggling was, even so, a ready source of income for the movement, as those involved were willing enough to pay tolls for permission to move their goods.

ISIS had other sources of supply. These included financial support from abroad, particularly sympathetic wealthy individuals in western Gulf states, especially Saudi Arabia, and it also had unexpected but very welcome windfalls, notably more than $400 million in Iraqi currency that was looted from banks when Mosul was taken.

The culmination of ISIS's expansion came with the appearance of its leader, Abu Bakr al-Baghdadi, in a mosque in Mosul on 5 July, and his declaration of an Islamic caliphate with himself as its head, stretching initially across substantial parts of Iraq and Syria but clearly with much greater ambitions. Even at this stage, ISIS differed substantially from the original al-Qaeda vision of a decade and a half earlier. The al-Qaeda of Osama bin Laden and Ayman al-Zawahiri was bitterly opposed to the near enemies comprising the apostate rulers in Egypt, Jordan and elsewhere in the region, with the greatest antagonism directed towards the House of Saud, the utterly unacceptable 'Guardian of the Two Holy Places'. It also supported separatist movements elsewhere, including in Chechnya and Thailand, and was bitterly anti-Zionist, as well as opposing the United States and its partner states – the far enemy.

The long-term al-Qaeda vision was of an evolving caliphate that would ultimately spread worldwide, perhaps in a century or more, but how this would materialise was less clear, the initial aim being to overthrow existing regimes and take control of states one by one – the Taliban's victory in Afghanistan being an example.

From the start, though, al-Baghdadi and the other leaders within ISIS saw the control of territory, rather than the overthrow of states, as the key to longer-term success, partly to ensure security, but mainly as a powerful symbol of a renewed Islamic entity with 1,400 years of history.

By 2014 al-Qaeda had little in the way of territorial control – its associate in Yemen notwithstanding, it was essentially restricted to a few districts in north-western Pakistan. Islamist militias in Libya, Egypt, Mali, Niger and other states might control some territory, and a few might have substantial control, including al-Shabaab in Somalia and Boko Haram in Nigeria, but while such groups might well be powerful in their own right they are, at best, at a distance from the remaining al-Qaeda leadership, and in no way under its control.

For ISIS, control of territory was an early priority. It was not even a means to an end but an end in itself. The leadership correctly saw the potency of establishing a proto-caliphate, and its steady acquisition of territory in Syria from 2012 onwards, coupled with its rapid takeover of a substantial part of north-western Iraq, showed at a stroke that a caliphate was actually being created. Islamists controlled land and people, and on a substantial scale – this was a development without parallel in the modern history of Islamism, but one that also adds to the potential of future paramilitary movements.

This last point, about the future, is relevant to my broader theme, and therefore this chapter will look at the rise, resilience and potential of ISIS. This book argues that a future in which the core global problems stem from a thoroughly dysfunctional economy and critical environmental constraints is one in which revolts from the margins will become the norm. Developments in the post-9/11 world, and especially the rise of ISIS, are unambiguous markers of the forms of insecurity that will await us if the underlying problems are not addressed. Moreover, the persistent failures of presumed military solutions to ISIS, al-Qaeda and other extreme movements point to the risk of future failure without a change in thinking.

To assess ISIS's capabilities, intentions and prospects, it is essential to understand how it was able to emerge, apparently from nowhere, and to have such a major effect. Remember that in Barack Obama's election campaign in 2008 he argued that Iraq was a 'bad war', that it had little connection with al-Qaeda and 9/11 and therefore little relevance to US interests, at least in terms of the human costs and financial outlays. Once in power, Obama was able to plan the withdrawal, although the administration aimed to keep a much smaller force of combat troops in the country.[1] The al-Maliki regime in Baghdad would not countenance a continuing US military presence unless the troops were subject to Iraqi law, but since that was not acceptable to the United States the withdrawal was completed by the end of 2011.

Obama, early in his second term, could count this a major success, even if serious problems remained in Afghanistan – Iraq, at least, would no longer be a major issue. Contrast that with the sudden rise of ISIS in 2014 and the substantial engagement of the United States in a major air war from August onwards. At the head of a coalition of a dozen states, the United States was back in Iraq less than three years after its departure, and the intensity of the air war quickly exceeded anything in Afghanistan over the previous five years.

There are several reasons for this remarkable change, one of which has already been explored. This is the manner in which the 'shadow war' fought by US and UK special forces from 2004 onwards, which may have led to the curbing of the most potent element of the Sunni insurgency in Iraq, ended by leaving a cohort of hugely experienced, bitter and determined paramilitaries who had survived combat with the world's best-trained and -equipped troops. These men, many of whom also served time in the massive detention camps, were crucial to the subsequent growth of ISIS, and their significance should not be underestimated – the movement's rapid progress across northern Iraq during 2014 would not have happened otherwise.

There were other important factors that help explain ISIS's power and influence by early 2015, and when put together they show both how the movement grew and also why its potential was, and still is, persistently overlooked. These factors are particularly interesting because, taken together with that hugely influential combat-trained cohort, they worked in a synergistic manner. They included the Arab Awakening, the Syrian civil war, the policies of the al-Maliki government in Iraq, political attitudes in Europe towards fighting further wars in the region and, finally, wider geopolitical factors including Saudi–Iranian relations in the context of Russian and US regional security policy. Of all of these the development and chequered history of the Arab Awakening is the most important in understanding the sudden growth of ISIS.

ARAB AWAKENING, SYRIAN CIVIL WAR AND ISLAMIST OPPORTUNITY

The young Tunisian street vendor Mohamed Bouazizi set himself on fire on 17 December 2010 in a desperate response to a life with no hope of advancement, and died from his burns two weeks later. His death prompted a chain of mass street demonstrations that became so intense that the autocratic regime of Zine el-Abidine Ben Ali collapsed after they peaked on the weekend of 8–9 January 2011. Opposition elements linked to the Muslim Brotherhood had been in jail for many years or driven underground by the regime, and the rebellion was largely secular and stemmed partly from hatred of the sheer autocracy of the government and the elite that gained so much from the system, but also partly from the lack of economic opportunity for so many Tunisians, not least many tens of thousands of young unemployed graduates.

This 'Arab Awakening', as it came to be called, spread rapidly to Egypt and across much of North Africa and the Middle East, aided by 24-hour TV news channels and the widespread use of new social media. Within a month the regime of Hosni Mubarak in Egypt had collapsed, following an extraordinary series of demonstrations, especially in Cairo's Tahrir Square, with this seeming to mark the start of a region-wide transformation away from autocracy and towards more representative governance. It appeared to be a time of great promise, but with huge risks too. In my own analysis for ORG towards the end of January 2011, as the demonstrations in Egypt were reaching a climax, the elements of promise and uncertainty were both addressed:

> The coming weeks and months will determine whether the traumatic political changes in Tunisia lead on to a stable and more accountable government, and whether the Tunisian experience is repeated elsewhere. If Tunisia does make a successful transition, then other elite regimes may possibly recognise the need to promote emancipation and democracy, and there might just be peaceful trans-itions elsewhere. That is the most optimistic assessment [...] What is well-nigh certain is that the combination of the deep socio-economic divisions across the region and the gathering impact of environmental constraints mean that in the absence of human security-orientated political change, there will be severe instability and suf-fering, even if that is over the next decade rather than the next year.[2]

One of the most significant aspects of the rapid political changes in the first three months of 2011 was the possible impact on al-Qaeda. The movement appeared to have been in retreat worldwide in the three years leading up to Osama bin Laden's death in May 2011, and if the Arab Awakening were to succeed, with a progressive transition towards more representative democracy achieved in part by non-violent protest, it could be a very serious setback for the al-Qaeda aim of working for the violent overthrow of apostate non-Islamist autocracies.

If, on the other hand, the transition stalled – if autocratic regimes held on and even increased the suppression of dissent – then the outcome might be very different. Those millions of people who supported non-violent change would see all too clearly that it was a failed response to their predicament. In such circumstances many might turn to more extreme alternatives, including a radical-Islamist approach. In such circumstances the al-Qaeda idea might be revived, with an added intensity born of desperation.

In the event, beyond Tunisia and Egypt the region's autocracies reacted in three different ways. Some, such as Saudi Arabia and Oman, combined repression with concessions: dissent was dealt with firmly, demonstrations were put down and organisers were jailed, but major economic reforms were made, commonly in the form of increased pay and pension rights for government employees. Some regimes such as Morocco engaged in a modicum of reform, which was just sufficient to ward off major dissent, although this may not work for much longer in Jordan. Others chose repression, including Bahrain, Libya and Syria. Bahrain's repression of its Shi'i majority was supported by Saudi Arabia and the United Arab Emirates, both of whom sent security personnel, whereas in Libya NATO supported rebel forces in a six-month war that led to the violent end of the Gaddafi regime and the lynching of its leader, even though he had become a favoured figure for some Western states in recent years, and his country a potentially lucrative market for arms sales.

With the collapse of the Gaddafi regime, Libya disintegrated into militia-riddled chaos, and during the course of 2011 many Western analysts thought that Syria's Assad regime might follow suit. There, the state had responded to non-violent street protests, mostly by young people gathering after Friday prayers, with systematic repression that resulted in many deaths. The 40-year regime of the Assads had depended on support from the

Alawite minority, an Islamic sect leaning towards Shi'ism, but also had tacit support from successful Sunni business interests and Christian and other minorities, all of whom feared chaos if the regime collapsed.

The Assad regime had strong support from Iran and also from Putin's Russia, with the latter regarding Syria as its last major ally in the region – the Russian Navy's only facilities on the Mediterranean coast are in the Syrian port of Tartus. This support, combined with harsh repression and a fragmented secular opposition, meant that by the end of 2011 the regime remained entrenched in power in spite of a rapidly increasing death toll and huge displacement of people seeking shelter and an escape from the violence. It was also aided by the reluctance of Western states to intervene, primarily because of the disastrous outcomes of the wars in Afghanistan and Iraq. This would later be demonstrated by the failure of the United Kingdom's Conservative-led coalition government to get a parliamentary majority for the possible use of force against the Assad regime late in 2013.

From the start of the regime's violent repression of the rebellion, Assad repeatedly claimed he was faced with terrorists and that all states should recognise the threat. To an extent this was a self-fulfilling prophecy, in that during the latter part of 2011 and into 2012, Islamist elements in the rebellion came to the fore. Moreover, the Assad regime actually aided this process by releasing many hundreds of Islamists from prison early in 2011. This gave a substantial boost to the extreme tendency within the insurgency, and one of the key groups, the al-Nusra Front, claimed responsibility for its first substantive attack in January 2012. A number of smaller Islamist militias also gained ground but the most significant development was the growth in Syria of what is now known as ISIS, which had regrouped in Iraq following al-Zarqawi's killing in 2006 and the serious losses that were due to the intense operations of JSOC, especially during Operation Arcadia (see Chapter 3).

The drawdown of US forces in Iraq during 2011 coincided almost precisely with the intensification of the Syrian civil war, and as ISIS extended into Syria it could also expand decisively in Iraq. By late 2012, while it was growing in strength in Iraq, its achievements in Syria were remarkable. In spite of an often violent rivalry with the al-Nusra Front, which retained its al-Qaeda orientation, it gained territory centred primarily on Raqqa, but rapidly extending towards the Iraqi border.

Of particular assistance to ISIS has been the Assad regime's recognition that if such an extreme jihadist movement represents a substantial part of the rebellion, then the regime can present itself not as a ruthless suppressor of dissent but as a bulwark against a movement that is even more brutal and dangerous than those linked to al-Qaeda. One result of this is that much of the regime's effort in the civil war has been directed against the more secular elements of the rebellion, effectively aiding ISIS and indirectly leading to an evolving assessment in Western intelligence circles that the Assad regime might be the lesser threat to Western interests.

TRANSFORMATION IN IRAQ

Meanwhile, changing political and security circumstances in Iraq have provided the movement with many opportunities for consolidation and expansion. Two elements relate particularly to the government of Nouri al-Maliki.

The first is the issue of interconfessional conflict between Sunni and Shiʻa. During the Saddam Hussein era power had rested principally in the hands of the leader and those close to him, especially the 'Tikrit clan' from his home city and surrounding towns and villages. More generally, though, his regime persistently favoured the Sunni minority, to which he and the Tikrit clan belonged, over the Shiʻi majority. This was so deep-rooted that when al-Maliki came to power at the head of a coalition of largely Shiʻi parties, this favouritism was reversed. Although al-Maliki was under some pressure to reach out to the Sunni minority, he was deeply reluctant to do this, since further electoral success depended largely on the Shi'a. This marginalising of the Sunni became even more apparent as the Iraqi security forces progressively took control during the US withdrawal in 2011, with a marked increase in bitterness on the part of the Sunni clans, not least in Anbar Province and especially in previous centres of rebellion against the Western occupation, such as the city of Fallujah.

Over the period 2011–12, this kind of conflict grew rapidly, much of it originating in attacks on governmental targets and Shi'i communities and commonly involving powerful truck bombs delivered by suicide bombers. Coming often from ISIS, which had been effectively under the control of Abu Bakr al-Baghdadi from early 2010, the overall intention was to increase Shi'i anger at the Sunni minority, thereby radicalising that minority in its hatred of the regime. Within this was the more specific intention of targeting Iraqi security personnel, killing them and their associates and thus undermining morale.

The second element was that al-Maliki himself had continual doubts over the loyalty of elements of the Iraqi officer corps, and repeatedly replaced competent senior officers with his own men, however incompetent they might be. Even though the United States was putting considerable resources into training and equipping the army, this remained an Achilles heel once the US forces had withdrawn.

Another factor that was key to the rapid growth of ISIS was a specific series of operations it mounted in Iraq, mainly during 2012. As was emphasised earlier, much of the redevelopment of ISIS depended on highly motivated, experienced and skilled paramilitaries who had survived the shadow war against Western special forces, either avoiding capture or being released from prison when the US forces withdrew. One key element among this community was the many hundreds of paramilitaries who were not released, but were handed over to the Iraqi government as being too dangerous.

For ISIS under al-Baghdadi, this was a crucial group, encompassing people who were essential if it was to prosper. As a result, and with its forces sufficiently consolidated in Iraq and making progress in Syria, ISIS engaged in a year-long programme called 'Operation Breaking the Walls', beginning in July 2012, to release these high-value prisoners from the jails.[3] This met with considerable success and culminated in an extraordinary attack on Abu Ghraib prison, a few miles west of Baghdad, on 21 July 2013. Abu Ghraib had been best known for the reported abuse of inmates when under US military control, but its subsequent role in al-Maliki's Iraq was as a high-security prison for the most dangerous prisoners, including many associated with ISIS. According to one report:

> The deadly raid on the high-security jail happened as Sunni Muslim militants are regaining momentum in their insurgency against the Shia-led government.
>
> Suicide bombers drove cars packed with explosives to the gates of the prison on the outskirts of Baghdad on Sunday night and blasted their way into the compound, while gunmen attacked guards with mortars and rocket-propelled grenades.
>
> Other militants took up positions near the main road, fighting off security reinforcements sent from Baghdad as militants wearing suicide vests entered the prison on foot to help free the inmates.
>
> Ten policemen and four militants were killed in the ensuing clashes, which continued until Monday morning, when military helicopters arrived, helping to regain control.
>
> By that time, hundreds of inmates had succeeded in fleeing Abu Ghraib, the prison made notorious a decade ago by photographs showing abuse of prisoners by US soldiers.

'The number of escaped inmates has reached 500, most
of them were convicted senior members of al-Qaeda and
had received death sentences,' Hakim al-Zamili, a senior
member of the security and defence committee in parliament, told Reuters.[4]

Less than a year later, as ISIS moved right across north-western
Iraq, it conducted more prison raids. In May and June 2014 it
released 1,500 prisoners from detention centres in Mosul and 300
from a prison in Tikrit. Some of these were common criminals,
but they included more extreme jihadists who had not been freed
in the Abu Ghraib breakout the previous year.

Overall, these actions greatly boosted the paramilitary capabilities of ISIS, but there was still another factor that helped it
consolidate its advantage and to do so in a manner that combined pragmatism with the kind of flexibility not expected from
a dedicated and single-minded extreme movement. This was its
willingness to undertake informal but stable agreements with
groups for which ISIS had little or no liking. The most evident
example of this was the working together of three groups in Iraq
throughout most of 2014.

One was the core paramilitary element of the movement,
which was at the forefront of the fighting and particularly effective
because of a field leadership drawn from people who had survived
the special-forces operations of the Iraq War. But two other groups
were crucial, one being the militias drawn from Sunni clans,
especially in Iraq's Anbar Province. Their hatred of the al-Maliki
regime was more than enough for them to accept that ISIS was the
immediate way to curb the power of the state to marginalise Iraq's
Sunni minority. The other was drawn from surviving Ba'athists,
many of whom had originally been at the core of Saddam Hussein's
power. When that regime fell, the great majority of the elite units
chose not to oppose the US forces, which had an overwhelming
firepower advantage, and went to ground. The most significant

elements of these groups were drawn from four brigades of the Special Republican Guard, together with battalions attached to the old regime's intelligence and security ministries. A pattern emerged as ISIS made its rapid progress across north-western Iraq, in which its own fighters would take control of towns and cities but would then move on, leaving most of the power in the hands of Ba'athists and clan militias. By this means, fewer than 5,000 paramilitaries were able to occupy cities such as Mosul, as well as many smaller towns

One other factor is relevant: the impact of Israel's Operation Protective Edge against Hamas and other militias in Gaza during July and August 2014, just as ISIS was expanding its territorial control across northern Syria and north-western Iraq. The Israel factor has been discussed in Chapters 2 and 3, to the extent that it may seem a fixation, but when we consider the fact that Western observers find it very difficult to understand the impact Israel has, and its value to a movement such as ISIS, the emphasis is not so surprising. From the perspective of the government of Benjamin Netanyahu, the firing of unguided rockets into southern Israel had become utterly unacceptable, even if few hit populated areas and casualties were minimal. What was important was the psychological impact of the uncertainty about where the rockets might land, and the seeming inability of Israel, a regional military superpower, to prevent them, even with its impressive surveillance and intelligence capabilities and its vaunted 'Iron Dome' missile defence system. For the Israelis, therefore, it was essential to put a stop to this obvious aggression, and this required considerable use of force, which would be centred on air power. In the event, after weeks of air strikes and ground incursions, Israel eventually withdrew, and an uneasy ceasefire took hold, but the representation of the conflict in the Arab media across the Middle East favoured extreme jihadist movements such as ISIS. From an Arab perspective there was nothing that Hamas could do to stop the Israelis from destroying buildings, apparently at will, killing old men, women and children in the process. TV images, widely screened across the region, of Israeli settlers bringing their armchairs and picnics to sit on hills overlooking Gaza and watch the killing of Palestinians had a potent impact, not specifically on ISIS but on the wider Arab mood. In such circumstances, the one movement that seemed to be making progress against unacceptable regimes such as that of Nouri al-Maliki was surely worthy of support. What appeared to the Israelis to be the appropriate policy to contain a threat from the margins of Gaza had a much wider impact right across the region and beyond.

This mood persisted after the end of the war, and continued towards the end of the year as it became obvious that Israel was doing all it could to delay and hinder the repair and reconstruction of the thousands of buildings in Gaza damaged by Israeli air and drone strikes and artillery. It also connected with anger against the regime of Abdel Fattah al-Sisi in Cairo, as it, too, hindered reconstruction, an attitude stemming largely from al-Sisi's view of Hamas as being almost synonymous with the despised Muslim Brotherhood. By early 2015, radicalisation within Egypt was progressing, especially in Sinai, with every prospect that Egypt could experience sustained instability.

PROSPECTS FOR ISIS

By mid-2015 ISIS had consolidated its position, even if it was facing increased military action that was sufficient to prevent its further advance in Iraq. As of the time of writing (early 2016), its leadership and most advanced levels of political organisation are located primarily in Syria, especially in the city of Raqqa, and it has developed a robust structure that has a number of components. Its position is certainly challenged by the intensive air war being waged against it, although most of the emphasis of the air operations is on preventing further advances in Iraq.

The intensity of the war was fully reported through ISIS's own media outlets, especially the many forms of new social media that it has become particularly adept at utilising, even if there is virtually no reporting of the war in the Western media. In November 2015, US Central Command (CENTCOM), which is running the air war, reported that in the first 15 months of the campaign some 57,000 sorties had been flown, and that 8,300 air strikes had attacked 16,075 separate targets, killing 20,000 ISIS supporters.

Even so, there is little evidence that ISIS as a paramilitary and political movement is in retreat. Indeed, US estimates of the number of fighters available to ISIS remained at 20–30,000 by the end of the 15 months, the same as at the beginning of that time. Moreover, over broadly the same period, the US assessment of the number of recruits to ISIS from abroad rose from 15,000 from 80 countries to 30,000 from 100 countries. The intense air war is not defeating ISIS.

This is partly explained by the degree of organisation and the extent of paramilitary experience that ISIS now possesses. Within Iraq, as discussed above, ISIS's success in 2014 was aided by Sunni clan militias prepared to work with it against the common enemy of the al-Maliki government, and also by the willingness of former Ba'athists from the Saddam Hussein regime to be involved in the political governance of towns and cities that were overrun. There is much more to it than this, though, and a better understanding of ISIS's status and potential can be reached by looking at both the make-up of its key people and the extent of their support base.[5]

At the core is the leadership of al-Baghdadi, the proclaimed caliph, who has a number of established deputies. This leadership is closely linked to a system of religious authority rooted principally in the Sharia Council and a separate advisory Shura Council. Power lies with the leadership even if it is constantly aware of the need for full religious legitimacy. The leadership is thoroughly imbued with its singular and rigidly narrow interpretation of Islam, and this remains at the heart of ISIS. The vision is closely allied to the al-Qaeda idea in one respect and different from it in another, a key to understanding ISIS and its distinctiveness.

The similarity is that both movements are fundamentally eschatological: they look beyond earthly existence to eternity. Both may be described as revolutionary movements, like others in history that have sought the overthrow of leaderships or regimes, and like many others their aims are seen as best achieved through violence, since existing regimes threatened by revolutionary movements will inevitably use force against them. They see no prospect of a peaceful transition. Both are highly unusual since revolutionary movements are more commonly rooted in a political ideology such as neo-Maoism, nationalist or ethnic identities, or a combination of these. Such movements typically anticipate progress within years or decades and certainly within the lifetimes of the key leaders and ideologues. Neither al-Qaeda nor ISIS has this limitation, and they each look a century or more ahead. Like al-Qaeda, ISIS is in it not just for the long term but for the very long term – indeed, for eternity. This does not mean that every supporter, every fighter, has this outlook. As in any movement there are many different orientations, and there will be plenty of paramilitaries within ISIS seeking power, status or retribution. But the movement as a whole was and is rooted in an ultra-long-term view. This is the culture of the leadership and it permeates planning, tactics and internal politics.

The difference concerns the two organisations' territorial ambitions. Al-Qaeda has been focused mainly on the revolutionary downfall of the unacceptable regimes of the Arab-Islamic world, the so-called 'near enemy'. In a sense it has been territorial in its outlook, but in a state-centred manner. The overthrow of existing regimes and their replacement by acceptable Islamist alternatives have been at the core of its thinking, and the support for the Taliban regime in the mid- and late 1990s was an obvious example of this. Destroy unacceptable regimes, replace them with 'proper' regimes, and the revolution will spread outwards. At some stage a caliphate will be established.

For ISIS, the fundamental policy is radically different, and this got its clearest expression in the very early establishment of a caliphate by al-Baghdadi, with himself as the new caliph, in the Mosul mosque in June 2014. ISIS does not relate to an existing state, but has been carved out from territory that stretches across two states, ones that its protagonists remind us were 'Crusader creations' following the Anglo-French Sykes–Picot reorganisation of the post-Ottoman Middle East during World War I. The symbolism of establishing a caliphate should not be underestimated. From the perspective of its leadership it is a hugely important development, one that represents a direct challenge to the international status quo in which the region is controlled by outsiders. In their eyes it represents a seismic change in world affairs.

ISIS and its repression, violence and extremism may be anathema to the overwhelming majority of Muslims across the world, but the idea of a new caliphate does strike a chord with some, who see Islam as having been encroached on and marginalised by the West. All three of the 'religions of the book' – Judaism, Christianity and Islam – have had or still have elements of political organisation within them. There are passionate Zionists who are utterly convinced that Judaism can only be secure with the establishment of a singularly strong Jewish state, and this is what Israel must become. Political Christianity is highly variable in its intensity, but permeates many countries to a greater or lesser extent, and in the past has had periods of absolute control. Legacy elements include 'Christian democrat' parties in Europe, but there are also much more politicised elements, including movements such as Christian Zionism. This sees the future as being utterly bound up with the role of the geographical territory of Israel in the 'end times' and constitutes a powerful political force in the United States, one that is closely allied to, if not part of, the Israel lobby.

If ISIS were actually a sub-state paramilitary group devoid of a population base, it might be difficult to counter but would be acting primarily in the shadows. But ISIS is far from this, and the geographical element does much more than distinguish it from al-Qaeda. Thus, in northern Syria it is now a fully functioning political entity, in which the leadership outlined above controls a broadly based economy with an array of income sources. These include support from abroad, primarily from individuals in western Gulf states, and the results of the successful looting of Iraqi banks during the takeover of Mosul and other cities. It controls around 6 million people in an area which, while poor, has an active rural economy dependent primarily on crops grown under irrigation, although winter rainfall is sufficient in many areas to provide rain-fed crop production. This was, after all, part of the 'Fertile Crescent', one of those parts of the world that saw the origins of agriculture and the early growth of towns and cities.

Although accurate information on the economic and social functioning of ISIS is limited, there are clear indications that the municipalities are working, that there is the basis of a health service, that schools are open, albeit with a controlled and limited curriculum, and that routine policing goes on. There are basic social services and a functioning fiscal authority, backed up by numerous other networks. Northern Syria and north-western Iraq are areas of pronounced informal economies, including numerous smuggling routes that may be tolerated as they can readily be taxed, not least through roadside control.

The economy of the ISIS-controlled territory – its proto-caliphate – has proved to be far more robust than most external analysts expected, and this is essential in determining its longer-term prospects. ISIS is well organised, and one of the least-recognised aspects of this is a technocratic capability that owes much to the presence of Ba'athists, primarily from the Saddam Hussein era, who have the necessary experience of running urban and rural communities, organising education, health and social services, and ensuring that roads are repaired and sewage systems function.

ISIS also benefits from the production of petroleum products in a number of small and scattered oilfields. The wellheads in these fields feed into mini-refineries producing a limited but viable range of products, commonly transported by tanker. Such a dispersed system is advantageous in the face of air strikes. A large oilfield feeding from wellheads through pipes to central processing and refinery facilities is far more vulnerable to air attack than numerous small sites. These may well be hit, and the wellheads and mini-refineries damaged, but the make-up of these systems is relatively simple. Because of this, repairs may be readily undertaken if basic engineering facilities are available.

This points to the nature of the region, where, in any large town, let alone a city the size of Raqqa, one might find numerous small engineering workshops, which may be scattered through a neighbourhood and frankly difficult to pinpoint. It is worth remembering that during the 2014 Israeli war in Gaza, there were small workshops functioning and able to produce crude rockets right through a period of intense surveillance and facing the risk of immediate air and drone attack. Gaza, though, was a remarkably constrained environment, in which, at least during the war, supply from outside was virtually impossible, or else strictly controlled. ISIS in northern Syria, and to an extent in north-western Iraq, is in a very different position and will remain so unless there is a massive increase in US surveillance and air assault. Given the Israeli experience, even that will most likely be insufficient to undermine seriously the economic functioning of the state.

Perhaps most important of all in that regard are two elements that are commonly overlooked: bureaucracy and law. The indications are that in terms of political organisation, ISIS has a working bureaucracy that underpins its technocratic competence, and that this bureaucracy is sufficiently robust to survive a substantial level of military action against it. ISIS also has a legal system, dealing not just with crime but with a variety of civil disputes. In short, ISIS may be an extreme Islamist paramilitary movement that is dependent on often brutal control, but it is rooted in a functioning state. It is not alone in this: parts of rural Afghanistan operate in this way, where there is a largely acceptable system of courts; the same has been true in Somalia, and remains so in those areas still controlled by al-Shabaab, and even in north-eastern Nigeria there is some order among the disorder.

Even so, nowhere else matches the degree of territorial integrity of ISIS, and nowhere else is there an extreme movement which combines this with a remarkably effective paramilitary organisation. Indeed, this last element is seminal to the nature of the movement. It is very likely the case that the more senior elements of the paramilitary forces have less of a religious outlook and more of a secular one, some of them stemming from Ba'athist politics, but the organisation also benefits hugely from the fact that many of its key personnel gained combat experience against the best-trained, -equipped and -motivated of the US and UK armed forces in Iraq during the first decade of the twenty-first century. It is the combination of a motivated and ruthless leadership and a powerful paramilitary force, located together in a relatively secure and substantially functioning economy, that makes ISIS such an unusual creation.

In terms of international impact, ISIS is the most prominent of the extreme Islamist movements that have developed in the past two decades. It is seen by Western states as the greatest threat to the wider region – North Africa, the Middle East and South Asia – a threat to their interests across the region and also a risk to their own security, not least through a fear of paramilitary attacks. This last element has been more commonly applied to al-Qaeda and its loose offshoots, with memories still strong of the Madrid and London attacks, as well as of 9/11 itself, but there is a rising concern over so-called 'lone-wolf' attacks, or those undertaken by groups returning from the Middle East. A particular concern developed in southern Europe in early 2015 as several groups paying allegiance to ISIS gained control of territory in Libya. The fear was that they would infiltrate people among the thousands risking the dangerous voyage across the Mediterranean.

While the links between ISIS and groups in North Africa, the Sahel, South Asia and the core of the Middle East have been the principal concerns, even if many of those links are informal, al-Shabaab in Kenya as well as Somalia and Boko Haram in West Africa have also been factored in to the overall rise in extreme Islamist paramilitary movements. In the context of these developments it is appropriate to assess where ISIS stands and what its longer-term potential might be. This is fraught with difficulty given the many complex factors involved, and it is worth remembering that only a few years ago, in 2011, the consensus among counter-terrorism analysts was that al-Qaeda and other extreme Islamist factions were in decline. The Obama administration believed it was safe to consider withdrawing from Iraq and was debating how best to weaken the Taliban sufficiently to negotiate a withdrawal from Afghanistan, confident that it would not remotely be able to return to power. Osama bin Laden was dead, and 'al-Qaeda central' in Pakistan hugely diminished by drone and special-forces operations. The worst was over.

That assessment has been comprehensively taken apart. Instead, we need to be more rigorous in judging prospects, and to be willing to turn the entire analysis around and see it from the position of ISIS. In doing so, it is possible to identify a number of advantages for the movement, some of them factors that apply to most extreme Islamist groups, and others that are specific to ISIS itself. It is also possible to extend the analysis to problems facing the movement, again at both specific and generic levels. Overall, there are seven trends that aid ISIS, three of them dominant. These are the ability of ISIS to present itself as defending Islam under attack; the long-term impact of the Saudi promulgation of Wahhabism; and the ability of ISIS to gain support from those on the socio-economic margins. These are worth examining in turn.

It is particularly difficult from a Western standpoint to understand the perception that it is Islam that is under attack, that is in retreat in the face of aggression and that must be defended. This is not simply to do with recent Western interventions in Afghanistan, Iraq, Libya, Somalia, Yemen and elsewhere, but in relation to a much longer timescale. In this view, the high period of Islam was over the first 1,000 years, and especially during the equivalent of the European early Middle Ages. In one sense, it is seen as having been downhill since then, a particularly disastrous period being that of the collapse of the Ottoman Empire and the parcelling up of most of the Arab world in the 1920s, which led to nothing less than a neocolonial era in which local leaders were tolerated by the United Kingdom, France and the United States.

In other words, this is the mirror image of the common Western perception that it is Islam that is on the offensive, and that it threatens the free world with a clash of civilisations that can only be countered with the use of force. In a rather fractured and disconnected way, this Western version originated with the Iranian Revolution of 1979, but morphed seamlessly into the sub-state threat from al-Qaeda, especially after the 9/11 attacks, even if that movement was poles apart from Shi'i Iran.

This world view, of Islam under attack, is deeply rooted among that small minority of Muslims who see the need to fight, but it is felt at a more nuanced level by far more people. Not that this is unique to Islam – in particular, the rise of the West-dominated free-market system of the post-Soviet era is seen across the Global South as an uncomfortable and even unacceptable aspect of the world of the early twenty-first century. This, in turn, is part of a much wider phenomenon that brings in elements of a sense of marginalisation, alienation and cultural frustration. This can lead to stronger emotions, extending to anger and deep resentment at a perceived situation on the margins of economic well-being. It is within the extreme Islamist world view, though, that it translates into the need for violent resistance.

ISIS therefore has the consistent aim of presenting the movement as being in the vanguard of Islam under attack, using a wide range of means of communication, especially social media. In its more extreme, yet not uncommon, variant this narrative extends to bitter opposition to the apostate Shi'a and also to those many elements of Sunni Islamic governance that are not true to ISIS's particular fundamentalist interpretation of Islam. The protector of Islam under attack is an image that gains further strength from the extent of Western military intervention, and has a certain appeal to a small minority of Muslims outside the region as well as many more within. It has a particular appeal to young men and women in their late teens and early twenties, at that stage in life where a 'mission' may have a particular psychological attraction, who are influenced by peer groups, seductive advocacy and a voluminous digital environment.

Take one example. In Western Europe in the spring of 2015 there was widespread concern that groups of young Muslims were travelling to Turkey and then into Syria to join ISIS, some to help in hospitals, others presumably to fight and maybe die, and some young girls, the so-called 'jihadi brides', to marry paramilitaries. Among Western publics this was impossible to understand, even if some could see the vulnerability of young people to proselytising, especially those from a social environment on the margins of society in terms of perceived life chances.

This, though, cannot possibly explain joining an appallingly violent movement that engages in beheadings, massacres and many other acts of extreme violence. All of these have been reported widely in the Western media, but what was reaching potential recruits was a very different picture, of an element of Islam that was under constant attack. While ISIS propagandists are supremely adept at presenting a very narrow view, they are aided by what is almost completely missing from the Western narrative of a crucial conflict with a hugely dangerous movement. This was the fact that there was an intense war going on across Syria and Iraq in which hundreds of Muslims were being killed by coalition air strikes every week, reaching a death toll of more than 22,000 by the end of 2015. The ISIS propagandists have used this relentlessly and with considerable success. If the idea can be maintained of a noble cause, in the aid of which death is just one part of an eternal process, then even the brutality can be discounted as a necessary means of opposing the forces of evil in the form of apostates, traitors and the far enemy.

A second long-term factor that has indirectly aided the rise of ISIS, and will help determine its future prospects, is the promulgation of the Wahhabi tradition by Saudi Arabia over several decades.[6] The origins of this tradition lie with one of the most noted Islamic scholars of the early fourteenth century, Ibn Taymiyyah. His most relevant belief in the current context was that Islam must remain true to the very earliest days of the faith, in the seventh century CE. His thinking was developed by Muhammad ibn Abdal-Wahhab in the eighteenth century, in what is now Saudi Arabia. Wahhabism stems from the latter's teachings and is the strongest religious orientation within present-day Saudi Arabia, as well as the ideological inspiration for the expansion of Saudi influence over most of Arabia. It can be described as a puritanical form of Salafi Islam, which seeks its inspiration from the earliest days of the faith and which itself is deeply conservative. This is an interpretation in which Allah is at the centre of worship, which eschews reverence for all others, practises an austere lifestyle and diminishes the status of women. Many Muslims would argue that this is not a true representation of the earliest days of Islam, but Wahhabism does attract considerable support.

Wahhabism was deeply embedded in Saudi Arabia, but it came to the fore after the Iranian Revolution in 1979–80, being seen as a crucial way of counteracting the revolutionary potential of revitalised Shi'i Islam in Iran. From 1980 onwards, the vigorous export of this belief system was an important element in Saudi foreign policy, much aided by the considerable oil wealth of the kingdom. Moreover, while not connected directly with US–Saudi relations, the support for Wahhabism was a very valuable counter to revolutionary Iran, seen in Washington as the primary threat to US influence in the Middle East, and also to Soviet control of Afghanistan in the early 1980s.

During the 1980s and 1990s, much of the emphasis in exporting Wahhabism was directed at South Asia, especially Pakistan, where numerous madrasas (religious schools) were supported. In the 1980s this was in parallel with US and Saudi support for the mujahidin fighting the Soviets in Afghanistan. While a minority of the original mujahidin were fighting from religious rather than nationalist motives, that element grew after the Soviets withdrew, developing into the Taliban movement, which drew heavily on young men with madrasa educations.

Financial and other Saudi support for Wahhabism has continued unabated and extends across the Middle East and South Asia, and into North Africa and the Balkans. It is by no means the basis for ISIS, however. Indeed, the leadership of that movement may commonly regard the Saudi royal family as inadequate for the role of 'Guardian of the Two Holy Places'. What this support has done, though, is aid greatly a climate of Sunni thinking across the Middle East that would be regarded by most Muslims worldwide as being excessively puritanical and not true to the greater spirit of Islam.

In the current context, this puritanical millenarianism helps to underpin ISIS's thinking and translates into support, especially from young men seeking a cause. In this sense it is of continuing help to the developing movement but, more importantly, this applies to any Islamist movement that may espouse violent opposition to Western states, Israel and the corrupt leaders across most of the Middle East. It is not peculiar to ISIS and is an outlook that could long outlast that movement. It is a further indication of why

ISIS is so significant, both in its own right and as a marker of other extreme movements in the future.

The third long-term trend, the issue of majority marginalisation, extends to a number of countries across the region, especially those without significant oil-export income, including Jordan, Morocco and notably Egypt. Indeed, marginalisation was one of the main factors, along with anger at autocracy, that fuelled the Arab Awakening itself. If this uprising had presaged a region-wide transition to more democratic governance, and if that transition had brought in policies designed to counter marginalisation, then the prospects for extreme movements such as ISIS might have been severely damaged.

That has not happened, making it easy for the Islamist proselytisers to claim that only their violent approach will work. It helps explain, for example, why a country that is slowly making a successful transition to representative governance, Tunisia, is also providing ISIS with more young recruits than any other state, relative to population. The problem in Tunisia is illuminated by the fact that there is 30 per cent graduate unemployment there: the prospect of hugely constrained life chances is a powerful inducement, born of frustration and bitterness, for people to join ISIS.

As with the promulgation of the Wahhabi world view, such marginalisation is certainly not the fundamental reason for the rise of ISIS, yet it is a sustained advantage for the movement. It may not even be a matter of relative deprivation, but relative exclusion, that is the issue. As long as it persists, it will be an aid to the development of extreme responses, whether in the form of ISIS or of a successor movement.

Of the remaining four of ISIS's advantages, two have already been discussed: the symbolism of controlling a territorial proto-caliphate and the value of having a paramilitary core with experience of fighting Western forces in Afghanistan, Iraq and elsewhere. The movement has two further advantages – one immediate and one much more long-term. The first relates to the violent retaliation that Sunni communities across north-western Iraq are experiencing from Shi'i militias loosely allied to the Iraqi Army. In those few parts of Iraq where the army–militia combinations have regained some territory, a picture emerges of the burning of villages, the disappearance of young men and the dispersal of whole communities. This may be understandable as revenge for the former treatment of Shi'i communities in the Saddam Hussein era, but does nothing to prevent ISIS propagandists from latching on to such atrocities and ensuring that Sunni clans increase their support for the movement.

Finally, there is the issue of detention and radicalisation. Camp Bucca and many other detention centres provided potent environments for the proselytisation of detainees. This was the experience of such centres in Iraq but it is a phenomenon that has much wider salience. Although it may not be specific to ISIS, the holding of many hundreds of young men, and some women, in prisons across the Western world is providing great opportunities for spreading the word, especially in prison systems such as that of the United Kingdom, where staffing levels and the quality of warders' training have declined markedly. While this may not aid ISIS directly, if that is the movement that has the highest international profile in pursuit of an extreme Islamist perspective and in resisting Western aggression, then that is the movement to which the young people will tend to gravitate.

ISIS is not without its vulnerabilities, however, including the problem of maintaining domestic acceptability in its own territory, where the response to the initial bringing of order out of chaos may translate slowly into opposition to a rigid and even brutal rule. ISIS is also rather narrowly hierarchical in its organisation, meaning that the leadership has considerable power, and the detention – or more likely the killing – of leaders may lead to significant structural and propagandistic damage. When bin Laden was killed in 2011 he was of little importance within the al-Qaeda movement, holed up in an Abbottabad compound. Even the symbolic value of his killing was short-lived. This is less the case with the current leadership of ISIS, and when such a death occurs it leaves a vulnerability that might last many months rather than weeks.

ISIS has two other problems, one being the size and diversity of the coalition facing it. The direct elements are a number of Western states, led by the United States but including France, the United Kingdom, Canada, Australia, Belgium, Denmark and others, together with most of the states of the western Gulf region. Indirectly, it is facing an Iran that is determined to prevent any extreme Sunni paramilitary movement developing influence across its border and threatening the viability of Iraq, its closest regional ally. It is also facing a Russian leadership that, on this issue, is cautious, however much it may relish Western discomfort, since it has its own concerns about violent Islamists in the Caucasus Emirate. Even China, because of the Uyghur issue, will do little to interfere with the war against ISIS.[7]

The other problem for ISIS is the brutality of so many of its actions. These may frequently constitute straightforward terror-ism – textbook behaviour to instil fear in a constituency far greater than those actually attacked – but the beheadings, immolations and other atrocities can have a direct impact on potential recruits and, much more significantly, anger Muslims who might otherwise have some sympathy with the need to oppose Western actions in the Middle East. There is little evidence of this at the time of writing, but the cumulative impact of the atrocities will most likely be to reduce support, not among those people who are fully in tune with its aims but among a much larger constituency across the Middle East.

What is frequently forgotten is that there are many tens of thousands of family connections between those living under ISIS rule and others beyond that geographical area. The internet, telephones and other forms of communication are regularly used and there is far more direct travel into and out of areas controlled by ISIS than is commonly realised. Thus, information about actual living conditions under ISIS rule is readily available and widely communicated. Insofar as it is possible to generalise, most towns and cities are orderly and organised, and the levels of crime and corruption are often much lower than before. If people obey orders strictly they survive and, to an extent, thrive, at least in the short term. If ISIS survives for some years, though, maintaining order ultimately through brutal force, then it stands to lose the reluctant support it currently enjoys unless it moderates the rigidity of its rule. ISIS's control of substantial territory is a recent phenomenon but it has so far succeeded in surviving against a sustained and wide-ranging air war, but that does not mean that its leadership can be sure of long-term survival, let alone expansion.

Although ISIS has evolved initially in a markedly more territorial form than al-Qaeda, it became clear in the early months of 2015 that there had been a further development of strategy in the form of a greater commitment to transnational actions, especially when they could be directed at the far enemy or its interests. This was apparent from the attack on the Bardo Museum in Tunis in March 2015 that killed Western tourists, and the assault shortly afterwards, in June, in the tourist resort of Sousse. Towards the end of the year there was an attack on a Russian tourist jet after it took off from Sharm el-Sheikh airport in Egypt, which killed all 224 people on board, and multiple attacks on a rock-concert venue and restaurants and bars in Paris that killed 130 and wounded more than 360. Further attacks followed in Istanbul, Djakarta and Brussels early in 2016.

THE CHOICE

ISIS is not in imminent danger of defeat and, as a single organisation, may have some years ahead of it, though not necessarily focused on its proto-caliphate. Since ISIS is regarded as a very serious threat, the question for the United States and its coalition

partners is whether sustained military action is the most appropriate course, given that it appears unlikely that the movement
can be suppressed by air attacks alone. Even more difficult is the
question lurking behind this entire approach: does ISIS actually
want war with the West?

In spite of the losses that the movement sustains in the persistent air assault, it is also clear that ISIS attaches huge importance
to presenting and emphasising a narrative in which it is the one
force that protects Islam from the Crusader attack. The risk, therefore, is of giving it what it wants, and this is a problem with two
added elements. One is that the antecedents of ISIS, dating right
back to the mujahidin in 1980s Afghanistan, were rooted in the
idea not just that the old Soviet Union was defeated and evicted
from Afghanistan but that this was the greatest single factor in
destroying one of the world's superpowers.

While the current US leadership is cautious not to get embroiled
in a ground war in Syria and Iraq, that attitude may not last.
Indeed, there are already indications that special forces are being
used extensively in both countries. The next administration in
Washington, or the one after that, or even the one after that, may
take a very different view and see no alternative to seeking the
complete military defeat of the movement. ISIS is simply not in
it for the short term and might relish that possibility.

Moreover, even if ISIS was to be defeated in Syria, Iraq and
Libya, what it has already shown is what is most significant – that
it is possible to establish a 'true' caliphate. This, its leaders no doubt
believe, will remain as a testimony to what can be achieved in the
face of what they proclaim to be a sustained Crusader–Zionist
threat to Islam.

In any case, what is clear is that some of the most senior and
experienced Western military leaders foresee a long war. In July
2015, the outgoing vice chair of the US Joint Chiefs of Staff,
Admiral Sandy Winnefeld, likened it to a generational struggle; the
following month, the retiring US Army Chief of Staff, General Ray

Odierno, said that the war against ISIS was a ten- to twenty-year problem.[8]

Moreover, the core of ISIS is rooted in its eschatological dimension, seeing this as the great global millenarian conflict that will stretch over decades and even go beyond this earthly life. Indeed, in its view, it may well presage the end days of humankind. This makes it and related extreme Islamist movements very different from a more traditional revolutionary movement, which would typically operate on a much shorter timescale, with a leadership confident of achieving success in years or decades and certainly not centuries. ISIS stems from a radically different mindset. In comparison with that, the term of office of a US president is little more than the blink of an eye.

6

IRREGULAR WAR

Fundamental to understanding ISIS and its proto-caliphate in Iraq and Syria is the recognition that while the movement's emphasis is on territorial control, and while it differs in this respect from al-Qaeda, its very success in gaining and controlling territory has made it attractive to a broad range of extreme Islamist movements. This does not mean that this single proto-caliphate will spread out across Africa and Asia, with an element of coordinated global organisation, but it does mean that something is happening that is far more significant than even the ongoing violence in Syria and Iraq.

The core argument of this book is that we are moving into an era of revolts from the margins, stemming from an economically divided and environmentally constrained world. In this global context we should not see ISIS as a specific movement that must be confronted and destroyed, believing that, once this is achieved, all will be well. This view misses the point. Rather, the way in which ISIS has spread and evolved into a transnational movement should be seen as an instance of a phenomenon that is likely to be repeated in the future, perhaps in very different circumstances that stretch far beyond the Middle East.

Moreover, such circumstances may have nothing whatsoever to do with Islam, but may instead be rooted in quite different religious, ideological, nationalistic or ethnic elements of identity – leading to an age of insurgencies rather than a clash of civilisations. This means that understanding the process of evolution as it applies to ISIS has a more general relevance if we want to get some idea of how future conflicts might develop and how, in particular, they might be avoided, or at least ameliorated.

As al-Qaeda diminished in importance after 2010, it left a very powerful legacy in the form of a potent idea about the renewal and violent expansion of a very narrow interpretation of Islam. Even if ISIS had not evolved from al-Qaeda in Iraq after 2006, there would have been ongoing concern among Western politicians and military leaders over the rise of a number of other movements. One of the most startling has been Boko Haram in northern Nigeria, especially after the death of its first leader, Mohammed Yusuf, in police custody in 2009.

This movement was founded by Yusuf in 2002 and grew slowly in significance, not least through its ability to attract disaffected youths in the north-eastern parts of a country that had seen far less development than the oil-rich south.[1] By 2009 the group was becoming a major security threat to the Nigerian government and a joint police–army task force acted strongly to suppress it. By July of that year, some 700 people had been killed and Yusuf captured. He died shortly afterwards, and in the following five years Boko Haram grew in intensity and capability, only coming to worldwide attention after major bomb attacks or the kidnapping of hundreds of schoolgirls in 2014.

By 2015 Boko Haram was seen as by far the most potent paramilitary movement in West Africa. The authorities acted repeatedly against it, but the levels of violence used and the civilian casualties that resulted did much to increase its support. It had killed more than 5,000 people, mostly civilians, and the war had displaced 1.5 million people. It controlled at least 25,000 square miles of territory in its home state of Borno, and had links with Islamist factions in neighbouring Mali, Chad and Cameroon, and looser connections with al-Shabaab in Somalia.

Boko Haram initially aligned itself with al-Qaeda, but in 2014 its leadership embraced ISIS.

To the north of Nigeria a number of small Islamist militias had become active across the Sahel, but these were less significant than the militias in Libya as the security of that state deteriorated after the termination of the Gaddafi regime by a rebellion dependent on NATO air strikes. By mid-2015 Islamist militias were controlling a number of Libyan towns, including ports on the Mediterranean coast, and several of these were pledging allegiance to ISIS. Support also came from paramilitary groups in Sinai opposed to the government of the Egyptian president, the former military commander General al-Sisi.

Extreme groups elsewhere in the world have either affiliated themselves with ISIS or developed along similar lines, including groups in Yemen, Afghanistan, Pakistan and India. There is also one in Russia, the Caucasus Emirate, a movement that gets very little attention in the West but is a continuing security problem for the Putin government, which uses severe methods of control that have so far had little effect.[2] Al-Shabaab in Somalia may appear to be in retreat in the face of wide-ranging military action, principally by Kenyan, Ugandan and Ethiopian troops, but has proved capable of major attacks in Kenya, including the assault on the Westgate shopping mall in Nairobi in September 2013 that killed 67 people, and the massacre of 147 students at Garissa University College in April 2015.

Down the East African coast in Kenya and Tanzania, often termed the 'Swahili Coast', Islamist movements have developed with links to al-Shabaab that draw support from a widespread perception of relative neglect.[3] This is especially the case in Kenya, where the view among disaffected and often unemployed young men is that the neglect has been in marked contrast to progress in central Kenya, especially in the capital, Nairobi.

Of the many developments in southern and south-western Asia, perhaps the most significant has been the allegiance to ISIS now being expressed by some militias in Afghanistan.[4] This is a contributing factor to the decision by the Obama administration to maintain a force of at least 10,000 troops in the country after the intended final withdrawal date of December 2015. Although this seemed to conflict with Obama's original hope of withdrawing all regular US forces from Afghanistan before he leaves office in early 2017, there was still the possibility that the forces remaining by that time might be down to a couple of thousand, involved principally in protection of US diplomats and other civilian personnel. By the end of 2015, however, it was clear that this was not to be, and that it would be necessary to maintain many thousands of troops in the country long after the end of the administration.

Repeatedly we find that the extreme movements that relate to the core ISIS idea of a new caliphate stem in part from a perception of external control, that Islam is under threat, and above all of exclusion from that element of society that holds the reins of power and benefits persistently from its position. It is a perception or actual experience of being marginalised from the mainstream, especially when that 'mainstream' is a minority of society. This is a remarkably strong underlying motive, whatever the more specific impact on the followers of such movements of a narrow version of Islam that they may see as providing the providential answer.

Within this context, the spread of extreme Islamist movements is in marked contrast to what was expected from the war on al-Qaeda and the 'axis of evil' after 9/11. It is a further illustration of how that experience has been little short of disastrous. Even in 2011 it was abundantly clear that the original optimism expressed by President George W. Bush in his January 2002 State of the Union address and his 'mission accomplished' speech of 1 May 2003 was little more than wishful thinking. A careful and wide-ranging assessment in June 2011, the 'Costs of War' report by the Eisenhower Research Project at Brown University, showed that in the War on Terror as a whole:

- At a conservative estimate the overall death toll in Iraq, Afghanistan and elsewhere, including civilians, uniformed personnel and contractors, was at least 225,000.
- There were 7.8 million refugees created among Iraqis, Afghans and Pakistanis.
- The wars will cost close to $4 trillion and are being funded substantially by borrowing, with $185 billion in interest already paid and another $1 trillion likely by 2020.[5]

Since then the number of people killed has increased greatly, especially in Iraq. The group Iraq Body Count, which seeks to record actual casualties rather than relying on surveys, put civilian casualties in Iraq by December 2015 at somewhere between 147,000 and 167,000, and total casualties at 224,000.[6] Civilian deaths in Afghanistan have proved far more difficult to assess, but in 2014 alone UN sources reported 3,699 deaths and the total for the war as a whole was more than 18,000.[7]

The Afghan casualties are those directly due to actual incidents of violence, whether aerial bombing, artillery strikes or, in most cases, attacks by the Taliban and other AOGs. They do not include people dying later from their injuries or the far larger numbers of people dying from the effects of sudden refugee movements, especially in the winter of 2001–2. Put together, the casualties from both wars will be far higher than suggested by the 2011 Costs of War study and will probably approach 300,000, about 100 times greater than the number of people killed in the 9/11 atrocities.

Perhaps most remarkable of all is the acceptance among all the major Western security and intelligence agencies that they are not succeeding, even after nearly 15 years, in containing the challenge of extreme Islamist paramilitary movements. In April 2015, during a question-and-answer session at Harvard's Belfer Center, the director of the CIA, John Brennan, expressed the view that the War on Terror was essentially never-ending, and a few weeks later a book by the former deputy director of the CIA, Michael Morrell, confirmed that, in the words of the *Washington Post*, 'U.S. intelligence agencies badly misjudged al-Qaeda's ability to take advantage of political turmoil in the Middle East and regain strength across the region after Osama bin Laden was killed.'[8]

Although a few Western politicians now recognise the formidable problems that have arisen in the wake of the War on Terror, very few are willing to understand, let alone acknowledge in public, the extent of the failure. Moreover, there is scarcely any acceptance of this in the wider military–industrial complex. Privately, one finds that some recently retired senior military figures are quite candid, but they are very few and far between. Instead, defence industries are more concerned with developing new methods of warfare that will meet the challenges raised by the recent failures. Moreover, since so many recently retired senior armed-forces personnel and defence civil servants rapidly take up consultancies or board memberships with arms companies, or else work for think tanks funded from such sources, their primary interest is in the technologies and defence postures required to support new methods of control, and the income they help ensure.

In part this is down to the sheer profitability of the arms industries and in part it is due to what is more accurately termed the 'military–industrial–academic–bureaucratic complex'. Furthermore, this complex is by no means limited to Western free-market states, and takes different forms in different systems. During the Cold War era, for example, Western military corporations were mirrored by the various design bureaux in the Soviet Union, which covered aircraft, missiles and other forms of weaponry. In the West, in particular, there has been a marked trend in recent years to consolidate military companies into a handful of huge transnational corporations, each of which maintains very well-resourced lobbying enterprises, especially in the larger markets, centred, for example, on Washington, London, Paris or Riyadh.

Some academic centres and a handful of think tanks provide analysis that is independent of funding from defence sources, but there is a further factor, especially in Western states, that limits any real change in thinking: an overriding public perception of the threat of terrorism. This is one of the long-term effects of 9/11, which demonstrated that a hugely powerful state was susceptible to attack by otherwise weak groups, especially if the people involved were willing to give their own lives. To put it at its crudest, 9/11 showed that it was no longer possible to 'close the castle gates' against a dangerous 'outside', the implication being that the 'outside' had to be controlled.

In part this could be done by a far greater emphasis on home-land security, and the period since 9/11 has seen an extraordinary increase in resources in this area. In addition to tighter border controls and greatly increased airline- and aircraft-security pro-cedures, most Western countries have substantially reinforced their counter-terrorism forces, and this has involved far greater coordination between the police, security services and intelligence agencies.

In the United Kingdom, for example, a number of Counter Terrorism Units (CTUs) were established in 2007, three of which cover England, based in Manchester, Leeds and Birmingham, with a fourth set up in 2009 for the Thames Valley and the south-east. Other units cover Wales, Scotland and Northern Ireland, and over all of this is a much larger central group in London. The term 'unit' sounds like a small affair but the regional CTUs are substantial organisations in their own right, with a thousand or more people based at the centres and others linked with police forces in a particular region. While primarily police organisa-tions, they work very closely with MI5, MI6, other agencies and the Home Office, and each CTU includes personnel from such agencies.

A cautious estimate is that the United Kingdom as a whole has 12–15,000 people engaged solely in counter-terrorism activities, the really big increase, involving at least a doubling of the numbers involved, having come in the wake of the London bombings in July 2005. This increased again following the May 2015 general election, with the Conservative government of David Cameron announcing a substantial strengthening of counter-terror legislation.

Enhancing internal national-security forces is seen as just one part of a much larger process of countering Islamist paramilitary movements, but this runs right up against the deep and enduring failure of the approaches that have been pursued since 9/11, principally in Afghanistan and Iraq but extending to many other countries, especially Yemen, Somalia, Mali, Libya and Syria. It is here that there has been a subtle change in approach, stemming primarily from the evident failure of the methods initially adopted, especially regime termination and subsequent military occupation in Afghanistan and Iraq.

WAR – BY REMOTE CONTROL

When George W. Bush formed his administration in January 2001, he brought Donald Rumsfeld in as secretary of defence. Rumsfeld was very much the assertive realist, determined to maintain US military superiority, but he believed that an improved defence posture should go alongside a determination to bring high-tech means of military control to bear on the conduct of war. The phrase around the Pentagon was 'war lite' – the aim being to fight wars using very few boots on the ground and with much greater emphasis on 'force projection'. This might take a variety of forms: US Air Force actions with strike aircraft, strategic bombers or stand-off missiles; the use of the expeditionary capability of the US Marine Corps; the use of the immense firepower of the US Navy's carrier battle groups with their strike aircraft and sea-launched cruise missiles; or the US Army's deployment of special forces units in low-profile operations. It might also involve the use of surrogate forces. From this perspective, Vietnam was very much a thing of the past, and even the more recent use of ground troops in Iraq in 1991 was an anomaly in the transition to high-tech warfare.

In the early stages of both conflicts after 9/11, this view prevailed and seemed to work admirably. The Taliban regime in Afghanistan was gone within three months, aided by special forces, CIA operatives, intensive aerial bombing and the use of Northern Alliance militias as surrogate ground troops. Iraq was even more successful, with the Saddam Hussein regime collapsing within three weeks. In both wars, though, success turned to disaster as tens of thousands of troops had to be deployed to try to maintain security in the face of determined insurgencies. 'War lite' had become 'war heavy': tens of thousands of civilians were killed, millions of refugees were forced from their homes and sustained trauma is likely to affect future generations.

In Iraq, for example, over a seven-year period more than 4,000 coalition personnel were killed and more than 20,000 seriously injured – many of them maimed for life. War costs were estimated to run to $3 trillion. The impact on the country was massive, with at least 120,000 people killed, several hundred thousand injured and close to 4 million displaced. During the war more than 120,000 people were detained without trial, some of them for years, and there were frequent instances of prisoner abuse and torture, which cost the United States considerable moral authority among many of its Western allies.

Within ten years of the 9/11 attacks, the era of 'boots on the ground' had come to an ignominious end and a combination of new technologies and a reworking of counter-insurgency doctrine led to new versions of 'war lite'. By the time of the NATO air intervention in Libya in 2011, major ground-force operations to terminate the Gaddafi regime were not even considered. The regime was subjected to intense air attacks by NATO, averaging 50 each day, until it capitulated to rebel forces. The orientation to war by remote control had increased substantially after 2008 but it was not new, since stand-off weapons, special forces and the use of private military companies had been significant in a number of late-twentieth-century wars. What was new was the emphasis on this, and the substantially increased use of these methods of warfare.[9]

In the public eye the best known of these have been armed drones such as the 'Predator', the 'Reaper' and their Israeli equivalents. The Predator came into service in an unarmed reconnaissance form during the late 1990s, and was used first in the former Yugoslavia and then in Afghanistan. Early in 2001, some months before the 9/11 attacks, an armed version of the Predator, equipped with Hellfire missiles, was tested, and the following February a Predator was deployed in an attack in Afghanistan. Since then a much more powerful drone, the Reaper, has been widely deployed and used, principally by the United States but also by the United Kingdom, and most recently by France.

Armed drones, or 'unmanned combat aerial vehicles' (UCAVs), have been used by the United States and its allies in the Sahel, Libya, Syria, Iraq, Somalia, Yemen, Afghanistan and Pakistan, and by Israel in Gaza and probably Syria. The sudden expansion of their use was such that, in the three-year period to November 2012, the United States mounted 1,160 armed-drone attacks in Afghanistan alone, and there have been many hundreds more elsewhere, especially in Pakistan and Somalia. More recently, armed drones have been used by the United States and the United Kingdom in Iraq and by the United States in Syria. They continue to be used in Afghanistan, Somalia, Yemen and Pakistan, and there are indications that France may use the Reaper in its counter-terror operations in Mali and other parts of the Sahel. Armed drones are frequently weapons of choice since their use need not be transparent, they are far cheaper than strike aircraft and they do not risk the lives of air crew.

Elite special forces have been used by many states in the past 80 years and especially by the United States in Latin America during the Cold War, but their use has been substantially expanded.

They tend to be very low profile because special forces get little or no publicity, but enough information has entered the public domain to show that the numbers involved have undergone a remarkable expansion since the War on Terror started to have unexpected consequences. The clearest example of their use was JSOC's operations in Iraq, discussed in Chapter 3, but this is the tip of the iceberg.

In the United States, the various special forces were brought into a unified military command, USSOCOM, which was established in 1987, partly as a consequence of the failure of special forces in 'Operation Eagle Claw' – an attempt seven years earlier to free more than 60 American hostages held at the US embassy in Tehran by supporters of the Iranian Revolution. From a strength of just under 43,000 in 1979, USSOCOM had increased to 63,600 by 2012 and is expected to have peaked at 71,000 by the end of 2015. This will not be far short of the size of the entire British Army by the end of the decade. The United Kingdom's special forces are much smaller and are focused mainly on the SAS and the Special Boat Service (SBS), but they are supported by other units, including reconnaissance and signals units and the SFSG, a new force established in 2006 as part of the United Kingdom's expansion of special forces, which draws on the Royal Marines, the Parachute Regiment and the RAF Regiment.

Special forces have been widely deployed over the past decade, not just in Iraq and Afghanistan but in Syria, Yemen, Pakistan, Somalia and Mali. A common feature of special-forces operations is secrecy. In early 2015, for example, the countries involved in the air war in Iraq were insistent that troops would not be involved directly in combat operations. There would be no boots on the ground, except for trainers and advisers. The secrecy was broken, however, when a Canadian Army source admitted that there had been three occasions in the early months of 2015 when Canadian special forces had been directly involved in firefights with ISIS paramilitaries.

The pattern of extensive night raids that was at the heart of the shadow war in Iraq was repeated in Afghanistan, where by 2013 up to a dozen raids were being conducted every night. The issue proved so controversial that President Karzai at one point demanded the withdrawal of all US special-forces units.

The third main element of remote-control warfare is the much-increased reliance on private military and security companies (PMSC). While such companies perform a vast range of functions, right through to security guards and prison warders, there has been a rise in the number of well-armed contractors available for direct combat. Most are drawn from infantry battalions, but many are ex-special forces. There is a preponderance of UK- and US-based companies, which dominate the market with a 70 per cent share, but personnel come from many other countries, notably Ukraine and South Africa.[10]

In 2012 there were reported to be 20,000 foreign PMSC personnel in Iraq and Afghanistan alone, even though US combat troops had withdrawn from Iraq, the United Kingdom was due to leave Afghanistan within two years and the United States planned to withdraw the great majority of its forces by the end of 2014. PMSC are considered to be of substantial value to governments seeking to avoid troop deployments overseas that might not have public support, and their activities have the political advantage of being low profile, with little obvious accountability and much scope for deniability.

They have a particular value in anti-piracy operations, especially in the Arabian Sea and off the coast of East Africa. Because of the need to have well-armed private military personnel on ships paying for protection, and because states prefer to avoid having private armouries on their territory, it became common practice after 2010 to have what amounted to floating armouries. These are ships that may formerly have been tugs or fisheries-patrol vessels but are now operated by private companies and house substantial armouries. They also provide accommodation for personnel between operations. Some are what are known as 'flag of convenience' ships, meaning that they are registered in countries different from those of the shipowners, which may have looser regulations and conduct few, if any, inspections of armouries.[11]

The move to remote control has other elements, including the use of cyberattacks if opponents have sufficiently sophisticated communications and other systems of economic and social interaction to make them vulnerable. In the longer term there is also the move towards what tends to be called 'Prompt Global Strike' (PGS). This involves the development of long-range, highly accurate and very fast conventionally armed missiles that can be used over intercontinental ranges to destroy the fixed targets of an opponent. Originally envisaged in the form of systems such as the Trident D5 submarine-launched ballistic missile, retrofitted with a conventional high-explosive warhead, a PGS system would be capable of delivering a powerful conventional charge over a distance of 5,000 miles or more within 30 minutes. More recent ideas revolve around the development of air-breathing aerodynamic hypersonic vehicles that may reach speeds of 4,000 miles an hour or more over a range of many thousands of miles, and will have pinpoint accuracy and be able to adjust course and target in flight. As in most fields, the lead actor is the United States, but it is followed by China, which has a particular interest in hypersonic systems.[12]

From the perspective of governments that have been involved in wars since 2001 with radically different consequences to the successes originally anticipated, the progressive move towards war by remote control has many advantages. These include relatively low cost, far lower casualties, far less media attention and consequent unwelcome visibility, greater deniability and a far lower risk of debate. Armed drones, in particular, can be sold to an electorate as effective means of control that do not risk air crews getting killed – a clear win–win situation. All in all, security by remote control must surely be the appropriate way forward, given the dismal military failure of recent years. Indeed, this is increasingly seen as one of the most effective ways of fighting future wars, especially those that might occur in far-off places and that originate in revolts from the margins, which may still have a formidable impact on the interests of elite states, especially when dedicated paramilitaries are willing and able to take the wars back to those states themselves.

THE SEDUCTION OF REMOTE WAR

Already, though, there are many questions arising from the move towards remote-control warfare. Three issues relate immediately to armed drones, one being that they are already proliferating, in a process that is likely to accelerate in the next five years. The main developers and exporters so far have been the United States and Israel, but the United Kingdom, France, Russia, China, India, Turkey and Iran are among the countries that have active programmes. As the use of armed drones increases, so does their potential use, the precedent being set by the United States and Israel making for some substantial dilemmas. Both states have used drones to kill individuals considered to be security risks in what amount to targeted assassinations.

For the states themselves the legal justification is their own security, but if that is the case then the same must surely apply to other countries. If the United States can kill people in Somalia or Syria, then China could do the same in Myanmar, India in Kashmir, Turkey against Kurds in Syria, or Iran in Iraq. Russia may argue that it has the right to use armed drones in eastern Ukraine or Georgia. Thus, for the moment, armed drones may look attractive to the United States, the United Kingdom, France and Israel, but precedents have been set, and in a proliferating world in which there is an absence of any arms-control process, we should expect drone warfare to constitute a major, yet uncontrolled, trend.

The idea that the more powerful states will be able to direct how weaker states embrace and use remote-control warfare without broad international agreement is simply untenable, not least because of the rapid spread of the technologies and their progressive commercialisation. In the five years from 2010 to 2015, numerous types of drone designed for many different commercial activities became available on the open market, including some capable of transporting significant payloads that would be highly dangerous if they were weapons.[13] Over the same period many commercial developments in the area of public-order control, including anti-riot agents, have begun to become available in forms that may be deliverable by drone.[14] It might be argued that powerful high-technology states will always be able to stay ahead, but paramilitary movements have been remarkably successful in the past 30 years at opposing superior numbers of well-trained and well-armed forces, including the mujahidin in 1980s Afghanistan and, more recently, the Taliban and ISIS. The diverse experience gained and the entrepreneurial capabilities demonstrated clearly suggest that it is hugely dangerous to underestimate the blowback potential of what appear to be highly useful means of control. Moreover, we can assume that paramilitary groups will soon develop their own capabilities. Reconnaissance drones have been used by ISIS in Iraq, and by Hezbollah over Israel, much to the embarrassment of the IDF.

The second issue with drones is a marked lack of accountability, in that the public assessment of casualties is far more difficult than it has been in recent conventional wars. This is despite the fact that the militaries that conduct armed-drone strikes have comprehensive information on the casualties they cause since it is essential for them to know that they have killed the 'right' people. Post-attack reconnaissance, mainly through drones, signals intelligence and some human intelligence, gives them full details of outcomes, not least because of the need to undertake repeat attacks if the first attempts fail. While they do this, though, they go to considerable lengths to avoid any mention in public of the consequences.

This is not specific to drone attacks, but a feature of modern air warfare. In 2011 the RAF was involved in many months of air raids in Libya as part of the coalition process of supporting anti-Gaddafi elements. At the time the United Kingdom did not use armed drones in Libya, and the attacks involved precision bombing and stand-off missiles from strike aircraft. The details of the raids were distributed to the UK media, right down to the nature of the targets struck and the effects of the attacks. They might involve tank transporters, artillery positions, barracks, psychological-warfare centres or air defence positions, but the curious thing about the otherwise detailed press releases was the complete absence of any information about casualties. One would think that all Libyans in Gaddafi's forces had some kind of sixth sense warning them of an impending attack, even by a supersonic missile, and could run like hell from their positions and escape unharmed. In reality, many Libyans were killed in the RAF attacks and it is highly likely that there were civilians among them, but this was simply unreported in the UK media.

In the absence of information there is less likely to be informed media coverage of what is happening within conflicts, and consequently less chance to debate and question the conduct of wars. There will, instead, be an assumption that the approach is correct and likely to be successful. This is already at variance with the experience of drone attacks in recent years because of the manner in which they lead to profound anger and resentment within communities on the receiving end.

In particular, it is the actual experience that is so potent. If armed drones are being used in a conflict, then a very common pattern is for them to conduct high-altitude surveillance for perhaps hours at a time. The sound of the engines can be heard at ground level, but when a Hellfire missile is finally fired at a target it is supersonic and therefore silent in the vicinity of the target. This means that anyone within earshot of a drone knows that at any instant they might be killed without warning. This may result in intense worry and trauma but it can also readily lead to deep and sustained anger – even more so if it is an external state that is undermining the sovereignty of the country concerned.

Resentment also stems from the actions of special forces, especially night raids leading to targeted assassinations. They may seem useful to the personnel undertaking them and may appear to deliver results, but all too often the outcome is an increase in the degree of radicalisation of individuals and communities. Moreover, and this is perhaps the strongest argument in the case of special forces, there is the experience of JSOC in Iraq, where many thousands of suspected radicals were imprisoned for long periods of time in places such as Camp Bucca, which became hugely effective recruiting and proselytising detention centres – universities not of crime but of extreme ideology.

Finally, perhaps the most substantial question mark over the whole issue of war by remote control is that although it has been progressively developed in Afghanistan and Iraq, applied rigorously in Libya and utilised in many other environments, after the best part of a decade of a transition away from thousands of boots on the ground it is a military posture that is signally failing to bring ISIS and similar movements under control.

IRREGULAR WAR AND THE WEAK AGAINST THE STRONG

Writing in the immediate aftermath of the end of the Cold War, Roger Barnett, a professor emeritus at the US Naval War College and a former submarine commander, wrote perceptively about the changing international security environment. His subject was the evolving role of the US Navy, but he had a particular concern with the future potential for small groups to have an effect out of all proportion to their size and apparent lack of power. He focused on a series of changes in technology and possible causes of conflict, and among others he identified the following:

- Widening economic differentials between the economic North and South;
- Impact of high-technology weapons and WMD on the ability – and thus the willingness – of the weak to take up arms against the strong;
- Inequitable distribution of world food supplies and the dislocation of millions of people because of famine, wars and natural disasters;
- Use of force or of terrorism to attempt to redress grievances or resolve problems.[15]

Barnett's comments stick in the memory and are readily reflected in the situation we face today, well over two decades later, but also relate to the actual experience of that whole period.

Earlier sections of this book have pointed to many instances of small paramilitary groups having a considerable impact, even before 9/11. The use of city-centre bombs by the LTTE is one example, and another is the attempt by Algerian extremists to crash an Airbus A300 on the centre of Paris in 1994. Although not aiming to cause huge casualties, the targeting of the British economy by PIRA from 1992 to 1997 had a far greater impact on the UK government of the day than was ever acknowledged, and was largely responsible for the substantial focus on Northern Ireland of the incoming Labour government of Tony Blair in 1997. The first World Trade Center attack in February 1993 could have been ten times worse than 9/11 and caused considerable concern in domestic security circles, even if politicians were reluctant for this to be discussed.

All these, and many other examples, are indicators of precisely Barnett's point: the ability of the weak to take up arms against the strong. In many ways this is a consequence of the organisation of modern-day industrial and commercial societies and their considerable fragilities. The PIRA campaign killed few people and the total direct damage over several years may have been little more than £2 billion, but its indirect impact in terms of increased security spending was very much greater, and even more worrying at the time was the risk that London would lose out to Frankfurt as the financial heart of Western Europe.

In all manner of ways, modern, highly organised and integrated states have numerous nodes of vulnerability, often increased by the success of accurate and responsive systems of distribution. The whole concept of 'just in time' logistics that has become central to the retail process is thoroughly dependent on uninterrupted pathways of supply, especially within countries. Internationally, the concentration of maritime transport into high-capacity container ships and Very Large Crude Carriers (VLCCs) using very few ports provides for many weak points in the entire supply process.

If a single airport hub such as London Heathrow or Paris Charles de Gaulle were rendered unusable for just a few months as a result of a radiological attack, it would affect the whole economy of a country. The United Kingdom has just two high-capacity north–south road and rail routes, making it possible to ensure severe delays through narrowly focused attacks. Other systems are similarly vulnerable. While some communications systems involve quite robust networks with few hubs, others do not: many distribution systems are more hierarchical, with oil and gas terminals and their links to national or international distribution systems being examples.

After 9/11 the US security system modelled a series of possible attacks designed to focus on particular weak spots. One example that was illustrative of thinking was the release of anthrax spores into the ventilation system of the New York Stock Exchange. In place of anthrax one might envisage sarin or VX nerve agent, but in those cases the appearance of symptoms in those first affected would be so quick that the exchange might be evacuated before there were really substantial casualties. With anthrax, on the other hand, individuals would not know they had been infected until symptoms appeared some hours later, the delayed action being a considerable aid to increasing the impact of an attack.

One of the complications of current societal and economic changes is the impact of the digital revolution and its relevance to rebellions. Moore's Law of 40 years ago (which predicted that computing performance would continue to double every two years) has largely held good, and this allows for immense storage of data and vastly increased connectivity.[16] Devices connected to the internet exceed the global human population in number and are projected to grow to about 50 billion by 2050.[17] Of all the radical and extreme groups of recent years, ISIS has proved to be the most competent in its use of digital media, but the wider security concern is the potential ability of groups to stage cyberattacks.

ISIS has undertaken some attacks of this kind but these have so far been primarily for publicity purposes. The potential for future attacks by ISIS or other groups is considerable. Most of the concern for states and commercial enterprises is about attacks by other states or commercial rivals, but governments are investing heavily in meeting what they perceive as future threats from sub-state actors.[18] The range of possibilities is wide and extreme groups may have a particular focus on highly disruptive attacks that affect infrastructure, leading to a high economic cost. There is a particular concern about potential attacks on 'supervisory control and data acquisition' (SCADA) systems, which are widely used for the control of industrial and distribution processes, where successful interruption could have considerable economic consequences.

In broad terms, this is an area where the capabilities of extreme groups may remain lower than that of states or large commercial enterprises, but the issue is that narrowly targeted attacks that involve lateral approaches may have much greater effects than anticipated. It is in this context that the PIRA use of economic targeting in the United Kingdom back in the 1990s is so significant. It caught the authorities largely by surprise, not because of the technologies involved, which reflected standard PIRA capabilities, but because of the intended and actual political impact. On a much more devastating scale, this was also true of the 9/11 attacks themselves. It is this that makes the risk of cyberattack so potent.

EXPERIENCE AND ITS IMPLICATIONS

As discussed earlier, one of the most notable features of paramilitary movements of the past three decades has been the accretion of experience. Tactics and methods used in Afghanistan in the 1980s led to a cohort of experienced paramilitaries, with lessons applied in the civil war against the Northern Alliance a decade later. Then paramilitary fighters going to aid the insurgency in Iraq brought that thinking with them; much further experience was gained and some of it spread back to Afghanistan. More recently, the experience of the early years of the century has been applied in both Iraq and Syria, where even more experience is being gained. All this feeds into paramilitary methods used in many locations of conflict, from Libya to Chechnya, Mali to Yemen, Somalia to Nigeria, and many others. To this we can add the historical experience of groups in targeting centralised economies, including PIRA in the United Kingdom, the LTTE in Sri Lanka and Shining Path in Peru.

The 9/11 attacks showed the capacity of determined groups to cause thousands of deaths and incite a full-scale War on Terror extending eventually across many countries in the Middle East and South Asia. Trillions of dollars have been spent, hundreds of thousands of troops have been used and three regimes have been terminated. At least 250,000 people have died; hundreds of thousands have been injured; millions have been displaced and failed states created. Yet in spite of the use of very well-armed and

well-trained Western forces and their local allies, extreme movements are far better established, and in more countries, than at
any time in the past two decades. While this is partly due to more
causes for revolt, not least a widespread perception of exclusion
and marginalisation, it is also a reflection of a combination of
numerous technological developments, interconnectedness and
the globalisation of economies and communications.

By any analysis the War on Terror has been a conspicuous failure, but it continues as what appears to be the only way forward.
Boots on the ground may have been replaced by remote-control
warfare, but the solution is seen in Western security circles almost
entirely as the use of intense and persistent military force, with
little attention paid to the underlying reasons why the wars have
developed. It appears more and more to be a case of keeping the
lid on, rather than of turning down the heat – 'liddism rules OK' –
and there is very little sign of any serious new thinking.

On its own, and just in relation to the response to al-Qaeda and
its successors, this would be a matter of serious concern, but one
of the aims of this book is to put the experience since 9/11 in the
longer-term context of overall global trends – especially transnational marginalisation and environmental limits. As these give rise
to deep frustration in the majority margins across the world, there
is every risk that the lessons that should have been learnt from the
disasters of recent years will be missed, and that attempts will be
made to maintain control and keep the world safe by force – with
disastrous results as elite states and communities seek to maintain a tenuous security. The final two chapters, therefore, return
to the theme outlined at the beginning of this book. Chapter 7
concentrates on analysing the factors that could move us towards
an age of insurgencies involving techniques and technologies of
war that cannot be controlled by traditional military means – an
era at risk from multiple revolts from the margins. Chapter 8 then
provides a tentative guide to how the 'crowded glowering planet'
that Edwin Brooks warned us of can be avoided.

7

A GLOWERING PLANET?

A couple of years ago I received an invitation out of the blue from an Oxford college to contribute to a seminar on security risks likely to arise from weak and failing states and affecting the United Kingdom. Someone was required to lead off with an overview of world trends in the light of the many problems of violence and insecurity that were evident across the Middle East and South Asia. The idea was that a number of highly experienced regional and country specialists would then provide the detail. The organiser promised an experienced and relevant audience but was reluctant to be specific as to its make-up. I assumed it to be diplomats and civil servants.

Even though I did not know the backgrounds of the participants, it seemed a very interesting theme, coming at a time when the wars in Afghanistan and Iraq seemed at last to be winding down but Syria was heading into chaos. Perhaps worse than this from a UK perspective was the disaster that was unfolding in Libya, where NATO's role in terminating the Gaddafi regime had left a country that was not just weak and failing but the scene of daily violence. At the very least, participating in the seminar would be informative, and the value of 'leading off' was that I had a free hand to cover the broader issues but the privilege of listening to some highly knowledgeable specialists in particular regions.

In the event, the participants turned out to be a substantial number of senior officers from the SAS, including the commandant, together with other special-forces, MI6 and Defence Intelligence Staff personnel. The seminar was one of a series of occasional, privately funded sessions designed to enable the United Kingdom's elite military and security forces to keep their thinking ahead of world trends.

While the United Kingdom's special forces are centred on the SAS and the SBS, they have been expanded in recent years with the addition of the SFSG, and also include the Special Reconnaissance Regiment, with all four of these groups including a squadron from the 18 (UKSF) Signal Regiment. As we saw in Chapter 6, this expansion is mirrored by similar developments in other Western armed forces, but this particular meeting at the Oxford college was almost entirely UK-oriented, and its purpose was to look well ahead of the crises at that time – well beyond the horizon of the 'War on Terror' – and work out what major problems there would be in the years and decades to come.

The great majority of personnel in the SAS and other special-forces groups stay with their units for many years and even for their entire careers, especially the NCOs, but officers may serve more limited periods before continuing their careers elsewhere, quite commonly ending up in some of the highest ranks of the armed forces. One former Chief of the Defence Staff spent part of his time in the SAS running President Jomo Kenyatta's bodyguard in Kenya. Long known in SAS trooper slang as 'Ruperts', such officers are not particularly disrespected, are disproportionately public-school educated and comfortable with talking to senior politicians when required. In short, this is part of the British armed forces that would be at the centre of the country's military posture, not just by being engaged in future conflicts but also by helping to populate the leadership of tomorrow's army.

It was an interesting session with a well-informed group of people, but it was clear that their remit was limited to looking ahead to the problems they would have to face over the next decade or more and at what would be required to maintain the security of the United Kingdom and its partners in the face of new threats. Their role did not appear to extend to examining the underlying causes of those threats and how they might be avoided. Their concern was not with the reasons for the weaknesses or failures of states and how to prevent them from becoming problems in the future, but with how to handle the consequences. The issue was essentially one of treating symptoms rather than causes, bearing in mind that their professional roles were, after all, to defend the realm.

This was all very reasonable and indeed one could readily argue that they were being responsible in looking ahead. This was their nature, and it was a relevant part of their career progression to be as good as possible at working out where the threats would arise and how to respond to them. Looking beyond the problems, at how to prevent them in the first place, was not really part of their job. This is not a reflection on their professionalism, or indeed that of other elements of the security apparatus, but it does point to a serious gap in our analysis of the problems that lie ahead. It does not seem to be sufficiently in our nature to do otherwise.

Take an example from that seminar. One of the points I put to them related to the main argument of this book: that there are likely to be two fundamental trends in world security, both of them potential drivers of severe conflict unless we can control and reverse them. One is the increasing marginalisation of the majority of the world's people caused by the workings of the neo-liberal system of international economic activity, which tend remorselessly to concentrate most of the fruits of economic growth in the hands of a transglobal elite of about 1.5 billion people. I argued that this was likely to lead to much human suffering, resentment and anger as people on the 'majority margins' saw that they had little prospect of a decent life. The other trend was climate change: it is now well-nigh certain that climate change is going to lead to huge problems of food supply and also to far more dangerous episodes of extreme weather, with profound political and social effects. These will affect the stability of countries with intrinsically weak economies, with the very strong possibility of multiple revolts from the margins.

Neither point seemed to gain much traction with the participants, perhaps because they were concerned with effects rather than causes, even though a comment from the next speaker reinforced the issue of climate change. She was a senior staff member of Islamic Relief, a large UK-based charity that raises around £100 million a year, with much of the aid going to countries across North Africa, the Sahel and the Middle East. She told the seminar that one theme that is already frequently raised by Islamic Relief's field officers is that climate change is not a future issue but already with us, especially in its effect on food production across much of the Middle East and North Africa.

Reflecting afterwards on the seminar, I was reminded of that prescient warning from the economic geographer Edwin Brooks, quoted in Chapter 1, when he warned of a future that we might all wish to avoid, of 'a crowded glowering planet of massive inequalities of wealth buttressed by stark force and endlessly threatened by desperate men in the global ghettoes'.[1]

At least the participants at that Oxford seminar were thinking about the future, and this itself was an interesting reflection on their approach, given that the United Kingdom's special forces had been at the heart of the wars in Iraq, Afghanistan and Libya. But there was little evidence that any connection was being made with that experience – that they were considering whether the 'War on Terror' had any relationship with what might be to come.

Brooks's argument may have been made more than 40 years ago, but there have been clear indications more recently that revolts from the margins might be one of the most enduring elements of the dystopian world he described. In an analysis written before the 9/11 attacks, I argued that such challenges could not be predicted to come from any one source:

What should be expected is that new social movements
will develop that are essentially anti-elite in nature and
draw their support from people on the margins. In different
contexts and circumstances they may have their roots in
political ideologies, religious beliefs, ethnic, nationalist or
cultural identities, or a complex combination of several of
these [...] What can be said is that, on present trends, anti-
elite action will be a core feature of the next 30 years – not so
much a clash of civilisations, more an age of insurgencies.[2]

In practice, the past 15 years have been dominated by just one
kind of revolt from the margins: extreme movements drawn from
one of the world's major religions – Islam; but there has also been
a thread of neo-Maoism that has been particularly entrenched
in South Asia, especially in Nepal and India. This is commonly
overlooked because of the sheer impact of the 9/11 attacks and the
wars that followed, but, as we have seen, a substantial part of the
turmoil that has affected the Middle East after the Arab Awakening
has been powerfully enhanced by the impact of marginalisation.

The aim of this chapter is to explore the current state and extent
of the underlying drivers of conflict – the increasing worldwide
socio-economic divide and the impact of environmental limits
on human activity, especially climate change – and what security
challenges will arise from these. In the face of such challenges,
what does the experience of failing to control al-Qaeda, ISIS and
the other manifestations of dissent tell us about the probable
outcome of trying to maintain order by traditional means? Is the
'control paradigm' realistic, or does the evolution of revolts from
the margins in a constrained and deeply unequal world mean that
other approaches are essential? The final chapter, Chapter 8, will
explore some of those approaches.

Western states have recently fought three disastrous wars – in
Afghanistan, Iraq and Libya – and then embarked on a fourth in
Syria and Iraq. The consequences for them have been pretty bad,

with around 10,000 of their people killed and more than 30,000 seriously injured, but these figures pale into insignificance in the face of the impact these conflicts have had in the countries concerned. The Afghan War is into its fifteenth year, facing a resurgent Taliban and an increasing ISIS presence; postwar Iraq since 2008 has been an unfolding disaster and has given a boost to a singularly violent and currently uncontrollable movement; and Libya has collapsed into multiple militias and endemic violence, with ISIS gaining a substantial foothold. The overall loss of life has been huge – at least 100 times greater than that in the 9/11 attacks – hundreds of thousands of people have been injured, many of them maimed for life, and the displacement of peoples across the Middle East and south-western Asia runs into many millions.

Even so, there is still a belief that traditional means of control work – witness what has recently been attempted in Syria and Iraq. There may be a move away from boots on the ground and towards control by remote warfare, whether drones, low-profile special forces, unaccountable private military companies or other means, but there is scarcely any evidence that these will be any more effective. It is this undying commitment to the control paradigm that bodes so ill for the next 30 years and requires a fundamental rethinking of ideas on international security. This rethinking needs to be rooted in an acceptance that the failure to recognise and understand the underlying challenges facing us, and to respond accordingly, will be the one factor that will ensure a deeply divided, resentful and angry world towards the middle of the century.

THE SOCIO-ECONOMIC DIVIDE AND THE MARGINS

By the end of the twentieth century there was a growing aware-ness that progress towards a wealthier world was not as advanced as many had thought, and that the benefits of the free-market approach that had evolved since the start of the Reaganomics era were not being delivered in the way that had been expected. This was believed to be due in part to the Asian downturn of the late 1990s, and also to the near-collapse of the Russian economy as it embraced 'turbo-capitalism'. Billionaire oligarchs there may have been, usually little more than robber barons benefiting from the chaos of the early 1990s and avidly grabbing much of Russia's resource base, but by the end of that decade there were close to 50 million people in Russia below the poverty line, alcoholism was rife, especially among middle-aged men, and life expectancy was plummeting.

Beyond this was a wider perception that the globalised free market was of great benefit to a minority of society but not working for the good of all, and the closing years of the century saw popular movements growing rapidly, especially across the Global North, and sometimes breaking out into large demonstrations that were violently suppressed, Seattle and Genoa being two examples.

Then came the election of George W. Bush, ushering in a renewed emphasis on a neoconservative world view and a commitment to the neo-liberal free market, as well as a comprehensive debunking of the threat from climate change. That was to last until 2007–8 and a renewed financial crisis originating in the toxic debts from banks financing unsustainable mortgages, but even that seemed to be overcome, albeit with severe austerity consequences.[3] Now, nearly a decade later, the issue of inequality has finally come back on the agenda, and at two levels. One is the acquisition of immense wealth by just a few individuals, frequently termed the 'one per cent', and this tends to be the focus of most discussion about inequality. While certainly significant, this actually masks recognition of the other level: the relative wealth of around a fifth of the world's population, with the marginalisation of most of the remaining four-fifths.

The difference between this fifth of the world's people and the rest can be illustrated in many ways, but the essential point is that the former controls or owns between 80 and 90 per cent of annual income and/or personal wealth. Figures cannot be exact because of variations in methodology, but the broad picture is clear enough: the majority of the world's people are relatively marginalised and the indications are that the gap is not narrowing but more likely widening. This immediately raises two questions. First, the terms 'margins' and 'marginalisation' normally imply a minority on the fringes of society, so can it really be the case that the *majority* are relatively marginalised? Second, how can this be happening when the world as a whole is growing richer and some of the UN Millennium Development Goals for 2015 have been reached or at least approached? The very idea of people on the margins simply does not gel with the ability of people to travel the world, the growth of skyscraper cities across much of Asia and Latin America and the rapid increase in employment in so many 'emerging economies'. In short, these factors create the impression that things are getting better, apart from in a few zones of protracted conflict.

It is useful to take these two questions in turn, starting with the concept of margins and marginalisation. What we are talking about here is not a minority fringe that is consistently excluded from the benefits accruing to most of society, but the majority of people, who are sharing inadequately the benefits of distorted economic growth. They are what should be thought of as the 'majority margins': not so much people who are desperately poor, but the far larger number who may be educated, literate and all too well aware of the state of society and that they have seriously limited life chances.

This is not to diminish the existence of serious impoverishment, which affects as many as a billion people, including 400 million children, nor the enduring problem of malnutrition.[4] These alone are manifestations of the fundamental failure of the world economy to increase equality, but they tend to be masked by the view that progress is being made, that almost everyone else is in an improving state, that middle-income countries are thriving and that wealth will duly trickle down to the poorest. The reality is different, with rich–poor divisions steadily being widened in almost every country. As a result, we are dealing less with the old rich country–poor country or first world–third world representation of three or four decades ago, but much more with a transnational elite of around 1.5 billion people, which is drawing away from the remaining 6 billion, the latter including the billion who are deeply impoverished.

That the old division between rich countries and poor countries no longer applies is illustrated dramatically in Joseph Stiglitz's most recent writing on this theme.[5] One reviewer of *The Great Divide* (2015) summarised the staggering degree of inequality in the US system, as described by Stiglitz:

> One-fifth of America's children live in poverty; the average wage of male high-school leavers has declined by 12 per cent in the past 25 years; and the pay of CEOs has swelled from 30 times the average worker's wage to 300 times.[6]

Nor is poverty limited to a cluster of very poor countries, even if they form a significant part of the worldwide divide. According to the '2014–2015 Global Food Policy Report' from the International Food Policy Research Institute, nearly half of the world's hungry, around 363 million people, live in the middle-income countries of Brazil, China, India, Indonesia and Mexico.[7]

Even that bastion of the neo-liberal economic system, the World Economic Forum, has raised the issue and done so by emphasising the evolution of a wealth–poverty divide that transcends individual states. Furthermore, the term 'poverty' is misleading, because we are dealing with far more than an entirely destitute community, but one that extends to billions of people who may have food, shelter, some education and quite probably work, yet see their prospects diminished by a system that persistently favours a substantial minority.

The second question raised above relates to the Millennium Development Goals and the argument that the fact that many of them are within reach must surely demonstrate that things are getting better. In many ways, personal wealth is higher than four decades ago, but that does not in any way diminish the fact that most people are not sharing adequately in the fruits of overall improvement. Working in a sweatshop factory for 60 hours a week for low pay may be an improvement relative to unemployment and living in a slum, but in the face of the growing wealth of the minority it is still a ready cause of resentment and anger, especially if the difference in wealth and poverty is growing.

Perhaps the most revealing way of considering this is the idea of a 'truly global poverty' measure of the kind proposed by Ravallion and Chen.[8] David Hulme, in his seminal book *Global Poverty: Global Governance and Poor People in the Post-2015 Era* (2015), summarises this approach as seeking to count

> both absolutely poor people and relatively poor people [...]
> the global poor are conceptualized as (i) those who cannot
> meet their basic needs in terms of a universal standard,
> and (ii) those who experience relative deprivation or social
> exclusion because their per capita income/consumption
> is low compared with the average levels in their country.
> This measure captures absolute poverty in the developing
> world (i.e. $1.25-a-day poverty), relative poverty in the
> developing world and relative poverty in high-income
> countries [...] It indicates that the truly global poverty rate
> has reduced much more slowly than the absolute global
> poverty rate.[9]

Most significantly, Hulme points out that while the global poverty rate may be declining slowly, the relative poverty rate in high-income countries has increased, and has more than doubled in the developing world.

Three or four decades ago sociologists discussed the 'revolution of rising expectations' taking place in the market-driven, rising-income countries of the West, where all sectors of society could look to significant improvements in their incomes and well-being. Now the greater risk is of a 'revolution of frustrated expectations', not least in the Global South. This is, as already argued, one of the drivers of the Arab Awakening, and certainly underpins the motives of young men in northern Nigeria who embrace Boko Haram. It has played a major part in the Zapatista rebellion in Mexico and has been an underlying cause of the neo-Maoist upsurges in Peru and Nepal.

Most indicative of all is the neo-Maoist Naxalite rebellion in India, scarcely covered in the Western media but seen within the Indian security establishment as the greatest threat to the internal security of the world's most populous state. The Naxalites were initially focused on the town of Naxalbari in the north of West Bengal in 1967, and the movement was assumed to have been largely suppressed following prime minister Indira Gandhi's launching of 'Operation Steeplechase' four years later. Instead the movement took root and spread south across eastern India. In 2006 the Indian government estimated the Naxalite strength to be 20,000 armed supporters, and persistent attempts to suppress it have so far failed.

There has been some decrease in activity since 2011 but with sudden outbreaks of violence, including the killing of 15 security personnel in a single attack in March 2014.[10] Even more violent was the killing of Congress Party politicians on 25 May 2013, when their convoy of 17 vehicles was returning through Naxalite-controlled territory from a political rally.[11] Much of the support for the Naxalites has come from the Adivasis, the tribal peoples of India, especially in those districts affected by mining and new industries, but more generally in reaction to their perceived long-term marginalisation. In recent years some Naxalites have moved into more conventional politics, albeit on the radical fringe, but the rebellion remains potent and serves as an enduring example of a revolt from the margins.

Despite the existence of al-Qaeda, ISIS, Boko Haram, the Caucasus Emirate and other Islamist groups, violent reactions from the majority margins in the form of large-scale extreme movements are still relatively rare. Much more common are high crime rates, especially within megacities, as well as social protests, some of which come from unexpected sources. A significant, if little-noticed, development has been the growth in popular protest in China, a phenomenon that, like the Naxalite rebellion, gets very little coverage outside the region. This has occurred slowly over the past ten years and comes mainly from people who have become increasingly bitter at their life chances in a country of 875,000 dollar millionaires, where the rich are prone to flaunt their wealth. What adds to this is anger at corruption in public life, which is often linked to the acquisition of excessive wealth. Together these factors have resulted in numerous strikes and frequent riots, and therefore a substantial expansion in the state's paramilitary forces in order to control dissent.[12]

A major reaction to a situation of marginalisation, one that has had a high profile in recent years, is the often desperate attempt to move to a better environment. This has been a long-term process, especially with emigration from Europe to North America and the old imperial dominions of the former British Empire. More recently there has been substantially increased pressure from Central America on the United States, South East Asia on Australia and the Middle East on Western Europe. Most notable, though, are the attempted migrations from North Africa into southern Europe. When such trends emerge, the reaction from within the receiving states is commonly an anti-immigrant stance rooted in those sectors of society that see their own positions as being potentially diminished by incomers. They offer ready support for political movements that utilise fear to increase their own power.

In response to an influx of desperate migrants who travelled across the Mediterranean from Libya to Italy in the early months of 2015, the European Union tried, in the face of difficulty, to get member states to take a modest quota of refugees. In this context, the decision to establish the European Union Naval Force Mediterranean (EUNAVFOR Med) to take action against people smugglers, their boats and networks, was widely supported. According to *Jane's Defence Weekly*: 'The 28 EU nations have set aside EUR 11.8 million (USD 13.1 million) from their CSDP [Common Security and Defence Policy] operations common fund to cover EUNAVFOR Med's start-up phase, plus an initial mandate for 12 months.'[13] From later in 2015, south-eastern European countries were faced with hundreds of thousands of desperate people trying to escape conflicts in the Middle East and western Asia, principally from Syria. While some EU countries have opened their borders to tens of thousands, others have been resolute in keeping migrants out or rushing them through to other countries. At worst this has resulted in the spectacle of new fences being erected on borders, topped with razor wire and protected by riot police. This situation has been exploited by right-wing anti-immigrant parties to improve their own electoral prospects, the effect being to increase the despair and anger among would-be immigrants, who are so often acutely in need.

All of these elements – paramilitary movements, large-scale social protests and increased migration – are harbingers, given that there is no sign that the issue of relative marginalisation is being addressed in any kind of consistent and effective manner. Indeed, the trend is in the opposite direction, which will itself be a factor aiding the development of radical and even extreme movements. But it is when the issue of marginalisation interacts with the second main driver of change – environmental limits – that a clearer picture of Brooks's 'crowded glowering planet' emerges.

ENVIRONMENTAL DEGRADATION

A global system embodying deep socio-economic divisions and majority marginalisation risks persistent instability and violence, especially if it leads to irregular wars involving extreme movements that cannot be controlled by traditional means, but the response from the margins is going to be greatly magnified if there are limits to conventional forms of economic growth. Such limits stem from environmental factors, and have the potential to make the impact of socio-economic divisions far worse. Even regional environmental limits – including marine pollution, declines in soil fertility (especially through salinisation), loss of richly biodiverse habitats, species extinctions, and air and water pollution – can have profound social effects, but beyond all these is the overarching issue of the human impact on the entire world ecosystem, the biosphere.

The first clear instance of this was specific and could be controlled by international action. This was the impact of chlorofluorocarbon (CFC) pollutants on the upper atmosphere, leading to a breakdown of ozone. This was highly significant since the ozone layer normally filters out medium-wave ultraviolet solar radiation, which would otherwise be deeply damaging to living organisms. The response to the problem after its recognition in 1983 was the Montreal Protocol of 1987, which started to phase out CFC production and use, but the several decades it will take for the full repair of the ozone layer is itself an indicator of the 'lag effect' common to global processes.

Vastly exceeding the challenge of ozone depletion is the impact of fossil-carbon release through the burning of natural gas, oil and especially coal, leading to increases in carbon-dioxide concentration and atmospheric temperatures. This issue had been widely recognised by the late 1990s, but was largely sidelined after the 9/11 attacks. Even eight years later, at the United Nations Climate Change Conference in Copenhagen in December 2009, scarcely any progress was made towards the decarbonisation of economies, even though the evidence of climate change and the link with carbon pollution was overwhelming.

Resistance to accepting climate change and to the need for radical decarbonisation was deeply ingrained in the Bush administration, and aided by emphatic climate-change denial from fossil-carbon companies, especially transnational oil corporations, and from those committed to neo-liberal economics. This was not least because decarbonisation would require concerted governmental and intergovernmental action, which would necessarily involve controls on the free market, something such ideologues could not possibly accept.

By the beginning of the second decade of the twenty-first century, attitudes were changing in the wake of more and more empirical evidence of climate change, most notably the extraordinary decrease in Arctic sea ice and the increase in the intensity of severe weather events. Among the denial community there has been a slow and singularly reluctant acceptance that the climate is changing, but an insistence that this is due to natural factors, including climate cycles, rather than any human influence. Even that view is becoming less tenable in the face of mounting evidence.

The reality of the situation was ably expressed by the American Association for the Advancement of Science (AAAS) in a report published in 2013. This can be summarised as follows:

- About 97 per cent of climate scientists agree that human-induced climate change is happening. Global temperatures are increasing and sea levels are rising. Extreme weather events are happening more frequently and climate change is the likely cause.
- There is now the risk of pushing the climate system towards sudden, unpredictable and potentially irreversible changes with hugely damaging impacts.
- The sooner action is taken the lower the risk and the cost.

- Carbon dioxide persists in the atmosphere for 'decades, centuries, and longer', so continuing emission of carbon dioxide increases warming and associated risks.[14]

In the context of international security, there are three key points to consider. One is that the rate of climate change appears to be accelerating, especially in some regions such as the Arctic and the northern subtropics. The second is that the entire process is proving to be markedly asymmetric. The most commonly accepted prognosis is that this trend will persist and that, in broad terms, the greatest impacts will be on the polar regions, the tropics and subtropics, with substantially more warming on land than over the oceans. Furthermore, there are predicted to be changes in rainfall patterns, marked by a relative increase over the oceans and the polar regions and a decline over tropical and subtropical land masses. Third, there is expected to be an increase in severe weather events, whether they be storms, floods, droughts or intense heatwaves.

It is the impact on the tropics and subtropics that is most significant. At the beginning of this chapter I mentioned the seminar involving UK special forces and the comment from a contributor from Islamic Relief that climate change was already a factor across the Middle East. This was emphasised by a study published in 2015 that pointed to evidence that the severe drought affecting Syria in 2007–10, which was probably linked to climate change, resulted in an exodus from rural to urban areas, adding greatly to the political instability that preceded the civil war.[15]

We are also moving into an era of 'positive feedback', as some climate-change trends actually speed the very process of which they are part. A well-known example is the 'albedo effect', whereby melted sea ice gives way to open water, which absorbs more solar radiation and therefore causes adjacent ice to melt faster. A more complicated example occurs when ice melts on glaciers or ice caps, even on the gigantic Greenland ice cap, seeping through crevasses and fissures down to the border between ice and rock, lubricating the flow of ice so that the glaciers or ice caps speed up their rate of slide.

Both of these processes are already under way. The third example may be in its early stages, but it has greater potential for acting as a tipping point. This is the thawing of Arctic permafrost, which initiates the decay of previously frozen vegetable matter, releasing methane, a far more potent climate-change gas than carbon dioxide. As it is released, the temperature increases, leading to a faster rate of melting. There are other examples of this kind of acceleration, some clear-cut and others less understood, but they all add to increased concern.

In spite of all of this evidence, the level of political literacy on climate change remains low, and this is made worse by some national attitudes. One of the most substantial recent barriers to a transition to ultra-low-carbon economies has been the attitude of three countries that have some of the greatest potential for fossil-carbon extraction and export: Russia, Canada and Australia. As recently as mid-2015, all three had governments with leaders who did not regard climate change as a problem; a further complication is that two of them, Canada and Russia, are among the very few countries that may benefit in the short term from the effects of climate change, as crops can be grown further north, and the loss of Arctic sea ice opens up new fuel and non-fuel mineral resources for exploitation.

Russia is one of the world's major oil and gas exporters and Canada has large supplies of oil in the form of tar sands, which require intense energy use to extract. Australia is in a slightly different position: despite having some of the world's largest reserves of coal – the most dangerous form of carbon – it is more vulnerable to the impact of climate change than either Canada or Russia. The latter fact may change Australian opinion, but that change would have to be substantial given the easy availability and high profitability of its mineral resources.

In late 2015 the Australian prime minister, Tony Abbott, was ousted; his replacement was Malcolm Turnbull, a politician less strident in his denial of climate change, even if Australian government policies have so far seen little sign of change. More important was the defeat in November 2015 of Canadian prime minister Stephen Harper by Justin Trudeau, leading to a marked change in policy on climate and energy issues. Even so, the previous combination of Abbott, Harper and Putin certainly set back international negotiations on climate change, much as George W. Bush's presidency had done in the previous decade.

THE SECURITY IMPACT OF CLIMATE CHANGE

The most important impact of climate change will be the reduction in the carrying capacity of some of the world's most important croplands, especially in the Global South. This, in turn, will mean a decrease in food production, both for local consumption and for export. This does not mean that the world as a whole will run out of food, but it most certainly does mean that poorer communities will not be able to produce enough; nor will they have the money to buy it. This will progressively add greatly to domestic economic and social pressures, hardship, suffering, resentment and anger, especially in states already on the economic margins and least well equipped to cope.

Moreover, the problem is made worse by the increasing frequency of extreme weather events, and the inability of poorer states to cope with them. A recent example is Typhoon Haiyan, which struck the southern Philippines in November 2013 and had the distinction of being the most violent storm on record ever to hit land, peaking at a sustained wind speed of 160 mph over a ten-minute time span, and an almost unbelievable 196 mph over a one-minute time span. Warnings were given and most sought shelter, yet the storm still killed 6,300 people. Although the Philippines is not the poorest of countries, 2 million people remained without secure shelter six months later.

Haiyan and similar intense weather events can be categorised as 'rapid-onset events', with an immediate impact in terms of issues such as migration, and it is estimated that more than 140 million people have experienced such displacement as a result of climate-related disasters since 2008. In the aftermath of such experiences, many people may eventually be able to resettle the areas evacuated and reclaim their lives, albeit often at great cost, although that is certainly not the case if inundation of low-lying coastal land results in salinisation of soil. Until recently it was not possible to determine whether extreme weather events were directly linked to long-term climate change, but evidence is now accumulating that this is indeed the case.[16]

What will most likely have a far greater impact is 'slow-onset change' such as long-term declines in rainfall and increases in temperature. As Steve Trent argues on the ORG's Sustainable Security blog:

> Research shows that slow-onset changes are significant drivers of permanent out-migration – one recent study estimates that an additional 2°C rise in temperatures could force up to 5% of Indonesia's population (12.4 million) to migrate by the end of the century. When people move across borders to cope with environmental change – whether to seek employment or as an act of desperation – international governance systems fail to recognise the key climatic driver of their movement.[17]

In short, if climate change is not prevented, the prognosis is for a progressive decline in the viability of many parts of the Global South. It is deeply ironic that the impact on these regions is likely to be far greater than that on the countries of the northern and southern temperate latitudes, which would be far more able to cope, given their greater economic resources.

PUTTING IT TOGETHER

When Brooks wrote of the 'crowded glowering planet' more than 40 years ago, his main concern was with economic differentials and broad issues of environmental limitations to growth. The experience of the past four decades shows that one particular issue – the evolving impact of climate change, especially on the Global South – is by far the most important of the environmental factors, and that this is greatly more significant when it is integrated into the failure of the global economic system to deliver greater equity and emancipation.

We already have the formidable problem of the 'majority margins', but it is those margins that will be most affected by climate disruption, as a result of their inability to cope with the effects – such as short-term extreme weather events or the long-term changes in the ability of large areas to sustain populations. The risk is of current levels of resentment, bitterness and anger escalating in the face of an inadequate response from elite minorities, whether within states or across borders. In such circumstances, current movements such as the Naxalites and some Islamist groups serve as warnings of future reactions, both within particular states and transnationally.

What cannot be predicted is whether we will ever face a coordinated international movement of opposition, the potential 'Southern Army of the Poor' described by Ronald Higgins in the the 1970s, but this is where the al-Qaeda/ISIS element may be particularly significant.[18] In this case it is rooted in a religious belief with a transnational following, but other elements of identity might prove just as significant, such as in the event of the reawakening of an organised, global neo-Maoist movement.

Overall, it is the link between environmental limits and a world economy not fit for purpose that underpins the security challenge. In the ordinary way, security professionals might argue that it will be possible to maintain stability without addressing the underlying drivers of conflict, even as we move into a period of greater uncertainty, fragility and angry reaction to marginalisation. This attitude is especially apparent in the thinking on climate change, the whole issue of which is increasingly treated as one of security. Thus, from the perspective of an elite-security mindset, climate change is a threat to well-being and the right response is to maintain stability in the face of this threat. According to this view, it is the proper duty, indeed the fundamental responsibility, of those charged with the security of a civilised society to maintain that society as it is, and against whatever threats and challenges arise as a consequence of climate change.[19]

This is where the experience of the 15 years of the War on Terror is so relevant, demonstrating as it does the huge difficulty of maintaining stability in an era in which apparently weak movements have been able to exploit the vulnerabilities of advanced and well-armed states. ISIS, al-Qaeda and Boko Haram are cases in point, but the individual strategies of other groups, including PIRA's use of economic targets, are further examples. Similarly, although the rapid development by a middle-ranking but determined regime such as that of Saddam Hussein of a range of chemical and biological weapons is not something that could be easily replicated by a sub-state group, it is still an indicator of a path that could be followed in the future.

It appears to be very difficult for security establishments to embrace the idea that sub-state movements might be beyond their control, in spite of the exceedingly difficult experiences since 9/11 in the three failed and tragic wars in Afghanistan, Iraq and Libya. This is made even more problematic by the extent, power and influence of those establishments, which are part of a global military–industrial complex that consumes around $1,700 billion each year. For the component corporations, military spending provides for eminently profitable endeavours. Furthermore, the development of the 'military–industrial–academic–bureaucratic complex' over many years, and its embedding in society, may make it impossible to comprehend the idea of the obsolescence of established forms of war. The notion that movements such as ISIS and Boko Haram are simply not amenable to traditional military solutions is simply too difficult to contemplate.

Instead, the primary concern is with maintaining military budgets, and this is achieved through extensive lobbying, as well as support for appropriately oriented policy research. It is further aided by the internal interconnections in the great majority of states with sizeable military budgets. Throughout the system there is an established process whereby senior officers and civil servants, especially those connected in any way with research, development and procurement, move seamlessly at the end of their professional careers into well-paid consultancies and even board memberships. In this revolving-door system, industry personnel are also frequently seconded to government departments.

One of the requirements of this system is to be able to identify threats that demand military systems and forces. As a result, the 45-year Cold War was one of the best periods in history, for it, followed by the 1990s, with their risk of a 'peace dividend', proved worrying for many in the security establishment. The War on Terror was therefore hugely important in raising budgets, even if much of the equipment required was hardly at the sophisticated end of the spectrum. Even so, with the War on Terror now expected to have cost well over $3,000 billion over its first 15 years, it was a useful source of revenue, and has been joined recently by the thoroughly welcome increased threat from Russia and possibly China, and the considerable rise in military spending by the oil-rich states of the Gulf.[20]

All in all, there remains the cosy belief that there is little need for any kind of change in attitude, in spite of all the evidence to the contrary. It is as though the development of irregular warfare has not been happening, and the very idea of elite centres of power losing control is unthinkable.

8

A POSSIBLE PEACE

We have ahead of us a period of at least two decades in which three challenges face us. One is that the worldwide economic system – the neo-liberal model of free-market capitalism – is not delivering sufficient equity and emancipation. It is simply not fit for purpose, yet deeply entrenched and therefore likely to prove singularly difficult to modify. This, though, is essential in the interests of building a much more stable and just society, one that can respond to climate disruption, let alone the more practical motive of avoiding the evolution of violent responses. The second challenge is climate change, which, if not countered, will lead to huge problems of insecurity and fragility in what is a thoroughly connected world. Moreover, responding to this challenge requires a radical move towards ultra-low-carbon economies long before the more severe effects of climate disruption are felt. That is a formidably difficult and electorally unpopular task for political leaders rarely noted for their wisdom, who commonly have to seek re-election every four or five years. Thirdly, we have to control an integrated culture of militarism that sees military solutions to evolving challenges as the most appropriate responses.

It seems simple: stop climate change, transform the global economy and sideline militarism – all in the space of a couple of decades! When it is put like that, our reaction might be to throw up our hands in despair, because these goals seem so unachievable. In practice, though, it is what has to be done, and there are actually quite a few reasons for optimism. Before reviewing those, it is helpful to look at the longer-term challenges facing us.[1]

A WIDER PERSPECTIVE

The biosphere or global ecosystem is remarkably complex, having evolved over several billion years and including a diverse range of life forms. One of these life forms – humanity – has had an astonishing impact on the biosphere, and this has occurred over a remarkably brief period compared with the millions of years of its own evolution – let alone the several billion years over which life itself has evolved.

The further you go back into prehistory the less precision there is about dating the developments, but our ancestors have probably been toolmakers, as distinct from merely users, for around 2 million years. Even so, our impact on the environment has been minimal until the very recent past – no more than the blink of an eye in evolutionary history. As recently as 12,000 years ago we were still hunter-gatherers, spread widely across the world but very few in number and living mainly in very small communities, because of the need for groups to hunt and forage over a wide area.

At that time the worldwide population was probably no more than 5 million, smaller than any of today's major cities, and that did not change until we began to learn how to farm, both by domesticating wild animals and by growing early food crops. These 'hearths of domestication', as they are known, were developed in different parts of the world over several thousand years and led to an extraordinary increase in the ecological carrying capacity of previously natural systems and their ability to support human communities. With the development of agriculture, people began to live more commonly in settled communities, and towns and then cities developed where the soils were exceptionally rich and much more food could be produced, as in major river basins and deltas. Between around 12,000 and 7,000 years ago the world's population grew from 5 million to more than 80 million.

This was the first great transition. There was a second, even greater expansion, which began 300 years ago with the advent of the industrial and agricultural revolutions of the eighteenth and nineteenth centuries. In this more recent era there were hugely increased environmental impacts, although they were mainly on a local, national or regional scale rather than a global one. Even so, the cumulative effect of these, especially changes in land use, meant that the biosphere as a whole was being affected by human activity, something further increased by the surge in population in the twentieth century. As has already been discussed, though, it is only in the much more recent past that humanity has had a truly global impact on the biosphere. This was shown first by the problem of ozone depletion, and now involves the much more entrenched and fundamental problem of carbon emissions and climate change.

This second great transition continues, and within it are two aspects of human behaviour that present possibly the greatest challenges faced since the beginnings of human civilisation more than 10,000 years ago: a capacity for self-destruction and an ability to damage the entire global environment. Moreover, we are now in a period in our history in which these challenges are having to be faced. This period began in 1945, the dawn of the nuclear age, which ushered in the potential for immense destruction, and will last until around 2045, by which time we have to reverse the trend towards climate disruption with its huge global consequences. In a sense, this makes our current era what might be described as a 'century on the edge'.

Responding to our ability to destroy ourselves reveals a mixed message. Thirty years ago, at the height of one of the most danger-ous phases of the Cold War, there were more than 60,000 nuclear weapons in the world, almost all in the arsenals of the countries of the Warsaw Pact and NATO. There were also tens of thousands of tonnes of chemical weapons, again mostly held by these two alliances. The move away from reliance on these arsenals has been spectacular, but very far from complete. All the major nuclear powers are modernising their arsenals, albeit at much reduced levels compared to the Cold War years, and while conventions now ban both chemical and biological weapons, neither is fully effective.

In the case of nuclear weapons, instead of the small risk of an utter nuclear catastrophe that we faced during the Cold War – peering over the edge of the abyss – there is now a potentially slippery slope: a risk of proliferation and the possibility that sub-state groups may eventually find ways to develop and utilise such weaponry. Possibly in the very near future, sufficiently independent and robust groups may develop their own effective chemical and radiological weapons, especially if they control territory. In the longer term, they may develop effective biological weapons and, ultimately, crude nuclear devices, though this may be decades away unless they are aided by a state. It is therefore a mixed message.

There has been some progress in arms control, especially for chemical and biological weapons, but little in the way of formal agreements on nuclear weapons: there is no prospect of the coming into force of the Comprehensive Nuclear-Test-Ban Treaty, which was adopted by the United Nations in 1996 but not ratified by all member states, and none of the existing nuclear states seems inclined to consider a binding convention. We escaped a Cold War nuclear holocaust more by luck than judgement, and with a notable lack of wisdom. The risk of nuclear war may be much diminished, but it has not disappeared. Indeed, as noted above, nuclear-armed states are busy modernising their systems. All five major nuclear powers – the United States, Russia, China, France and the United Kingdom – are doing so, and India and Pakistan are actually increasing the size of their arsenals. Israel maintains a substantial arsenal, shows no interest in a Middle East nuclear-free zone and is even suspicious of the progress made in limiting Iran's nuclear capability. Meanwhile North Korea continues its slow progress down the nuclear path and this is readily used by the existing powers as yet another excuse to hold on to their arsenals.

After the end of the Cold War in the early 1990s, some hard-line strategists in the West argued surprisingly for moves towards a nuclear-free world, not least because of fears of nuclear proliferation. Support for such an approach had largely died away by the end of the decade, but the need for it has not just remained but intensified, with the growth of extreme movements with an eschatological dimension, for whom nuclear deterrence is irrelevant. Because we are not really serious about moving beyond a world without WMD, there is a significantly greater risk that future revolts from the margins will involve such systems.

The effects of the other challenge to human society, the threat of environmental limits, are slow but accelerating and potentially disastrous. They are many and varied and may be summarised in a crude but legitimate manner: the biosphere cannot withstand the impact of a population of more than 7 billion people that utilises resources and causes pollution at the rate of the current richest fifth; nor can it withstand anything approaching such an impact. We would need three planets, not one – and we only have the one.

Faced with the biggest single issue, climate change, we need to make radical changes in the next two decades and move towards at least an 80 per cent decrease in carbon emissions across the Global North, and combine these changes with a rapid transition to low-carbon modes of societal organisation in the Global South. This can be done, and there is time – just. Overall, this 'century on the edge' is immensely challenging, since it requires fundamental changes in economic and environmental policies and a greatly decreased dependency on conventional approaches to international security. Even so, given the rapid change that can be achieved in many other fields, and the speed with which new approaches can be implemented, it is certainly possible to see a way through. This final part of the book only begins to chart the changes necessary, since that would require an entire volume on its own, but it does aim to provide some pointers, with some emphasis on positive scenarios, bearing in mind that the pace of change can greatly exceed expectations.

RESPONDING TO CLIMATE CHANGE

After the lost first decade of the twenty-first century, and especially the failure of the Copenhagen summit in 2009, there has been a notable change in attitudes to climate change. This stems from several factors that, although largely independent of each other, are having a synergistic impact, and is reflected in the relatively optimistic outcome of the United Nations Climate Change Conference in Paris at the end of 2015. One is the continuing accumulation of evidence that the climate is changing and that the rate of change is exceeding expectations. There is the beginning of a sense of urgency, one that is going beyond the minority of people who have long been concerned with the issue, and starting to affect a far wider constituency. This is being boosted by the impact of more severe weather events, and the beginnings of an acceptance that these are linked to carbon emissions. Whenever a severe weather event occurs anywhere in the world, the question of its possible link to climate change is raised in a manner that simply was not seen only five years ago.

Then there is the wide range of technical developments that are altering the economic viability of renewable energy systems, with wind and solar power in some locations already getting near to grid parity in unsubsidised costs. For now, this applies primarily to especially attractive sites such as onshore locations that have plenty of steady 'clean wind' and are close to reliable grid connections, or particularly sunny places with solar arrays, but as systems become more efficient so the proportion of such sites will increase.

Efficiencies are increasing in two quite different ways: economies of scale are leading to radically lower production costs, and
technical improvements are allowing for more efficient capture
of renewable energy. Very large wind turbines of 8 megawatts or
more are now being developed, and the potential for new solar cells
is remarkable. Silicon-based photovoltaic cells are now heading
towards economically viable third-generation systems that capture
solar radiation across a broader range of the spectrum, and the
current development of entirely new systems based on perovskites
is particularly impressive. Perovskite photovoltaic systems were first
developed in 2009 with an efficiency of 3.8 per cent, but this had
increased to 20.1 per cent by 2014, an extraordinary improvement
in just five years. Even more efficient tandem-layered perovskite/
silicon-based sheets are now being developed, with start-up companies in several countries expecting to start marketing by 2017.[2]

One of the most indicative changes is the application of photovoltaic electricity generation to small, cheap, independent
systems that provide four to six hours of light at the end of ten
hours or so of daylight. For off-grid use in many parts of the
Global South they readily replace more dangerous and unhealthy
kerosene-based lamps and at a lower cost. In Africa as a whole
nearly 600 million people cannot access electricity supplies, but
barely five years ago cheap photovoltaic kits came on the market
and now they benefit 50 million people. Such speed of uptake
should not be surprising given the rapid spread of the mobile
phone and then the smartphone, and indicates just how quickly
change can happen.

There are many other areas of positive change, including intensive research and development of large-scale storage systems based
not just on batteries but on a range of novel technologies, and also
the development of undersea turbines, often powered by highly
predictable tide-related currents. Nor is this all for the future. In
the particularly windy month of December 2014, 43 per cent of
UK home electricity use was generated by wind turbines; in the

first six months of that year year 31 per cent of Germany's total electricity demand was met by renewables, and the figure was 41 per cent for Denmark. Electricity is only one form of energy use, typically making up a third of the total, so there is still a long way to go and still an excessive dependency on oil and especially coal, but all the figures quoted above were records for the countries concerned, and indicate what could be achieved with much greater short-term fiscal support.[3]

An analysis from Deutsche Bank in 2015 suggested that solar power is close to grid parity with coal under many circumstances, not just in ideal locations and climatic conditions. The Bank's study, 'Chasing the Chasm', predicts that the solar industry will grow tenfold in the next 20 years and will supply 30 per cent of global electricity power generation by 2050:

> Over the next 20 years, we expect over 100 million new customers to deploy solar and roughly $4 trillion of value to be created during this timeframe [...] we believe the solar industry is going through fundamental change and the opportunity is bigger than it has ever been before.[4]

All these examples give cause for optimism about the transition to ultra-low-carbon economies, and ultimately to the carbon-neutral future that is essential in responding to the global environmental challenge. It is a process that is inextricably linked with transforming the economic system into one that is not just low carbon but puts a premium on greater equity and emancipation.

One of the best markers of changing elite attitudes to climate change is the UK political magazine *The Economist*. Until about a decade ago, its prevailing editorial stance was one of a lack of interest, if not denial, providing plenty of space for the climate-sceptic community, much along the lines of most of the conservative press in the Global North. Bit by bit, though, the views of *The Economist* have altered: it seems to have been dragged, kicking and screaming, into accepting human-induced climate change as a reality. Indeed, it now reports on climate science and renewable technology in a way that was very largely missing before, and is often commendable in its breadth of coverage. One senses two possible reasons for this. It could be that the editorial team came under sustained pressure from its science journalists to take the issue seriously. It could also be that so-called 'green technologies' have become so mainstream and important that no self-respecting journal of economic rectitude can afford to do otherwise. Perhaps one day the magazine will undergo a Damascene conversion in its economic thinking, though that could take some time.

One of the features of climate change is the well-nigh certain increase in extreme weather events, such as extreme droughts, storms or hurricanes, which act like the canary in the coal mine of old – early indicators, in that case of a build-up of toxic methane, and warnings to change behaviour. Such events have occurred throughout history and work most effectively when it is already clear what should be done. London's 'Great Smog' of 1952 was an extreme, four-day air-pollution episode that killed at least 4,000 people, but it also helped convince the public authorities that clean-air legislation was essential. This was already planned, but it was substantially sped up after the disaster.

Nearly a century earlier, the 'Great Stink' of London had a similar effect. The hot summer of 1858 produced such a fetid, nauseous smell from the open sewer that was the River Thames that Parliament finally provided the funding for a proper sewage system for the rapidly growing metropolis. Again, such a system was already planned and its desirability known, but the severe episode brought its implementation forward by some years and also did much to banish the scourge of cholera from the city. A more recent example has already been cited: the rapid response to ozone depletion due to CFC pollutants, with an intergovern-mental agreement reached in less than five years following the full recognition of the danger.

In one sense this approach is somewhat pessimistic, in that it anticipates substantial disasters with much human suffering before adequate action is taken. This is a grim way of achieving progress, but it can be minimised if awareness of the problem and knowledge of the remedy are already at an advanced stage. One helpful, if lateral, definition of prophecy is 'suggesting the possible', and, in this context, the greater the awareness of 'the possible' the earlier the necessary action can be taken. Many of the examples cited here are indicators of what is possible. Moreover, if the changes are seen in the wider context of a divided and militarised world, which this book argues they should, then the impetus may be heightened.

ECONOMIC CHANGE

An effective response to climate change requires considerable optimism, but it may turn out to be much harder to respond to the failing world economic system, given the level of public apathy and disbelief that its faults can be addressed. To take just one example, in May 2015 five of the world's largest banks were forced by the US Justice Department to agree to

> pay about $5.6 billion and plead guilty to multiple crimes related to manipulating foreign currencies and interest rates [...] The Traders were supposed to be competitors, but much like companies that rigged the price of vitamins and automotive parts, they colluded to manipulate the largest and yet least regulated market in the financial world, where some $5 trillion changes hands every day, prosecutors said.[5]

The level of criminality in this case is staggering; it is probably the worst financial crime in history, yet even more astonishing is the probability that no one will be jailed for any part in this systemic behaviour, as well as the fact that there has been little public interest in what happened. The news was reported briefly in the Western media, with a little more detail in the financial press, but then the world moved on. It is this acceptance of an often criminal system that enables a deeply flawed industry to persist, and makes reform of free-market capitalism so difficult to envisage.[6]

This is not to say that there are no reforms available – there are many that run right across the sector. The first, obviously, would be the imposition of far higher levels of regulation, implementing hugely improved regulatory systems and far greater intergovernmental cooperation. There has been some modest tightening up since the 2007–8 financial crisis, but regulation is still woefully inadequate in the face of the cavalier attitude of immunity that pervades the financial world. A second reform would involve cracking down on tax evasion and tax avoidance, and establishing far higher tax rates for richer sectors of society and firm control of the insidious use of tax havens.[7] There remains a strong argument for applying a tariff system to the multi-trillion-dollar exchange market – the so-called 'Tobin tax', named after its inventor, the US economist James Tobin – which could raise many billions of dollars at even a minuscule tax rate of 0.25 per cent, and use the revenues for multilateral programmes of welfare support and low-carbon adaptation, especially in the Global South.

At the time of writing, negotiations between the United States and the European Union on the Transatlantic Trade and Investment Partnership (TTIP) have come into the public eye, and are being seen by many critics as an indication that trading power now resides far more with transnational corporate interests than with governments. One of the most controversial aspects of this is that the European part of the negotiating process is being conducted with high levels of confidentiality, to the extent that a final agreement will have to be accepted by the European Parliament in its entirety, even if parliamentarians have had little or no transparent involvement – the negotiations are currently being conducted by officials in association with the private sector.

Central to the controversy over TTIP, and indicative of the seepage of power from sovereign governments to corporations, is the provision within the agreement for the 'investor–state dispute settlement' process, which allows corporations to sue foreign states for damaging future profits, something that would involve adjudication in secret, without the possibility of appeal for states party to the treaty.

The questioning of TTIP may be an indication of growing concern, but it is only one example of the bias of the governance–commerce balance towards the corporate sector and the downgrading of any intergovernmental counter to such a trend. Another example is the decline in influence over the last four decades of two intergovernmental organisations: the International Labour Organization (ILO) and the United Nations Conference on Trade and Development (UNCTAD). The ILO has as its remit 'to promote rights at work, encourage decent employment opportunities, enhance social protection and strengthen dialogue on work-related issues', and was founded in 1919 'in the wake of a destructive war, to pursue a vision based on the premise that universal, lasting peace can be established only if it is based on social justice'.[8] It has worked consistently to further these aims, yet is continually sidelined in too many of the international negotiations relating to the rights of labour.

In the case of UNCTAD, the transformation is obvious: from being a potential beacon of the positive elements of trade and development in the late 1960s and early 1970s to being sidelined by the dominance of neo-liberal economic thinking. UNCTAD has simply receded into the background, long since overtaken by the WTO, where the power lies principally with elite countries. Yet the kinds of proposal that were developed in the mid-1960s under UNCTAD's first secretary general, the Argentine economist Raúl Prebisch, could have hugely improved the development prospects of the Global South. The original emphasis on primary commodity agreements, compensatory finance, tariff preferences, control of invisibles and other reforms was years ahead of its time, as was the consolidation of many aspects of these into the Integrated Programme for Commodities, the foundation of the 1974 UN declaration for the establishment of a 'New International Economic Order' (NIEO). That fell by the wayside by 1976, thanks primarily to opposition from the Global North, and within four years the era of Reaganomics and Thatcherism had dawned, which has led to the widening socio-economic divide of the past three decades.[9]

Reform across the board in all these areas is required, but inevitably it is seen as little more than a pipe dream. That may be the case, but it is also apparent that there are concerns that permeate well beyond the minority of radicals and progressives who continue to make a noise. The sudden emergence of controversy over the TTIP process in the middle of this decade is a marker of a growing awareness of the problems. There is also much to report in the way of new thinking and alternative approaches. An example of the former is the work of a number of think tanks busily engaged in 'suggesting the possible', such as the UK-based New Economics Foundation and its 'Great Transition Project'. This includes an 'econometric' model of the UK economy, designed to explore and develop an economic path that combines greater equity and emancipation with radical cuts in carbon emissions.[10]

There are also existing active alternatives, especially the world-wide movement of cooperatives and mutuals. Such organisations involve some 950 million people worldwide, and are particularly strong in the Global South, where in some states they account for a substantial part of GDP.[11] They have their faults but they are also effective business models, and although most cooperatives are involved directly or indirectly with farming, they and mutuals extend to many other activities, including retail trade, banking and insurance. Even in intensely competitive areas in countries that have embraced free-market attitudes more than most, they can compete and succeed. The employee-owned John Lewis Partnership in the United Kingdom, for example, combines a large department-store chain with a network of upmarket supermarkets that are leaders in their fields. Where I live in the north of England, the shop in our village is a cooperative; we can also buy motor fuel, gas and electricity from cooperatives, save through a mutual building society, insure with a mutual and bank with a cooperative.

There is therefore no lack of answers, but does that mean that the current system can be changed? One way this might happen directly links the world economy with climate change. Climate scientists now argue that it is essential to hold the world to a maximum temperature rise of 2°C, and to do this means that at least three-quarters of current reserves of fossil fuels have to remain in the ground. The issue is that much of what, in this view, are 'unusable' resources are already part of the global economy in the form of companies' stock-market valuations, which are based on the assumption that all remaining reserves will be exploited. This is known as the 'carbon bubble'.

The potential loss of value in the fossil-fuels industry due to this problem is estimated to be around $27 trillion. To put this into context, there were $0.7 trillion toxic-debt losses at the root of the 2007–8 financial crisis. The idea of writing off such a sum is currently unthinkable, but it will have to become eminently thinkable if climate disruption is to be taken seriously. This, though, is utterly denied by the world's fossil-fuels industry and most governments, even if it is beginning to feature in the form of the expanding divestment movement. As further changes to the world's weather occur over the next decade, a rethinking of attitudes to carbon emissions will follow. When this happens, the impact on the working of the world economy could be truly fundamental.

CHANGING THE MILITARY PARADIGM

The three major challenges we are facing are climate change, the wealth–poverty divide and the persistence of the control paradigm in military thinking despite multiple failed wars. If we meet the challenges and accelerate the process of moving to a more sustainable and stable world, we also have to face up to the third of these problems, which may be the most intractable: changing the military paradigm. Doing so is essential because of the risk of mistakenly believing that there are effective military responses to multiple insurgencies, and that there is no great need to address the environmental and economic issues underpinning them.

The argument presented here is that although responding to climate change is a huge issue and faces formidable obstacles, a great deal is already happening: the capacity for technological developments and the potential uptake of new systems are both very impressive and there is a sense in which opinion is at last starting to move in favour of radical action. Compared with this, drastically rethinking our economic future to ensure a much less divided world is more problematic; indeed, the 'business as usual' response to the 2007–8 financial crisis shows how little the system thinks there is a need for reform. Even so, there is some impressive new thinking and a great deal of good practice already out there, with many people in many countries addressing the need for change. It may be that a further serious shock, rather like an extreme weather event, will produce a tipping point, especially if its main effect is on elite communities.

That leaves the matter of the control paradigm, the outlook that permeates military thinking and practice and is hugely resistant to change. If much new work is going on in think tanks and universities on climate change and the need for economic reform, and if numerous practical initiatives are already being tried in these areas, the same cannot be said for thinking on security. There are exceptions, but they are few and far between, and the whole military–industrial–academic–bureaucratic complex is remarkably resistant to facing up to reality. The extent of the failure of the wars in Afghanistan, Iraq and Libya is simply not recognised and, instead, efforts are put into making new methods of control more effective – remote warfare being an obvious example. This is going to be the hardest nut of all to crack, and there are not many pointers as to how it can be done.

Two experiences point to the extent of the problem faced in confronting military certainties. A few years ago I attended an international conference of specialists in 'information warfare'. This was a couple of years after 9/11 and around a decade after the 'Black Hawk Down' incident in Mogadishu in 1993, when US stabilisation units mounted a special-forces raid to capture a militia leader, Mohamed Farrah Aidid. The operation went very badly wrong: two Black Hawk helicopters were shot down and 19 US soldiers were killed. President Clinton subsequently ordered the withdrawal of the US forces. The operation was one of the subjects of the conference, and one participant argued that it had actually been a success because of the manner in which hundreds of Somali militiamen had been 'hosed down' by US helicopter gunships. It was the choice of words and the way it went down well with the participants that had an impact on me: 'hosed down' – rather like firefighters tackling a conflagration. Perhaps the United States had sustained casualties but, by God, the cost to the Somalis was much greater.

In fact, it is estimated that around 1,000 Somali militiamen and civilians were killed by US forces; most had indeed been 'hosed down'. Such language was a throwback to the decimation of Apaches and others with Gatling guns in the Wild West, or to the 'gook kills' and free-fire zones of the Vietnam War. It simply was not possible for the military to comprehend that every Somali killed had scores of family and friends, every one of whom would be affected by the death. Multiply this by 1,000 and we might achieve some understanding of attitudes to the United States persisting in Somalia to this day.

The second experience is more recent. During an early stage in the writing of this book, towards the end of May 2015, there were reports over a couple of weeks that the war against ISIS in Iraq and Syria was going well for the US-led coalition. We were told that nine months of intense air attacks had targeted more than 6,000 sites and killed more than 8,500 ISIS paramilitaries. Iraqi government forces had retaken not just Tikrit but other territory; ISIS had lost a number of its key leaders to air strikes and armed-drone attacks, and there was every chance of Ramadi and even Mosul returning to government control in the coming weeks and months. Even Fallujah and the rest of Anbar Province could be regained from ISIS forces as the Iraqi government finally began to take full control after 18 months of chaos. Then, on Saturday, 16 May, we were told that there had been a successful Delta Force raid into the city of Deir al-Zour in Syria that had killed a very senior ISIS leader, Abu Sayyaf; on the same day one of the US generals running the war confirmed again that it was going well.

Thirty-six hours later the situation looked very different: the intention of the Deir al-Zour raid had been to capture Abu Sayyaf, not kill him. In fact, he was not one of the top leaders but a key economic organiser of the movement, described by one US source as the equivalent of Al Capone's accountant. As such, his knowledge of the entire organisation would have been priceless, and his capture and consequent 'robust interrogation' a real cause for celebration. Instead, he died in the fighting as the Delta Force troops faced considerable resistance. Furthermore, it became clear that Ramadi had fallen to a few hundred ISIS fighters, who had defeated elite troops of the Iraqi Army's 'Golden Brigade', who fled in disarray, leaving behind large quantities of weapons and equipment.

Whatever happens in the coming months and years, and whether ISIS thrives, just survives or declines, the conditions remain for other movements to arise anywhere across North Africa, the Middle East or South Asia. The lessons of three failed wars, with a fourth now in progress, are clear, and yet the belief still persists in clear-cut military solutions. Altering this deeply embedded attitude will be singularly difficult, even more so than changing economic thinking or responding to climate change, but has to be done. It is an area requiring intensive work, but there is little immediate evidence that much new thinking is under way.[12]

There are, though, some indicators of a way forward. First, the extent of the failures in Afghanistan, Iraq, Libya and now Iraq/Syria has to be analysed in detail, and acceptance of the implications must be argued for forcefully and repeatedly. Otherwise the outlook of the entire security complex and its deeply restricted world view will prevail. Second, the work of existing non-violent movements and their capacity to enhance positive change should be promoted. Some of the most notable movements for social change of the twentieth century were marked for their non-violent approach, yet their significance is scarcely recognised. The suffrage movement is an example, as is the US civil-rights movement after World War II. A considerable part of the impetus behind the decolonisation of the world from the 1940s onwards originated with the non-violent protest of Mahatma Gandhi and his followers in 1930s India, and the citizen movements across Eastern Europe in the late 1980s had a hugely influential role in the ending of the Cold War. Such an approach is not a panacea, and there were confrontational and even violent aspects of these complex movements, but the role of non-violence has been consistently underplayed in the face of much more powerful and profitable endeavours.[13]

Third, we can appreciate the considerable knowledge and experience that now exists in relation to mediation, conflict resolution and peace-building.[14] Fourth, closely allied to this, is the need for a greater commitment to effective intergovernmental action, involving broader agreement than is common in hastily assembled coalitions responding to particular challenges. The United Nations may have some effective specialised agencies, but its central organisation, especially the Security Council – whose composition reflects the global political situation of the period immediately after World War II – militates against good international leadership, something that is made far worse by a singularly inadequate capacity for conflict prevention and early intervention.

An idea long discussed but making little progress is that of a standing international force under UN auspices, which would comprise many different abilities and be able to perform multiple functions, but be rooted in a degree of permanency. The proposed United Nations Emergency Peace Service (UNEPS) has different variants, but most include a standing force of at least 10,000 personnel, who would be drawn from a number of member states, reflecting geographical, cultural and socio-economic diversity. Such a force might include capabilities in mediation and negotiation, disaster relief, health-crisis response, famine response, public-disorder management, peacekeeping and stabilisation – as well as, on hopefully rare occasions, direct intervention with agreed rules of engagement.[15]

UNEPS and other initiatives represent very different approaches to responding to international security challenges and normally get short shrift from the numerous vested interests in the security establishment. That makes them no less relevant – just more difficult to insert into mainstream thinking. What may change that is the experience of the last 15 years, and the lamentable consequences of old thinking and even older approaches. This is one of the core intellectual and analytical tasks for the next decade, one that, regrettably, is likely to be aided by further failures to address the underlying drivers of the new challenges.

PUTTING IT TOGETHER

This final chapter has ranged widely over issues of human activity – economic, environmental and military – but this has been necessary because the argument of the book goes way beyond a narrow analysis of the War on Terror. It would be possible to accept that the Western conduct of that war has been a disaster and to argue for the development of more effective ways of countering and defeating movements such as al-Qaeda and ISIS, involving new military approaches and better national and international defences against political violence. That might at first sight seem a reasonable approach, but the analysis presented here of the years of failure, which has occurred in spite of numerous changes in strategy and tactics, shows otherwise.

Instead, we have to recognise that ISIS and other loosely related movements are part of an historical shift towards revolts from the margins, and that such revolts are made more likely by the widening global socio-economic divide and the onset of climate disruption. This chapter has pointed out some of the changes that need to be made, but there is no pretence that this will happen without a great deal of endeavour and a near-revolutionary transformation in attitudes, especially among the world's elite communities. Much is already happening, though, and this gives real cause for optimism – the human community really does have the capacity for rapid change when really serious problems are recognised, and enough is known about the many alternative approaches, as this chapter has sought to show. Even so, time is short and it will be essential to accelerate the process in the period between now and 2030.

ENDING ON A CAUTIOUS HIGH

Can it be done? Perhaps it is best to end on a personal note.

For nearly a decade and a half, until around 1990, my research on international security focused on nuclear issues and the very real risk of what was called, in an anodyne phrase, a 'central nuclear exchange'. If a global nuclear war had been fought, hundreds of millions would have died, and perhaps billions in the years that followed, and yet the two power blocs prepared and trained for just such a conflict. In the early 1980s the risk was real and we now know that we were lucky on several occasions to avoid a global catastrophe. Yet catastrophe was avoided, and while we still face serious problems, these do not include worldwide nuclear disaster. Since 1990 it has been my fortune, or perhaps misfortune, to focus on the changing nature of international conflict and, in particular, on terrorism and political violence and how powerful states have tried and failed to address them.

When dealing with such subjects – potential nuclear annihilation, terrorism and political violence – over a long period (the best part of 40 years in my case), one has three options: drink, suicide or optimism. I don't drink (much) and have not so far felt suicidal, so I must have chosen optimism, even if that optimism has been a little misguided at times.

Shortly after I moved from London to Yorkshire, in the north of England, more than 40 years ago, I had occasion one April day to drive to the city of York, 40 miles away. With time to spare and preferring to avoid busy main roads, I took a country route that at one stage skirted the village of Saxton on the way to another village, Towton. This is not the Yorkshire of the Dales or the North York Moors; nor is it 'Brontë country'. Instead it is the rich farmland region of the Vale of York, and this road runs through undulating countryside given over mainly to large fields of wheat and barley, with few hedges or dry stone walls. At one point it rises briefly to a plateau, and down in the valley to the left is a small river, Cock Beck, which feeds into one of Yorkshire's best-known rivers, the Wharf, just outside the famous brewing town of Tadcaster.

As I drove along this deserted route through open country I saw by the side of the road what appeared to be a small monument next to a brief stretch of holly hedge. Curiosity got the better of me and I stopped to look. What was odd was that although the date on the monument was 1461, there was a small wreath of red poppies, as though some historic event were still being commemorated more than 550 years later, but there was nothing more to say what it meant. If you visit that site now, you will find the monument still there, but a small lay-by has been constructed for cars to park in, with some informative signs explaining the significance of the memorial, which marks the site of the Battle of Towton, fought on Palm Sunday, 29 March 1461.

In the latter part of the fifteenth century, England was locked in a bitter civil war – a fight for control of the English monarchy – between the rival Plantagenet houses of York and Lancaster. Known as the Wars of the Roses, because of the white and red rose symbols of the rival families, this conflict reached its conclusion at the Battle of Bosworth Field in 1485, which was won by the Lancastrians, led by Henry Tudor. This victory marked the beginning of the Tudor era.

Fought in a snowstorm and with the Yorkists' archers having the advantage of the wind behind them, the Battle of Towton was carnage, and the Lancastrians were killed by the thousand. It was estimated that 28,000 people died on that day, making it the bloodiest battle not only of the Wars of the Roses but ever fought in England, causing the deaths of around one in 30 of the entire able-bodied adult male population of the country. Allowing for the much greater population, that is equivalent to the total losses, not just of England but of the whole of the United Kingdom, throughout World War I being suffered in a single day, and in just one place. Furthermore, it was a singularly savage contest, in which some of the worst features of a civil war were evident: investigations of mass war graves in recent years by forensic archaeologists from Bradford University have pointed to the gross mutilation of bodies after death, such was the frenzy of the occasion.

The reason for ending with the Battle of Towton is that it provides a sense of perspective and points to the view elaborated by some historians, psychologists and others, and notably by the scientist and author Steven Pinker, that however great the problems of insecurity may be, and however substantial the risks we face, progress has been and continues to be made.[16] It is true in many fields, including human rights, education, health and nutrition, and not least in relation to the experience of war. Whatever the problems in the Middle East, North Africa, the Sahel, Ukraine, the Caucasus and elsewhere, the great majority of people in most of the world live in a state of at least partial peace most of the time, even in the face of many other challenges.

The next two decades are likely to prove pivotal in avoiding an unstable and insecure world, but there is immense potential for positive change and huge possibilities. In its own small way, Towton is a reminder of that and a sure source of perspective when circumstances require it, as they so often do.

NOTES

1. WORLD ORDER OR DISORDER

1   Tom Lasseter, 'Sides blur for U.S. troops trying to secure Samarra', *Houston Chronicle* (19 February 2006).
2   Edwin Brooks, 'The implications of ecological limits to development in terms of expectations and aspirations in developed and less developed countries', in Anthony Vann and Paul Rogers (eds), *Human Ecology and World Development* (London: Plenum, 1974), p. 132.
3   Paul Rogers, *Losing Control: Global Security in the Twenty-First Century* (London: Pluto Press, 2000), p. 98.
4   The United Nations Conference on Trade and Development (UNCTAD) was set up in 1963 specifically to address such issues, largely because of pressure from newly independent countries joining the United Nations. It worked tirelessly for more than a decade but made little progress against the entrenched trading policies of key Northern industrialised states. Its approach still makes sense half a century later: this is covered in Chapter 8.
5   This is quoted in James Stephenson, *The 1994 Zapatista Rebellion in Southern Mexico: An Analysis and Assessment*, Strategic and Combat Studies Institute Occasional Paper 12 (Camberley: Strategic and Combat Studies Institute, 1995), p. 9. Stephenson's paper is unusual for a military analysis of a conflict in paying particular attention to the social and economic conditions underlying the rebellion.
6   Rogers, *Losing Control*, p. 131.
7   Donella H. Meadows, Dennis L. Meadows, Jørgen Randers and William W. Behrens III, *The Limits to Growth* (London: Earth Island, 1972).
8   Rogers, *Losing Control*, p. 118.
9   Ibid., p. 131.
10 Richard Wilkinson and Kate Pickett, *The Spirit Level* (London: Penguin, 2009) and Thomas Piketty, *Capital in the Twenty-First Century*, trans. Arthur Goldhammer (Cambridge, MA: Harvard University Press, 2014).

2. COMING OUT OF NOWHERE

1   For a detailed account of this complex operation, published in the immediate aftermath of the operation, see Nadine M. Post et al., 'Anatomy of a building disaster', *Engineering News-Record* (8 March 1993).
2   'Full transcript of bin Ladin's speech', Al Jazeera [website] (1 November 2004). Available at http://www.aljazeera.com/archive/2004/11/200849163336457223.html.
3   President George W. Bush, State of the Union address, 29 January 2002. Available at http://georgewbush-whitehouse.archives.gov/news/releases/2002/01/20020129-11.html.
4   Ibid.
5   President George W. Bush, graduation speech at US Military Academy, West Point, 1 June 2002. Available at http://georgewbush-whitehouse.archives.gov/news/releases/2002/06/20020601-3.html.
6   Ibid.
7   Robert Schlesinger, 'Combat wounds proving less deadly', *Boston Globe* (31 August 2003).
8   For a detailed discussion of the Indian issue, see Richard Sobel, Peter A. Furia and Bethany Barratt (eds), *Public Opinion and International Intervention: Lessons from the Iraq War* (Dulles, VA: Potomac Books, 2012).
9   David A. Fulghum and Robert Wall, 'Israel refocuses on urban warfare', *Aviation Week and Space Technology* (13 May 2002).
10 Barbara Opall-Rome, 'U.S.–Israel army brass swap tactics', *Defense News* (15 December 2003).
11 Ibid.
12 Paul Rogers, *A War on Terror: Afghanistan and After* (London: Pluto Press, 2004), p. 113.
13 See Barbara Opall-Rome, 'Marines to train at new Israeli combat center', *Marine Corps Times* (24 June 2007).
14 Brian Everstine, 'Inside the B-1 crew that pounded ISIS with 1,800 bombs', *Air Force Times* (23 August 2015).

3. CONFLICTING NARRATIVES AND AN ENVIRONMENT FOR REVOLT

1   Pamela Constable, 'A wrong turn, chaos and a rescue', *Washington Post* (15 April 2004). Available at https://www.washingtonpost.com/archive/politics/2004/04/15/a-wrong-turn-chaos-and-a-rescue/c6fb50ff-0678-4a4b-9449-1b796b3ee559/.

2   Dexter Filkins, 'U.S. air raids took large civilian toll', *International Herald Tribune* (22 June 2002).

3   In one of the few positive recent examples of arms control, the Convention on Cluster Munitions was adopted in Dublin in May 2008 and signed in Oslo in November of the same year. It entered into force on 1 August 2010. Although it had been a prominent producer and exporter of cluster munitions, the United Kingdom was an early signatory, and subsequently destroyed its stocks. By March 2015, 116 states had joined the convention, but they did not include Russia, Israel or the United States. See www.clusterconvention.org.

4   Ruth Blakeley and Sam Raphael, 'Dirty little secrets' [paper presented at the British International Studies Association annual conference, Birmingham, 20 June 2013]. Available at https://kar.kent.ac.uk/44066/1/Dirty%20Little%20Secrets%20%5BBISA%20Paper%5D.pdf. The words in quotation marks at the beginning of this extract are those of a CIA officer to the Marty investigation, launched by the Council of Europe in 2005 to investigate the complicity of European states in rendition.

5   Thomas Fuller, 'Late special / confusion and death: allied forces burst into the heart of Baghdad', *International Herald Tribune* (8 April 2003). Available at http://www.nytimes.com/2003/04/08/news/08iht-attack_ed3__5.html.

6   Walden Bello, 'Endless war?', Focus on the Global South [website] (September 2001). Available at www.focusweb.org/publications/2001/endless_war.html.

7   Scilla Elworthy and Paul Rogers, 'The United States, Europe and the Majority World after 11 September' [ORG briefing paper, 2001]. Available at http://www.oxfordresearchgroup.org.uk/sites/default/files/sept11briefing.pdf.

8   Seth Hamblin, Gene Thorp and Doug Stevens, 'Ambush at Takur Ghar', *Washington Post* (6 March 2002).

9   Anand Gopal, *No Good Men among the Living: America, the Taliban, and the War through Afghan Eyes* (New York: Metropolitan Books, 2014), quoted in 'Creating enemies where there were none', Daily Kos [blog] (3 May 2014). Available at http://www.dailykos.com/story/2014/5/2/1294365/-Creating-Enemies-Where-There-Were-None.

10   Greg Grant, 'Afghan fighters import tactics honed in Iraq', *Defense News* (31 July 2006).

11   Mustafa Hamid and Leah Farrall, *The Arabs at War in Afghanistan* (London: Hurst, 2015), p. 23.

12   For a detailed analysis of this period in the context of the evolution of networked warfare, see Steve Niva, 'Disappearing violence: JSOC and

the Pentagon's new cartography of networked warfare', *Security Dialogue* 44 (June 2013), pp. 185–202.

13 For an account of UK involvement in these operations, see Mark Urban, *Task Force Black: The Explosive True Story of the SAS and the Secret War in Iraq* (London: Little, Brown, 2010).

14 Quoted in Ian Cobain, 'Camp Nama: British personnel reveal horrors of secret US base in Baghdad', *Guardian* (1 April 2013). Available at http://www.theguardian.com/world/2013/apr/01/camp-nama-iraq-human-rights-abuses.

4. WEAPONS OF MASS DESTRUCTION AND POLITICAL VIOLENCE

1 On the former point (that ISIS did not have weaponised chemical agents), see Missy Ryan, 'Islamic State militants do not appear to have seized any chemical weapons', *Washington Post* (15 October 2014). Available at https://www.washingtonpost.com/world/national-security/islamic-state-militants-do-not-appear-to-have-seized-any-chemical-weapons/2014/10/15/65f4bf86-54b1-11e4-ba4b-f6333e2c0453_story.html.

2 Sarah Sicard, 'ISIL determined to acquire biological weapons', *National Defense* (7 October 2014).

3 Information on the CWC and the work of the OPCW is available at http://www.opcw.org/.

4 The United Nations Office for Disarmament Affairs (UNODA) provides reasonably comprehensive information on the BTWC. Available at http://www.un.org/disarmament/WMD/Bio/.

5 Similarly, a 'megatonne' is equivalent to 1 million tonnes of TNT.

6 See George P. Shultz, William J. Perry, Henry A. Kissinger and Sam Nunn, 'A world free of nuclear weapons', *Wall Street Journal* (4 January 2007). Available at http://www.wsj.com/articles/SB116787515251566636.

7 For an overview of modernisation plans, see Hans M. Kristensen, 'Nuclear weapons modernization: a threat to the NPT?', *Arms Control Today* (1 May 2014). Available at https://www.armscontrol.org/act/2014_05/Nuclear-Weapons-Modernization-A-Threat-to-the-NPT. The US nuclear programme is discussed in Stephen Young, 'Obama's trillion dollar nuclear weapons gamble', *Defense One* (1 February 2015). Available at http://www.defenseone.com/ideas/2015/02/obamas-trillion-dollar-nuclear-weapons-gamble/104217/. Russia's plans are the subject of Adrian Croft, 'Insight: Russia's nuclear strategy raises concerns in NATO', Reuters [news agency] (4 February 2015). Available at http://uk.reuters.com/article/uk-ukraine-crisis-russia-nuclear-

insight-idUKKBN0L825A20150204. A wide-ranging survey of nuclear weapons issues is 'The unkicked addiction', *The Economist* (7 March 2015). Available at http://www.economist.com/news/briefing/21645840-despite-optimistic-attempts-rid-world-nuclear-weapons-threat-they-pose-peace.

8   Thalif Deen, 'Failure of review conference brings world close to nuclear cataclysm, warn activists', Inter Press Service [news agency] (23 May 2015). Available at http://www.ipsnews.net/2015/05/failure-of-review-conference-brings-world-close-to-nuclear-cataclysm-warn-activists/.

9   See Alberto Muti, Katherine Tajer and Larry MacFaul, 'Cyberspace: An Assessment of Current Threats, Real Consequences and Potential Solutions' [paper published by the Remote Control Project/ORG, October 2014]. Available at http://remotecontrolproject.org/wp-content/uploads/2014/10/Vertic-Report.pdf.

10 Ibid., p. 12.

11 Ibid.

12 Most of the information concerning the Iraqi biological and chemical warfare programmes came to light as a result of the diligent work of UNSCOM, established after the 1991 war, which was published in a series of reports to the UN secretary general. The main report in this series is 'Report of the Secretary General on the Status of the Implementation of the Special Commission's Plan for the Ongoing Monitoring and Verification of Iraq's Compliance with Relevant Parts of Section C of Security Council Resolution 687 (1991)' [UN Security Council report S/1995/864, 11 October 1995]. Available at http://www.un.org/Depts/unscom/sres95-864.htm.

5. ISIS AND ITS FUTURE

1   The intention was to maintain a force of around 10,000 military personnel, including some combat troops but concentrating more on air power. This would both ensure the security of the al-Maliki government and maintain influence with it, while also helping to prevent Iran having too much of a military or paramilitary presence. Given that one of the unspoken motives for the termination of the Saddam Hussein regime had been to provide a major US presence as a counter to Iran, this more limited force would at least see that an element of the original intention had been maintained.

2   Paul Rogers, 'Tunisia and Egypt in context' [ORG International Security Briefing, January 2011]. Available at http://www.oxfordresearchgroup.org.uk/sites/default/files/Jan11En.pdf.

3 For a succinct analysis of this aspect of the rise of ISIS, see Charles Lister, 'Assessing Syria's jihad', in Toby Dodge and Emile Hokayem (eds), *Middle Eastern Security: The US Pivot and the Rise of ISIS* (Abingdon: IISS/Routledge, 2014), pp. 71–98. Dodge and Hokayem's book (in which the Lister chapter is found) is itself a useful source of much pertinent analysis of wider developments in Iraq and the region.

4 Kareem Raheem and Ziad al-Sinjary, 'Al Qaeda militants flee Iraqi jail in violent mass break-out', Reuters [news agency] (22 July 2013). Available at http://www.reuters.com/article/us-iraq-violence-idUSBRE96L0RM20130722.

5 A number of sources are useful in understanding the structure of ISIS. They include Lister, 'Assessing Syria's jihad'; Abdel Bari Atwan, *Islamic State: The Digital Caliphate* (London: Saqi, 2015); Michael Griffin, *Islamic State: Rewriting History* (London: Pluto Press, 2016); Sami Moubayed, *Under the Black Flag: At the Frontier of the New Jihad* (London: I.B.Tauris, 2015); and Richard Barrett, 'The Islamic State' [Soufan Group paper, 2014]. Available at http://soufangroup.com/wp-content/uploads/2014/10/TSG-The-Islamic-State-Nov14.pdf. For a more general and lucid analysis of how ISIS grew so quickly, see Patrick Cockburn, *The Rise of Islamic State: ISIS and the New Sunni Revolution* (London: Verso, 2015).

6 Atwan, *Islamic State*, pp. 202–3.

7 For a detailed and informed analysis of the Uyghur issue see Nick Holdstock, *China's Forgotten People: Xinjiang, Terror and the Chinese State* (London: I.B.Tauris, 2015).

8 Dan De Luce, 'Is the U.S. ready for an endless war against the Islamic State?', *Foreign Policy* [website] (27 August 2015). Available at http://foreignpolicy.com/2015/08/27/is-the-u-s-ready-for-an-endless-war-against-the-islamic-state/.

6. IRREGULAR WAR

1 The context of the rise of Boko Haram is summarised in John Campbell, 'Boko Haram: origins, challenges and responses' [Norwegian Peacebuilding Resource Centre policy brief, October 2014]. Available at http://www.peacebuilding.no/var/ezflow_site/storage/original/application/5cf0ebc94fb36d66309681cda24664f9.pdf.

2 'Jihad in Russia: the Caucasus Emirate', *IISS Strategic Comments* xviii/9 (4 December 2012), pp. xii–xiv.

3 'Contagion of discontent: the Swahili coast', *The Economist* (3 November 2012). Available at http://www.economist.com/news/middle-east-

and-africa/21565641-muslim-extremism-spreads-down-east-africa%E2%80%99s-coastline-contagion-discontent.

4   This expression of support has extended to the more direct involvement of ISIS-linked paramilitaries in Taliban operations, notably the assault on the northern city of Kunduz in April and May 2015, which also involved Uzbek, Tajik and Chechen paramilitaries. See Mujib Mashal and Jawad Sukhanyar, 'Afghan troops rush to Kunduz amid Taliban assault', *New York Times* (28 April 2015) and 'Taliban allying with Islamic State in north, says Afghan official', *Newsweek Pakistan* (8 May 2015).

5   For a summary of the original report's findings, see 'Estimated cost of post-9/11 wars: 225,000 lives, up to $4 trillion', Brown University [website] (19 June 2011). Available at https://news.brown.edu/articles/2011/06/warcosts. More up-to-date statistics can be found on the Costs of War website. Available at http://costsofwar.org/.

6   See https://www.iraqbodycount.org/.

7   'Afghan civilian deaths hit record high', *Guardian* (18 February 2015). Available at http://www.theguardian.com/world/2015/feb/18/afghan-civilian-deaths-record-high.

8   See Justin King, 'CIA director: War on Terror will never end', *MintPress News* [website] (13 April 2015). Available at http://www.mintpressnews.com/cia-director-war-on-terror-will-never-end/204322/. And Greg Miller, 'Former CIA official cites agency's failure to see al-Qaeda's rebound', *Washington Post* (3 May 2015). Available at http://www.washingtonpost.com/world/national-security/former-cia-official-cites-agencys-failure-to-see-al-qaedas-rebound/2015/05/03/d68e7292-f028-11e4-8abc-d6aa3bad79dd_story.html.

9   The move towards remote-control warfare is the focus of a London-based research and policy project hosted by the ORG. Running initially from 2013 to 2016, the Remote Control Project has commissioned and subsequently published a number of research papers covering most of the fields concerned. See www.remotecontrolproject.org.

10 Sean McFate, *The Modern Mercenary: Private Armies and What They Mean for World Order* (New York: Oxford University Press, 2014), pp. 12–18.

11 Omega Research Foundation, 'Floating Armouries: Implications and Risks' [paper published by the Remote Control Project/ORG, December 2014]. Available at http://remotecontrolproject.org/wp-content/uploads/2014/12/FloatingArmouriesReport.pdf.

12 Philip Ewing, 'Arms race goes hypersonic', *Politico* [website] (11 August 2015). Available at http://www.politico.com/story/2015/08/russia-china-arms-race-goes-hypersonic-weapons-future-121230.

13 Chris Abbott, 'Hostile Drones: The Hostile Use of Drones by Non-State Actors against British Targets' [paper published by the Remote Control

Project/ORG, January 2016]. Available at http://remotecontrolproject.org/wp-content/uploads/2016/01/Hostile-use-of-drones-report_open-briefing.pdf.

14 Michael Crowley, 'Tear Gassing by Remote Control: The Development and Promotion of Remotely Operated Means of Delivering or Dispersing Riot Control Agents' [paper published by the Remote Control Project/ORG, December 2015]. Available at http://remotecontrolproject.org/wp-content/uploads/2015/12/Tear-Gassing-By-Remote-Control-Report.pdf.

15 Roger W. Barnett, 'Regional conflict: requires naval forces', *Proceedings of the US Naval Institute* (June 1992), pp. 28–33. The words here are a paraphrase.

16 Strictly speaking, Gordon E. Moore's original paper of 1965 predicted the doubling of the number of components per integrated circuit every year. Moore revised this to every two years in 1975. It largely held good until 2015 but is expected to tail off somewhat in the next decade.

17 'Towards 2020 and beyond' [briefing published by the Parliamentary Office of Science and Technology, 19 June 2015]. Available at http://researchbriefings.parliament.uk/ResearchBriefing/Summary/POST-PN-0500.

18 The standard introductory text on this subject is P. W. Singer and Allan Friedman, *Cybersecurity and Cyberwar: What Everyone Needs to Know* (New York: Oxford University Press, 2014). For an assessment related particularly to issues of remote warfare see Alberto Muti, Katherine Tajer and Larry MacFaul, 'Cyberspace: An Assessment of Current Threats, Real Consequences and Potential Solutions' [paper published by the Remote Control Project/ORG, October 2014]. Available at http://remotecontrolproject.org/wp-content/uploads/2014/10/Vertic-Report.pdf.

7. A GLOWERING PLANET?

1 Edwin Brooks, 'The implications of ecological limits to development in terms of expectations and aspirations in developed and less developed countries', in Anthony Vann and Paul Rogers (eds), *Human Ecology and World Development* (London: Plenum, 1974), p. 132.

2 Paul Rogers, *Losing Control: Global Security in the Twenty-First Century* (London: Pluto Press, 2000), p. 98.

3 For one of the most informative and delightfully readable accounts of this period, see John Lanchester, *Whoops! Why Everyone Owes Everyone and No One Can Pay* (London: Penguin, 2010).

4 Jim Lobe, '400 million children mired in extreme poverty', Inter Press

Service [news agency] (10 October 2013). Available at http://www. ipsnews.net/2013/10/400-million-children-mired-in-extreme-poverty/.

5   Joseph Stiglitz, *The Great Divide* (London: Allen Lane, 2015).

6   Victoria Bateman, 'In the market for fairness', *Times Higher Education* (30 April 2015). Available at https://www.timeshighereducation.com/ cn/books/the-great-divide-by-joseph-stiglitz/2019874.article.

7   International Food Policy Research Institute, '2014–2015 Global Food Policy Report' (Washington DC: International Food Policy Research Institute, 2015), pp. 14–15. Available at http://ebrary.ifpri.org/utils/ getfile/collection/p15738coll2/id/129072/filename/129283.pdf.

8   Martin Ravallion and Shaohua Chen, 'A proposal for truly global poverty measures', *Global Policy* iv/3 (2013), pp. 258–65.

9   David Hulme, *Global Poverty: Global Governance and Poor People in the Post-2015 Era* (Abingdon: Routledge, 2015), p. 139.

10 Suvojit Bagchi, 'Maoists kill 15 in Chhattisgarh', *The Hindu* (11 March 2014). Available at http://www.thehindu.com/news/national/maoists-kill-15-in-chhattisgarh/article5773315.ece.

11 'Out of the trees', *The Economist* (1 June 2013). Available at http://www. economist.com/news/asia/21578686-murderous-attack-highlights-neglect-indias-outland-out-trees.

12 Antoaneta Becker, 'Resentment rises in China with widening gaps', Inter Press Service [news agency] (11 October 2010). Available at http://www. ipsnews.net/2010/10/china-resentment-rises-with-widening-wealth-gaps/.

13 Brooks Tigner, 'EU agrees military mission against Mediterranean people smugglers', *Jane's Defence Weekly* (27 May 2015).

14 AAAS Climate Science Panel, 'What We Know: The Reality, Risks and Response to Climate Change' [paper published by AAAS, 2013]. Available at http://whatweknow.aaas.org/wp-content/uploads/2014/07/ whatweknow_website.pdf.

15 Colin P. Kelley, Shahrzad Mohtadi, Mark A. Cane, Richard Seager and Yochanan Kushnir, 'Climate change in the Fertile Crescent and implications of the recent Syrian drought', *Proceedings of the National Academy of Sciences* cxii/11 (2 March 2015), pp. 3241–6. Available at http://www.pnas.org/content/112/11/3241.full.

16 'Is it global warming or just the weather?', *The Economist* (9 May 2015). Available at http://www.economist.com/news/international/21650552-scientists-are-getting-more-confident-about-attributing-heatwaves-and-droughts-human.

17 Steve Trent, 'Climate refugees: human insecurity in a warming world', Sustainable Security [blog] (27 January 2015). Available at http:// sustainablesecurity.org/2015/01/27/climate-refugees-human-insecurity-in-a-warming-world/.

18　See Ronald Higgins, *The Seventh Enemy: The Human Factor in the Global Crisis* (New York: McGraw-Hill, 1978).

19　Nick Buxton and Ben Hayes, *The Secure and the Dispossessed: How the Military Corporations Are Shaping a Climate-Changed World* (London: Pluto Press, 2015).

20　See for instance 'Surge in jet purchases reshuffles fighter market', *Defense News* (11 May 2015). Available at http://www.defensenews.com/story/defense/air-space/strike/2015/05/10/fighter-surge-kuwait-qatar-egypt-india-rafale-hornet/26977289/.

8. A POSSIBLE PEACE

1　This perspective is explored in more detail in Paul Rogers, 'A century on the edge: from Cold War to hot world, 1945–2045', *International Affairs* xc/1 (January 2014), pp. 93–106.

2　'Crystal clear?', *The Economist* (16 May 2015). Available at http://www.economist.com/news/science-and-technology/21651166-perovskites-may-give-silicon-solar-cells-run-their-money-crystal-clear. See also Chelsea Harvey, 'This technology may be the future of solar energy', *Washington Post* (15 January 2016). Available at https://www.washingtonpost.com/news/energy-environment/wp/2016/01/15/this-technology-may-be-the-future-of-solar-energy/.

3　Mat Hope, 'Energy trends in 2014 and how they affect climate change', Carbon Brief [website] (29 December 2014). Available at http://www.carbonbrief.org/energy-trends-in-2014-and-how-they-affect-climate-change.

4　Deutsche Bank, 'Crossing the Chasm' [report, 27 February 2015]. Available at https://www.db.com/cr/en/docs/solar_report_full_length.pdf. See also Gerard Wynn, 'Solar closing in on cost of coal-fired power – Deutsche Bank', Climate Home [website] (5 March 2015). Available at http://www.climatechangenews.com/2015/03/05/solar-closing-in-on-cost-of-coal-fired-power-deutsche-bank/.

5　Ben Protess and Michael Corkery, '5 big banks plead guilty in anti-trust investigation', *International New York Times* (21 May 2015).

6　There is also the related issue of the difficulty for non-specialists in understanding the financial and banking system. A book that aids this is John Lanchester, *How to Speak Money: What the Money People Say and What They Really Mean* (London: Faber & Faber, 2014). A book that analyses the 2008 financial crisis and its aftermath is Paul Mason, *Meltdown: The End of the Age of Greed* (London: Verso, 2010).

7 See Nicholas Shaxson, *Treasure Islands: Tax Havens and the Men Who Stole the World* (London: Bodley Head, 2012), pp. 8–10.

8 'About the ILO', International Labour Organization [website]. Available at http://www.ilo.org/global/about-the-ilo/lang--en/index.htm.

9 In some circles the acronym UNCTAD was said to stand for 'Under No Circumstances Take Any Decisions'.

10 Information on the New Economics Foundation is available at www.neweconomics.org. For a broad discussion on economic growth see Tim Jackson, *Prosperity without Growth: Economics for a Finite Planet* (London: Earthscan, 2009) and John Blewitt and Ray Cunningham (eds), *The Post-Growth Project: How the End of Economic Growth Could Bring a Fairer and Happier Society* (London: Greenhouse and London Publishing Partnership, 2014).

11 Thalif Deen, 'Cooperatives as business models for the future', Inter Press Service [news agency] (26 November 2012). Available at http://www.ipsnews.net/2012/11/cooperatives-as-business-models-of-the-future/.

12 An exception is the ORG's 'Sustainable Security' programme. Information about this is available at http://www.oxfordresearchgroup.org.uk/ssp. Another initiative is the 'Ammerdown Invitation'. Information can be found at https://www.opendemocracy.net/author/ammerdown-invitation.

13 See April Carter, Howard Clark and Michael Randle (eds), *A Guide to Civil Resistance: A Bibliography of People Power and Nonviolent Protest* (London: Green Print/Merlin, 2013). It is also worth noting the remarkable example of Badshah Khan (1890–1988), a Pashtun exponent of non-violence and associate of Gandhi. See Heathcote Williams, *Badshah Khan: Islamic Peace Warrior* (London: Thin Man, 2015).

14 The most comprehensive guide to the theory and practice of conflict resolution is Oliver Ramsbotham, Tom Woodhouse and Hugh Miall, *Contemporary Conflict Resolution* (Cambridge: Polity, 2011). See also Hugh Miall, Tom Woodhouse, Oliver Ramsbotham and Christopher Mitchell (eds), *The Contemporary Conflict Resolution Reader* (Oxford: Polity, 2015). An informed analysis of peace negotiations, especially of the unofficial variety, is Gabrielle Rifkind and Giandomenico Picco, *The Fog of Peace: The Human Face of Conflict Resolution* (London: I.B.Tauris, 2014).

15 H. Peter Langille, 'Time for a United Nations emergency peace service' [submission to the High-Level Independent Panel on United Nations Peace Operations, World Federalist Movement, Canada, 26 March 2015]. Available at http://www.worldfederalistscanada.org/HPL%20UNEPS%20for%20H-L-Panel%20March%2018%202015%20fnl.pdf.

16 See Steven Pinker, *The Better Angels of Our Nature: Why Violence Has Declined* (New York: Viking, 2011).

SELECT BIBLIOGRAPHY

Abbott, Chris, Paul Rogers and John Sloboda, 'Global Responses to Global Challenges' [ORG briefing paper, 2006]. Available at http://www.oxfordresearchgroup.org.uk/sites/default/files/globalthreats.pdf.

Aldis, Anne, and Graeme P. Herd (eds), *The Ideological War on Terror* (London and New York: Routledge, 2007).

Atwan, Abdel Bari, *Islamic State: The Digital Caliphate* (London: Saqi, 2015).

Barrett, Richard, 'The Islamic State' [Soufan Group paper, 2014]. Available at http://soufangroup.com/wp-content/uploads/2014/10/TSG-The-Islamic-State-Nov14.pdf.

Benjamin, Medea, *Drone Warfare: Killing by Remote Control* (New York: OR Books, 2012).

Blewitt, John, and Ray Cunningham (eds), *The Post-Growth Project: How the End of Economic Growth Could Bring a Fairer and Happier Society* (London: Greenhouse and London Publishing Partnership, 2014).

Bruce, Steve, *Fundamentalism* (Cambridge: Polity, 2000).

Burke, Jason, *The New Threat from Islamic Militancy* (London: Bodley Head, 2015).

Buxton, Nick, and Ben Hayes, *The Secure and the Dispossessed: How the Military Corporations Are Shaping a Climate-Changed World* (London: Pluto Press, 2015).

Carter, April, Howard Clark and Michael Randle (eds), *A Guide to Civil Resistance: A Bibliography of People Power and Nonviolent Protest* (London: Green Print/Merlin, 2013).

Chandrasekaran, Rajiv, *Imperial Life in the Emerald City* (New York: Random House, 2007).

Cockburn, Patrick, *Muqtada al-Sadr and the Fall of Iraq* (London: Faber & Faber, 2008).

―――― *The Rise of Islamic State: ISIS and the New Sunni Revolution* (London: Verso, 2015).

Dando, Malcolm, *Bioterror and Biowarfare* (Oxford: Oneworld, 2006).

Dodge, Toby, *Iraq: From War to a New Authoritarianism* (Abingdon: IISS/ Routledge, 2012).

Dodge, Toby, and Emile Hokayem (eds), *Middle Eastern Security: The US Pivot and the Rise of ISIS* (Abingdon: IISS/Routledge, 2014).

Dodge, Toby, and Nicholas Redman (eds), *Afghanistan to 2015 and Beyond* (Abingdon: IISS/Routledge, 2011).

Elworthy, Scilla, and Paul Rogers, 'The United States, Europe and the Majority World after 11 September' [ORG briefing paper, 2001]. Available at http:// www.oxfordresearchgroup.org.uk/sites/default/files/sept11briefing.pdf.

Feste, Karen A., *America Responds to Terrorism: Conflict Resolution Strategies of Clinton, Bush, and Obama* (New York: Palgrave Macmillan, 2011).

Gopal, Anand, *No Good Men among the Living: America, the Taliban, and the War through Afghan Eyes* (New York: Metropolitan Books, 2014).

Graham, Stephen, *Cities Under Siege: The New Military Urbanism* (London: Verso, 2011).

Griffin, Michael, *Islamic State: Rewriting History* (London: Pluto Press, 2016).

Hamid, Mustafa, and Leah Farrall, *The Arabs at War in Afghanistan* (London: Hurst, 2015).

Higgins, Ronald, *The Seventh Enemy: The Human Factor in the Global Crisis* (New York: McGraw-Hill, 1978).

Hokayem, Emile, *Syria's Uprising and the Fracturing of the Levant* (Abingdon: IISS/Routledge, 2013).

Hokayem, Emile, and Hebatalla Taha (eds), *Egypt after the Spring: Revolt and Reaction* (Abingdon: IISS/Routledge, 2016).

Holdstock, Nick, *China's Forgotten People: Xinjiang, Terror and the Chinese State* (London: I.B.Tauris, 2015).

Houen, Alec, *States of War since 9/11: Terrorism, Sovereignty and the War on Terror* (London: Routledge, 2014).

Hulme, David, *Global Poverty: Global Governance and Poor People in the Post-2015 Era* (Abingdon: Routledge, 2015).

Jackson, Richard, *Writing the War on Terrorism: Language, Politics and Counter-Terrorism* (Manchester: Manchester University Press, 2005).

Jackson, R., L. Jarvis, J. Gunning and M. Breen Smyth, *Terrorism: A Critical Introduction* (Basingstoke: Palgrave Macmillan, 2011).

Jackson, R., and S. J. Sinclair (eds), *Contemporary Debates on Terrorism* (Abingdon: Routledge, 2012).

Jackson, Tim, *Prosperity without Growth: Economics for a Finite Planet* (London: Earthscan, 2009).

Jones, Seth G., *In the Graveyard of Empires: America's War in Afghanistan* (New York and London: Norton, 2010).

Kassimeris, George (ed.), *The Barbarisation of Warfare* (London: Hurst, 2006).

Lanchester, John, *Whoops! Why Everyone Owes Everyone and No One Can Pay* (London: Penguin, 2010).

—— *How to Speak Money: What the Money People Say and What They Really Mean* (London: Faber & Faber, 2014).

Lawrence, Bruce (ed.), *Messages to the World: The Statements of Osama bin Laden* (London: Verso, 2005).

McFate, Sean, *The Modern Mercenary: Private Armies and What They Mean for World Order* (New York: Oxford University Press, 2014).

Mason, Paul, *Meltdown: The End of the Age of Greed* (London: Verso, 2010).

Meadows, Donella H., Dennis L. Meadows, Jørgen Randers and William W. Behrens III, *The Limits to Growth* (London: Earth Island, 1972).

Miall, Hugh, Tom Woodhouse, Oliver Ramsbotham and Christopher Mitchell (eds), *The Contemporary Conflict Resolution Reader* (Oxford: Polity, 2015).

Molloy, Ivan, *Rolling Back Revolution* (London: Pluto Press, 2001).

Moubayed, Sami, *Under the Black Flag: At the Frontier of the New Jihad* (London: I.B.Tauris, 2015).

Moyo, Dambisa, *Winner Takes All: China's Race for Resources and What It Means for Us* (London: Allen Lane, 2012).

Muttitt, Greg, *Fuel on the Fire: Oil and Politics in Occupied Iraq* (London: Bodley Head, 2011).

Pearce, Fred, *The Landgrabbers: The New Fight over Who Owns the Earth* (London: Eden Project Books, 2012).

Pearson, Graham S., *The UNSCOM Saga: Chemical and Biological Weapons Non-Proliferation* (London: Macmillan, 1999).

Piketty, Thomas, *Capital in the Twenty-First Century*, trans. Arthur Goldhammer (Cambridge, MA: Harvard University Press, 2014).

Pinker, Steven, *The Better Angels of Our Nature: Why Violence Has Declined* (New York: Viking, 2011).

Ramsbotham, Oliver, Tom Woodhouse and Hugh Miall, *Contemporary Conflict Resolution* (Cambridge: Polity, 2011).

Rashid, Ahmed, *Descent into Chaos: The United States and the Failure of Nation Building in Pakistan, Afghanistan and Central Asia* (London: Penguin, 2008).

—— *Taliban* (London: I.B.Tauris, 2010).

Reinert, Erik S., *How Rich Countries Got Rich and Why Poor Countries Stay Poor* (London: Constable, 2007).

Rifkind, Gabrielle, and Giandomenico Picco, *The Fog of Peace: The Human Face of Conflict Resolution* (London: I.B.Tauris, 2014).

Ritchie, Nick, and Paul Rogers, *The Political Road to War with Iraq: Bush, 9/11 and the Drive to Overthrow Saddam* (Abingdon: Routledge, 2007).

Rogers, Paul, *Losing Control: Global Security in the Twenty-First Century* (London: Pluto Press, 2000).

———— *A War on Terror: Afghanistan and After* (London: Pluto Press, 2004).

———— *A War Too Far: Iraq, Iran and the New American Century* (London: Pluto, 2006).

Scahill, Jeremy, *Blackwater: The Rise of the World's Most Powerful Mercenary Army* (London: Serpent's Tail, 2008).

Shaxson, Nicholas, *Treasure Islands: Tax Havens and the Men Who Stole the World* (London: Bodley Head, 2012).

Singer, P. W., and Allan Friedman, *Cybersecurity and Cyberwar: What Everyone Needs to Know* (New York: Oxford University Press, 2014).

Sobel, Richard, Peter A. Furia and Bethany Barratt (eds), *Public Opinion and International Intervention: Lessons from the Iraq War* (Dulles, VA: Potomac Books, 2012).

Starr-Deelen, Donna G., *Presidential Policies on Terrorism: From Ronald Reagan to Barack Obama* (New York: Palgrave Macmillan, 2014).

Stiglitz, Joseph, *The Great Divide* (London: Allen Lane, 2015).

Stiglitz, Joseph, and Linda Bilmes, *The Three Trillion Dollar War: The True Cost of the Iraq Conflict* (London: Allen Lane, 2008).

Taylor, Max, and John Horgan (eds), *The Future of Terrorism* (London: Frank Cass, 2000).

Urban, Mark, *Task Force Black: The Explosive True Story of the SAS and the Secret War in Iraq* (London: Little, Brown, 2010).

Vann, Anthony, and Paul Rogers (eds), *Human Ecology and World Development* (London: Plenum, 1974).

Wilkinson, Richard, and Kate Pickett, *The Spirit Level* (London: Penguin, 2009).

Williams, Heathcote, *Badshah Khan: Islamic Peace Warrior* (London: Thin Man, 2015).

INDEX